"Ron McIntosh's sharp, keen, and insightful approach to the wisdom he shares in "The Missing Ingredient" will provide a solid foundation in your life for finding your "missing piece". Having spent years dealing with how the mind and heart assimilate what become deeply embedded mental models of how the world works that are more often than not flawed mental models rooted in limiting beliefs, I appreciate the thorough manner in which Ron takes you as the reader through a carefully laid out step-by-step process to a place of flourishing and thriving from the inside-out.

Doing the "inner homework" that you need to do in order to become all that God intends doesn't have to be an arduous task. Once you understand how your beliefs structure your ongoing thought processes, attitudes, values, and affections that ultimately influence your behaviors, you are on you way to overcoming self-sabotaging patterns that have limited your ability to be and become all that you are supposed to be. Ron is masterful in laying out the journey for you. Read "The Missing Ingredient" for all it's worth, and the ␣␣␣␣ ′t and watch how transformation from the inside-out becom␣␣␣␣␣␣ ′u won't have to invite people to see; it will become ␣␣␣␣␣␣ ′rs will tell you how different you are without y␣␣␣␣␣␣ ′! Thanks Ron for sharing your brilliance in thes␣␣␣␣

␣. Mark J. Chironna
␣ Chironna Ministries
Church ␣␣␣␣␣␣␣␣ ␣ng Edge, Longwood, FL

"Some computer programs run in the background. Because they can drag or damage, they must be cleaned out. Our soul is like that. Things running in the background from childhood and other sources cripple our spirit. Reading Ron McIntosh's The Missing Ingredient can cleanse you of lies and false limitations, and also provide a clean slate to live the life you were destined to live.

One of the greatest advantages of Christianity is that it turns orphans into heirs. Correct interaction with Christ can't help but imbue confidence, faith, and audacious living. The enemy knew this active ingredient and the kind of spiritual giant it creates. He worked feverishly to counterfeit these truths. It is time to realize that new age and motivational speakers stole our fire, repackaged it, and sold the world a sad and inferior version of The Missing Ingredient. What are you waiting for? Buy it, read it, live it!"

—Mario Murillo
Mario Murillo Ministry
Best-selling Author of "Critical Mass"
Reno, Nevada

"This may be the single most important book you ever read! The Missing Ingredient, Ron McIntosh, and the power of God saved my life! The Missing Ingredient is a must read for anyone wanting to be more and achieve more in life. You were born to WIN! You deserve to WIN! You can WIN! You just need to discover The Missing Ingredient! Now is your time to live the abundant life and maximize your God-given talent and ability so that you can fulfill your calling and walk out your destiny!

This book will challenge you and equip you so that you can be THE BEST version of you and ultimately experience the abundant life just like it did for me!

Read this book! Expect to WIN! WIN ALL DAY"

—Jon Coneeley, "Coach JC"
Top Christian Motivational Speaker and Life Coach –
CoachJC.com
Author of "The Secret to Real Success"

"I worked for Ron McIntosh for five years and watched him live out these power principles every day. They are truly transforming and can move you into the super-achiever category. As a business consultant, I rarely see people rise to that level, but this book is a handbook to do just that! I absolutely love this book!"

—Lynette Lewis

"I have worked as a pastor or with pastors for 43 years now. After reading Ron's new book, I'm convinced that we have misunderstood discipleship as strictly learning about the Bible and not learning how to apply the principles of the Bible to our daily lives. This book is the best discipleship workbook I have ever read. If I had it to do all over again, this book would be my main resource of my discipleship program to change lives in the Kingdom. I will recommend it to all the churches I coach in the future. As you read this book, you will see what I mean. Enjoy."

—Bishop Gary McIntosh

"Ron has a way of communicating very complicated concepts from God's Word in a way that's easy to understand for everyone. He shares incredible truths from God's Word mixed with his personal experiences to help you tap into that same potential God offers all of us. This book is a book about discovering the life you were born to live and how to start walking in that LIMITLESS POTENTIAL that God has for you! I am so excited for this new book, and I believe it will bless you BIG TIME!"

—Paul Daugherty
Lead Pastor of Victory Christian Center
Tulsa, Oklahoma

"Ron McIntosh speaks my language! He is a theologian, a dynamic speaker, and a man of great faith. "The Missing Ingredient" is a book that I wish I would have written. Jesus really did come to give us abundant life and Ron has found the missing ingredient to the life of your dreams! In this book, he skillfully and clearly presents a way for the Body of Christ to live in a place of wholeness, joy, and abundance. If you are tired of living in a rut of emotional baggage and don't know what to do with the pain of your past or you know you are missing something vital in your day-to-day life, "The Missing Ingredient" is a must read!"

—Carol McLeod
Author of "Defiant Joy" and "No More Ordinary"

"Every day, we work on many things hoping to build a successful and significant life, but the majority of people haven't learned the ONE thing that can change EVERYTHING. Ron does a masterful job of communicating what every successful person enjoying a significant life wishes they learned earlier. This book can help anyone begin to make this season the best season of life!"

—Jim Graff
Pastor, Faith Family Church
President of Significant Church Network
Author of "Significant Life"

"As a fan of the *The Greatest Secret*, I was thrilled to find this updated and expanded text even more brilliant than its predecessor. In "The Missing Ingredient," Ron McIntosh asks hard-hitting questions about why we miss out on the success God desires for us. In this practical, scripture-based guide, McIntosh reveals the keys to real productivity in the church and in your life. Start reading now and watch His abundance manifest in your life!

—Simon T. Bailey
Leader of the Brilliance Movement
Best-selling author of *Release Your Brilliance*

"After years of knowing Ron McIntosh, I can say that he is a true jewel of a leader. He and his wonderful wife Judy live exemplary lives. Ron has hit upon a tremendous secret that "closes the loop" of why more people don't receive all that God has promised. I wholeheartedly suggest that you saturate yourself with the content of the book…apply every principle. Impact your heart, for out of it flow the issues of life. I believe you are next in line for a miracle."

—Larry Stockstill
Pastor of Bethany Church, Baton Rouge, LA
Author of "Laws of Increase" and "The Remnant"

"It pains me greatly to see people made in the image of God – children of God – living a subpar life. Jesus said He came to give us a full life, and that's what we should grow to expect. We don' realize it, but we live every day with self-limiting beliefs that hold us back. In Ron's book, "The Missing Ingredient," Ron explains that most of us are unaware of our self-limiting beliefs. As you immerse yourself in this book, not only will you discover things holding you back, but also how to truly transform your thinking. This is not a book you casually pick up and read, for each page will cause you to stop, ponder, and then intentionally put to practice what you just read. I've been eternally impacted by the discoveries Ron writes about in this book. How different the church would be if it truly understood the principles in this book!"

—Tracy Boyd
Pastor, Life Church
Naples, Florida

"Finally, someone has eloquently and clearly communicated how disease develops and provides a solution by bringing the spiritual world into the health and well-being of the people. A must read!"

—Dr. Greg Loman
Cofounder of Maximized Living

THE MISSING INGREDIENT

DISCOVER THE ONE THING

THAT CHANGES EVERYTHING

THE MISSING INGREDIENT

DISCOVER THE ONE THING

THAT CHANGES EVERYTHING

RON MCINTOSH

Published by Trilogy Christian Publishing
PO Box A
Santa Ana, CA 92711
Trilogypub@tbn.org
Phone: 714-425-4093

Cover design by Daniel Hook
Layout design by Christina Hicks Creative
christinahickscreative@gmail.com

Published in the United States of America
ISBN: 9781640880009

CONTENTS

DEDICATION

I want to take a moment to say a thank you to those who have made this work a reality. No one does a work like this on their own. You stand on the shoulders of many who have imparted into your life. To so many who have impacted me as a person (you know who you are) I say thank you to you all!

Writing is hard work and it is a collaborative effort. I first want to thank Rhonda Olson, who has encouraged me for 5 years to put what she considered life-changing principles into print. Her tireless interaction has encouraged me to "plow through" to a finished product.

To my Office Manager, Sue Scoggin, her tireless efforts to help put this work into a format that can be put into a finished manuscript are commendable. Your efforts and friendship are meaningful.

Most of all to my family. Without your continued love, encouragement and support, I would never take on such a task. Judy, your love is my greatest motivation this side of heaven. The very lives of my children, David and Shelly, Daniel and Laura and Jonathan motivate me to love God more. Your devotion to Christ inspires me.

FOREWORD

At this moment. you're holding a treasure in your hands. The information in this book is more precious than gold. It contains answers to the questions that have plagued the people of God for millennia. It will unlock mysteries whose answers have lain in plain site since the first recorded words of God, but have been hidden by religious interpretation. You can now know and utilize the One Missing Ingredient that changes everything!

There are many people who make reference to the heart, but have no real idea of that which they speak. They regurgitate words they have heard from others. But Ron McIntosh is a man on a journey, a life journey. He is not speaking theoretically, he is speaking experientially. He is one of the few voices you can trust to help you on this journey of living from the heart!

Through the pages of *The Missing Ingredient* you will gain much information. You'll have exercises for personal development. I can attest that this book is a wealth of treasure. But make no mistake: *The Missing Ingredient* is not a new formula. It is an explanation of the roles of the heart in all things related to God. The exercises are to help you develop your heart. But in the end, this book will only help you to the degree you put these exercise into practice.

The word "know" in the Greek New Testament is a knowing that comes by experiencing. It is not the knowing that comes by learning the information. It is the knowing that comes by believing and applying the information thereby developing a Biblically based personal experience! The way to manifest God's truth in your physical world is for you to first know/experience it in your heart.

Beliefs of the heart have many interesting dynamics. When we believe something in our heart, it changes our sense of identity. As a result of altering our identity, the capacity to do anything congruent with this identity becomes effortless. It doesn't take effort to do that which is based on identity. The person who believes they are righteous as a result of being in Christ will effortlessly live righteous. The same goes for peace, joy, success and health. We may all struggle or have failures from time to time but once something becomes real in our heart it actually takes effort to do or be anything else!

The only way to experience God and His promises prior to them manifesting in the physical world is in your own heart. As Ron so convincingly teaches, we must use our mind, thoughts, imaginations, memories and every other part of our being to experience God's promises as being real now, at this moment in order to influence our heart! Meditation is not faith; it is the precursor to faith. Meditation is not what makes the miraculous happen. Biblical meditation is where we make God's promises believable… not believable in a general sense but believable for us. *The Missing Ingredient* is like a train: the teaching and exercises will deliver you to the door of your heart, and then you have to get off the train and enter for yourself. Ron McIntosh will share the journey with you up to that point. But all he or any of us can do is lead you to the door. At that point you and Jesus have to step into that supernatural realm alone. Walking through this door is the end of your life as you have perceived it to be. It is the beginning of a view of life only shared between you and God!

Ron and I have been walking this path together and sharing our experiences for many years. We share a passion to lead people down a path that connects them to the life of God, in their heart! He is a voice I trust. He is a man of character. But in the context of this material, his most important qualification for writing this book is this: he is a man who is making this journey!

—James B Richards Ph.D., Th.D., OMD
Creator of Heart Physics
Author of Moving Your Invisible Boundaries

PREFACE

I was sitting in my associate's office when he asked a simple question "Is your book, *The Greatest Secret*, still listed on Amazon?"

I answered a simple, "I don't know" and set out to find out. As I researched Amazon, I started reading reviews of the book along with comments from other web sites as well. Here is a sample of what I found:

- "This is a book that answers all your questions. If you've ever asked yourself, 'Where am I missing it with God?' or 'Why am I not seeing the promises of God manifested in my life?' then read this book and you will get the answers and if you apply what you are reading to your own life you will see results. And, it doesn't hurt to read it again after the first time. Awesome material. Highly recommend it, if you want to excel in the Word of God."
  – Amazon customer

- "This book is a page-turner. I recommend it often and have purchased it several times over for our friends and clients … I especially liked the section which covered 'Breaking self-limiting beliefs.' In today's shifting landscape, I found it to be timely, powerful and practical."
  – Joe Boggess

- "Amazing! I love this book. I've heard of and read of others who teach on positive thinking, but none like this one. Ron McIntosh brings the power of positive thinking to the Bible and shows how it isn't just psychology --- It's a biblical principle for finding joy and abundance in your life. Read this book, read the Bible,

transform your mind and you will transform your life."
– Jere Galloway

- "This is the best version of a Christian self-help book. It takes principles of the Bible to improve life's outcome. . .I'm surprised I have not heard more buzz about it." – Scott J.P.

- "Every person should read this book! It'll transform your life, if you will follow its guidelines. Ron is an excellent teacher and writer. He takes Kingdom principles and makes them clear to understand and follow, that you may receive what Jesus promised—life abundantly" – Amazon customer

- "Absolutely life-changing. I'm only on Chapter 8 so far and this is by far one of the best development books I have ever read. I highly recommend this book to anyone who wants to understand the real Law of Attraction from God's Word." – Nicki Tompkins

- "I love this book! I've read it a couple of times and have recommended it to many friends." – Julie E.

- "Fascinating read! I'm actively engaged page by page." – Sharla

- "Great book! Should transform your life if you really absorb the material." – Peter Hughes

- "An outstanding enlightenment, clearly and simply written! A must read!" – Adrianne Braggs

- "I was told this book would change my life and it has. I have more joy, more hope and faith in Jesus and what the Father has done for us through Him. We have everything and don't even know it. We have the power to heal and change lives. The keys are in this book." – Jodie

- "This book will change your life! If you want to be filled with hope and joy no matter what happens in your life, buy this book and read it. You'll find out just how much power you have to change your circumstances through the keys that are available to you through Jesus Christ." – Jim Vandem

- "Great book! I have read this book over and over! It really challenges the way you normally think and frees your mind to think outside the box" – Kim Carlson
- " ... The Greatest Secret explains via the most recent discoveries of science, philosophies, health, psychology, cellular biology, etc. how things work together. Every point is documented with scripture. Next to the Bible this is at the top of my favorite books list." – Diana Huffman
- "I get excited every opportunity I have the chance to sit and read this book. I have experienced many revelations with the way the information is presented and backed up with biblical scripture and modern science. It's not only "thus said ... " but also how to apply the Word, grow and apply your faith into an action plan. This is a powerful little book you'll want to share with your loved ones." – Amazon 123

You may think this is a weird exercise in self-aggrandizement, but it is not. It simply re-energized me to get the missing ingredient into the hands of as many people as I can. If you've ever wondered why you don't see what you say you believe, this book will help you unlock the doors to living a life without limits.

Thus, I am writing *The Missing Ingredient* as an update to my previous book *The Greatest Secret*. In this new work, I take the existing work, amplify it, add to it and make it more practical with the help of some new research. Why? Because it is time to live a life without limits!

INTRODUCTION

THE MISSING INGREDIENT

Is success elusive, or is there something we don't know? Is there a missing ingredient we have overlooked to achieve success, prosperity, health and the abundant life Jesus promised?

The answer is, *yes!* The missing ingredient to abundant life categorically is, **heart beliefs** (what you believe in your heart). It is renewing your mind, establishing your heart and transforming your personal belief system. This is why what we say we believe, so rarely manifests itself with any degree of consistency. The only way to truly change your life is to change what you think in a way that changes your heart. You will always do what you think in your heart… *For as he thinks in his heart, so is he* (Proverbs 23:7 NKJ). This is why the launching pad scripture for this book is Romans 12:2, *And do not be conformed to this world, but be transformed by the renewing of your mind, that you may prove what is that good and acceptable and perfect will of God (NKJV). Conforming* is something you do to your life. It is behavioral modification. It works sometimes, but we mostly fall back into old patterns. *Transformation* is something God does to us. When our thinking becomes a heart belief it creates a permanent transformation that solicits the manifestation of the Kingdom of God. Conforming (*change*) comes from the outside/in. Transforming comes from the inside/out. The former is temporary and the latter is dominantly long lasting. Thoughts always precede actions. Dominant thoughts (**heart beliefs**) control your destiny. Heart beliefs are the missing ingredient to your breakthrough in life.

They are a missing ingredient because we have unwittingly overlooked them. As we re-examine the truth of scripture, prepare to experience real abundance—real abundance of feeling loved and fulfilled—abundance with real prosperity (giving and receiving in order to be a blessing to others), not just materialism. Real abundance is joy. Joy is not just an emotion guided by your circumstances. It is not just "joy because..." but joy regardless of the circumstances. Real abundance brings peace and not just peace because of a lack of storms, but peace in the midst of the storms as well. This is a book about breaking barriers in every corridor of your life. It is about the discovery of the keys that unlock the door to God's Kingdom.

Let me give you an example. My quest began some years ago when I began asking myself some tough questions about the productivity of believers and God's church. I asked myself,

- If the Body of Christ is the most powerful entity on the planet, why are we not more distinguished from the world than we are?
- If Jesus promised abundance (John 10:10), why aren't more of His people experiencing it?
- If God's message is one of healing and redemption (Isa. 53:4; Matt. 8:17; Lk. 44:18, 19; 1 Pet. 2:24) then why are so many Christians sick?
- If it is God's will to be set free, why are so many Christians hopelessly bound by fears, insecurities, discouragement and addictions of every kind?
- If God's will is for us to be successful in every area of our lives, why are so many believers mired in stagnation and defeat?
- Is success elusive or have we just missed something? Are we reaching our desires or getting what we don't want?

I began pouring over scriptures for hours at a time, searching for an answer. As I began searching verse after verse, I began to discover keys or kingdom laws to attract the kingdom of God to ourselves.

During this time, I had lunch with a highly recognized Christian leader from Tulsa. In between bites of fried rice, as we talked about the world and the church, he paused and looked across the table at me and asked, "What do you think God is doing right now?"

I pondered over the malaise of economic distress, terrorism, racism, and frustrating stagnation and I responded at what God was beginning to reveal to me: "I believe God is revealing keys to help people walk out of lives mired in mediocrity (after all, mediocre Christian is a contradiction in terms) and step into the abundance God has created for them. This abundance is not to be stopped in them, but to be poured out of their lives upon the culture and society around them." At the time, I wasn't even sure I truly knew what I meant, but I could sense an anointing on that moment.

The next day as I prepared for my staff meeting, God gave me an illustration to communicate this truth. As we gathered for the meeting I looked across the conference table at one of my key staff members. I said, "Liz, I want you to do something for me!"

Bright and positive, she responded, "Of course! What do you want me to do?"

I said, "Liz, I want you to go outside the door to this room. I'm going to lock the door behind you. Here's the key to the door to this room. I want you to unlock the door and come back into the room."

After some whimsical banter and stares of disbelief by some of the rest of the staff, she agreed to humor me and play along with my little ploy.

I locked the door behind her and I said loud enough for her to hear me, "Liz, use the key to unlock the door and come back into the room."

After some moments of trying, she protested and said, "I can't get the door to open."

"Try harder," I replied.

She tried to get the key to turn the lock for a while longer but the key didn't work. So I encouraged her to not give up but to make more effort. She prodded away for a few more minutes, but with no resolve. By this time, I could tell the staff was musing concerning this seeming insane exercise. Liz fiddled with the lock a few more minutes and finally decreed, "No matter how hard I try I cannot get this key to open the door. I think you gave me the wrong key."

"You're absolutely right," I told her. "I gave you the wrong key."

When I opened the door and Liz came in, I had everyone's attention (though I think some of them thought I was a hamburger short of a "Happy Meal"). Everyone's curiosity was peaked. I looked at them and related that this little exercise is a picture of what the church is experiencing today. Many believers are on the other side of a locked door. They believe God wants to open the door and bless them, because they are sincere and are trying hard. They tell themselves, "I go to church twice per week, I read my Bible on occasion and I am making an effort."

Here's the important fact I don't want you to miss. It doesn't matter how hard you try, or how sincere you are, you can't open the door unless you have the right key.

In this hour in which we're living, God is supernaturally revealing keys to bring about real productivity in people's lives. People are tired of the Gospel, no matter how true it is, that they can't get to work. Matthew 16:19 says it this way: *I will give you the keys to the kingdom of heaven. Whatever you bind on earth is bound (already bound-Amplified version) in heaven. Whatever you loose on earth, (must already be loosed-Amplified version) in Heaven.* Somehow the church has managed to reduce the magnitude of this verse to semantics in praying like, "I bind the devil," etc. While there is some truth to this thought process, this passage is more about "keys" or laws that govern access or attract the manifestation of the kingdom of heaven. Keys unlock something, in this case the Kingdom of God. The Kingdom of heaven (or Kingdom of God) is about the rule of God. However, it is not limited to that. It is also the location and resources of God and the system by which you access them in your life. Accessing kingdom resources allows believers to *dominate their environment* (Gen. 1:26) and *establish God's rule and reign on the earth* (Matt. 6:10). Keys unlock doors, in this case a door to the Kingdom of heaven. The word *bind* in this passage means to stop. The word *loose* in this passage means to start.

The greater meaning in this passage means when you learn the key kingdom laws and operate in them, you start the manifestation of the kingdom of heaven and you stop the devil's operation on the planet. However, it doesn't do any good to give keys to someone who doesn't know how to use them. I can have a ring of keys (*principle or laws*), but if I don't know the doors they fit they are useless. On the other hand, if I don't have the keys (*laws*) to open the doors I remain in frustration.

This missing ingredient is the key to unlock the door to the abundant life Jesus promised. Look at what the discovery of the missing ingredient did for Mary Ann at a recent Missing Ingredient Conference.

Mary Ann struggled with Ulcerative Colitis for 23 years. She had inflammation throughout her body, a leaky gut (the cause of many physical issues) and over 40 food allergies. During this conference, Mary Ann's heart was opened to what God could do in her life. She responded to an invitation for prayer for the manifestation of the Kingdom for healing.

As I purveyed the throng of people at the altar I asked, "What do you need from God?"

She shared the symptoms I related earlier, then she said, "I know I'm healed by the stripes of Jesus."

I responded to her, "It's time for it to manifest itself."

What she knew in her mind was transferring to her heart. I spoke to her body, and we continued the service. About two weeks later I got an email from the church office from Mary Ann's husband, Michael. She had just been retested by her doctor. Her test, according to Michael, amazed and shocked the doctor. Mary Ann's inflammation markers were now in the perfect range (not good or improved, but perfect). Just a couple of weeks earlier they were highly elevated and causing all kinds of issues in her body. Her food allergy test came back saying that she was no longer allergic to the 40 foods she had been prior! The **missing ingredient** transformed her circumstances and her body.

If you look around, you see people of all kinds who are feeling a sense of lack in their lives. People are hungry for the key to unlock the door to fulfillment and productivity. People are looking for the missing key (ingredient) that will open the doors to a life without limits.

Is this success elusive, or is there a missing ingredient that has been hidden beneath the surface of your Christian life? This book opens the door to a real, genuine Christianity that is a catalyst to living life and life more abundantly. It is time to discover the key that unlocks that door to the manifestation of the Kingdom of God and living a life without limits. The master key is renewing the mind, establishing the heart and transforming your personal belief system.

CHAPTER 1

LIVING A LIFE WITHOUT LIMITS

THEME: CREATE A NEED TO LIVE A LIFE WITHOUT LIMITS.

Lesson: We have a limitless gospel,
but we live a limited life.

Is success elusive, or is there something we don't know? Is there a missing ingredient we've overlooked that is the launching pad to the productivity and abundance we all desire and the manifestation of the Kingdom of heaven? Have you ever wondered why what you say you believe rarely manifests itself with any degree of consistency? Why is it that you are determined to change, but as usual you have short blasts of productive energy and then slide back to status quo (settling for the way things are now).

Why is it most of us seem to be at the same place year after year. . .the same place in our finances year after year. . .same place in our job year after year. . .same place in our marriage and family year after year . . .same place in our ministry year after year. . .same place or worse in our health year after year? How do I break the limitation off my life? How do I get from where I am to where I want to be?

Here is the problem: If the blueprint of your thinking is not set for success (Josh. 1:8), nothing you learn, nothing you know and nothing you do will make any difference.[1] This book will show you how to change your thinking by renewing your mind, establishing your heart and transforming your personal belief system. This is the missing ingredient to create heart beliefs, which we'll examine in the next chapter.

You'll discover this is the missing ingredient that is often overlooked to unlock the abundant life that Jesus promised (Jn. 10:10). Abundant love, abundant joy, abundant peace, abundant faith, abundant prosperity, abundant health, abundant marriages and families and more that God designed for you.

You might even be thinking, what is the abundant life that Jesus promised? John 10:10 says it this way, "I am come that they might have life and that they may have it more abundantly" (NKJV). What does He mean by "life?" The word "life" in Greek is "zoe." The term "zoe" means "life" in the fullest or the God kind of life.[2] The word used here for "abundant" means superabundant in quantity, superior in quality, excess, surplus, superfluity, superfluous, extreme, too much.[3] Wow! God wants you to have life that is too much. It is life with no degrees. It is a life fully blessed. It is living a life without limits!

However, even though we have a limitless Gospel, most of us lead a limited life. Let me give you an example of what I mean. Most of us believe healing is in the atonement (Jesus' death on the cross), which means it is God's will to heal us. Then why don't we see more healing than we do? We believe it is God's will to prosper us. Then why are so many Christians struggling? It certainly is God's will for believers to be free. Then why are so many Christians bound? Why do we often find ourselves stuck in the same place with the same struggles year after year?

Yet, here is the magnanimous, extraordinary will of God. In Ephesians3:8-10, Paul says, "And so here I am preaching and writing about things that are way over my head." If they are over Paul's head, they are certainly over mine as well. This simply means it's time to stop analyzing His Word and simply do what He says. Paul continues, "The inexhaustible riches and generosity of Christ." Here Paul talks about the inexhaustible riches of Christ. In other words, there is nothing that can expend God's supply and resources for our lives. . .the generosity of Christ. He desires to give us what we need out of an inexhaustible supply. "My task is to bring out into the open and make plain what God, who has created all of this in the first place, has been doing in secret and behind the scenes all along. Through followers of Jesus like yourselves gathered in churches, this extraordinary plan of God is becoming known and talked about even among the angels." (Ephes. 3:8-10 MSG; emphasis mine).

God's plan is for you to live an extraordinary life. The word extraordinary means to surpass the norm, to break away from status quo (people who settle for the way things are now), beyond usual, exceeding common measure, remarkable, amazing, unimaginable, beyond limits.[4] God's will is for your life to be amazing, remarkable, unimaginable, beyond limits. It is not a life that is at the same place year after year but one that explodes past the current limitations. Most people become preoccupied with life's situations and circumstances, and they lose sight of their own destiny.

STEPPING INTO YOUR DESTINY

The Apostle Paul gives us an initial key to launching into our God-given, God-ordained destiny. Hebrews 12:1-3 states, "Therefore, since we are surrounded by such a great cloud of witnesses, let us throw off everything that hinders ("weights" in KJV) and the sin that so easily entangles ("besets" in KJV) and let us run with perseverance the race mapped out for us. Let us fix our eyes on Jesus, the author and perfector of our faith, who for the joy set before us endured the cross, scorning the shame and sat down at the right hand of the throne of God. Consider Him who endured such opposition from sinful men so that you will not grow weary and lose heart."

I could go to extraordinary length of exegetical insight to unfold the meaning of this verse, or I can give you a simple illustration. Let's opt for the latter:

One of the first times I ever shared thoughts about this passage, I was in a large church in San Antonio. I proclaimed, "In this passage, Paul compares life to a race." I explained that I wanted to give them an illustration of how we cross the finish line of our destinies.

Boldly, I looked at the pastor and proclaimed, "I want you to find the best athlete in this crowd, and I'm going to challenge him to a race."

The pastor calmly surveyed the crowd of around 3,000 people and picked a young man in the first row. The crowd immediately howled with approval. Unbeknownst to me, but obvious to the congregation, this fine specimen of a human being was a professional basketball player in Europe. I sent out my charge, "I want to challenge you to a race!"

He looked at me and smiled. He was in his middle twenties, 6'3" and in excellent physical shape. I was, let's just say, somewhat older.

Then I announced, "Here are the rules. We'll line up here in front of the pulpit. I'll say, 'On your mark, get set, go!' We'll take off running across the front of the church, down the side, around back to the front of the church, and the first one to cross back across this pulpit area will win."

Then, I added, "Do you think you can win?" He smirked, looked at the crowd and solicited their support. Then I smirked and said, "I'm going to kick your tail!" Now the crowd really roared.

We positioned ourselves and I barked out, "On your mark, get set, go!" He bounded off the starting line with massive energy when I yelled out, "Hold it! Hold it! Come back here." Reticently, he returned to the starting point with an amused look on his face.

I looked at him and noted, "Did you notice in the passage it says to run without hindrances. I need a hindrance." I looked at a rather large man on the front row and deliberated, "I need you to be hindrance for me. Jump up on his back." Everyone roared with laughter. Then I mused to my opponent, "Do you think you can still take me?" He responded by taking off his sport coat to reveal a dress "Tee" and rippling six pack abs. Then, he removed his shoes and responded, "Absolutely!"

I got my hindrance in place. We positioned ourselves, and I rang out once again, "On your mark, get set, go!" He bounded off the starting point almost as if he didn't have a rather large man on his back. Once again, I cried out, "Hold it! Come back here!"

The crowd was rumbling with amusement. Again, he reluctantly came sauntering back to the starting point. I then emphasized, "This passage also said to not run with weights. I need a couple of weights." After securing two volunteers, I repositioned my hindrance on his back and asked my weights to securely grab his ankles from behind. At that point, I asked again, "Do you think you can take me now?" He shrugged his shoulders reticently, and we once again positioned ourselves. I looked over to the pastor and said, "This time you give the starting orders." He cried out, "On your mark, get set, go!" I bounded out while my star athlete struggled to even move. I started running backward as a not so subtle mockery of my opponent to the delight of the crowd. Finally, I stopped the proceedings and had everyone show appreciation for my volunteers, especially my race opponent.

Then I explained to the audience the point of this elaborate example. "Life is like this race. All we have to do is get around the track to the finish line, and on the other side of the finish line is abundant life. However, we've got so many hindrances and weights we can't get to our destination and find ourselves stagnated in our lives."

A lot of us live our lives unwittingly with the encumbrances of besetting circumstances, attitudes and actions. What is the hindrance mentioned in this passage in Hebrews 12? A hindrance is a non-sinful besetting circumstance or attitude. That includes fear, anger, discouragement, depression, bad information, worry, anxiety, bad relationships or ignorance. This would also include double-mindedness or the biggest one of all – subconscious self-limiting beliefs. (When I say not sinful, I understand that whatever is not of faith is sin – Rom. 14:23b. Here I am speaking of deliberate actions).

What are the weights? A weight is a sin. Really, there is only one sin – unbelief. The rest of what we call sin is simply the manifestations of unbelief. These would include lust, pornography, adultery, hate, alcoholism, drugs, etc. Jesus says I have life and life more abundantly (Jn. 10:10) for you. But you have unwittingly burdened yourself with hindrances and weights. The chief of which is self-limiting beliefs. This book is designed to show you God's process to dismantle hindrances and launch you into the abundance you are designed for in your life.

The main Greek word for sin is "hamartia." Most people define sin as, "to miss the mark." However, this is only a portion of the definition. It really means to miss the mark of the prize.[5] Sinful acts or attitudes cause us to miss the mark of the prize. We become distracted from the things of God's abundance we most desire.

The biggest problem among serious people (believers) is the inability to change. Many believers have the same or similar problems for a lifetime. Instead of growing into increasing abundance, they find themselves in a cycle of a blast of energy toward change, followed by a return to status quo. Here's what I mean. How many times have you seen someone legitimately touched at an altar and one month later right back at the same place? We see people get born again and yet find themselves falling back into lust. People desire to go to a new level, but find themselves backing off of new challenges. They want to go after new ideas, but lack the peace and confidence to try. They desire a good marriage, but they have the inability to adapt. They have a vision, but lack the faith to try it. They sometimes hate who they are, but lack the self-control to change.

Therefore, they remain stuck in their depression, stuck in lack, stuck in pornography, stuck in bad relationships, stuck being overweight, stuck in life and worst of all stuck in mediocrity. You might be thinking how mediocrity could be the worst of all? It is because a mediocre Christian is a contradiction in terms. God made you for abundance.

The answer to all of this is found in this one important key – your outside world is a direct reflection of your inward world. In fact, your outside world corresponds directly to your inward world. This is why two people can sit and listen to the same principles and one person is transformed and the other is not. Why is it that of the people who go to seminars of any kind (secular or spiritual), less than ten percent ever apply one thing they hear (this is even after they have spent big dollars for it)?[6] You are where you are today because of the decisions you have made up to this point. Your outside life will directly correspond to your inside life. At this moment, you are manifesting in your life what you truly believe on the inside.

It's time to be honest with yourself. Are you where you want to be in your life, finances, career or ministry? If life has thrown its fair share of disappointments your way, it is not too late to change all of that! God is ready and waiting with all of heaven's resources to help you. The key is transforming your inside world to manifest a new outward world. The way you transform your inside world is to renew your mind, establish your heart and transform your personal belief system. Often people think this is simple memorization of key truths. It requires something far beyond this to transform your total decision-making. Once truth is solidified in your heart (heart beliefs – the missing ingredient), it allows you the freedom to use the Kingdom of Heaven's keys and to experience its resources.

THE KINGDOM LAWS

There are six laws of success and the process of faith. These six laws are the key to transforming your inside world to manifest God's Kingdom to your outside world:

The **Law of Capacity** (Matt. 25:14-25): A person can only receive from God in direct correlation to his ability to receive from God. (We will deal with this at length in Chapter 10).

The **Law of Control** (Gen. 1:26): People are positive in life to the dimension that they are in control of their lives.[7] This is the principle of Spiritual Authority. The problem is most people feel out of control in their lives.

The **Law of Expectation** (Heb. 11:1): What you expect in your heart with conviction becomes self-fulfilling prophecy.[9] Your steps are literally ordered by your expectations. Some psychologists suggest that 85% of our actions are the results of our expectations. In other words, what we do or do not do is the result of what we expect the outcome to be.

The **Law of Belief** (Heb. 11:1): What you believe in your heart with confidence becomes your reality.[8] Everyone manifests what they believe. They either manifest abundance or they manifest scarcity.

The **Law of Attraction** (Matt. 16:18, 19): You attract to yourself people, ideas and resources according to your most dominant thoughts.[10] This is the process of the manifestation of God's Kingdom in your life. This law causes what is potential to become reality. You will recognize people, ideas and resources according to your most dominant thoughts.

The **Law of Correspondence** (Rom. 12:2): Your outside world corresponds directly to your inside world. In other words, what is without comes from what is within.[11] This is the dominant law. All productive manifestations in your life are the product of your inner world, which is the result of a renewed mind, an established heart and a transformed personal belief system.

GOD'S LAWS REFLECTED IN NATURAL LAWS

I have a brilliant friend from Huntsville, Alabama, Dr. James Richards. One day he was sharing with me how God's laws are reflected in natural laws. If you understand how natural laws work, you will understand how God's laws work. Romans 1:20 shows us this process, "For since the creation of the world, God's invisible qualities–His eternal power and divine nature–have been clearly seen, being understood from what has been made." In other words, nature's laws are simply reflected in God's eternal laws. We can see this in four examples from the Laws of Physics.

The Law of Entropy is a basic law that says things left unattended tend toward chaos. Isn't that true for most of our lives as well? We may have serious issues we're trying to deal with, but we often hope they'll go away if we ignore them long enough. The truth is that problems don't go away by ignoring them. In reality, they tend toward chaos. Yard work doesn't go away by ignoring it; the weeds take over and it gets worse. In the same way, your self-limiting beliefs don't disappear by themselves. Once they are logged in your subconscious mind, they work automatically to make those negative beliefs come to pass. Unfortunately, these thoughts often sabotage us and leave our lives in mediocrity or worse, total chaos.

Another of these natural laws is the Law of Cause & Effect. This law states that everything happens for a reason. Nature is neutral. It doesn't favor one person over another. Conversely, if anyone learns to operate in God's laws, they will work for them. So many people believe these laws will only work for the rich and famous and not for the common person. God honors faith whenever and wherever He finds it. It is in this day and time that He is raising up a people who understand the missing ingredient – you can be radically transformed by His laws and experience a new level of living.

We can find another example in Physics called the Law of Hysteresis. Hysteresis is the tendency of material to revert back to its original shape once the pressure changing it is removed. In Psychology, they call it "set-points" or self-limiting beliefs. When we hear a new truth, we change for a season. But when the pressure of that word is removed, we revert back to our old lifestyle. God intends for you not only to be changed for a season, but transformed into a new level of achievement and productivity forever.

Another law, the Law of Motion, states that anything in motion stays in motion unless acted upon by an opposite and equal force. If I were to roll a ball on a flat plain, it would roll forever, unless acted upon by a contrary force, such as gravity or friction. Similarly, in your life there are certain negative traits that are in motion, and will continue to be, unless they are acted upon by an opposite force. Things you want changed don't just disappear – all change for good must be intentional. You must cooperate with truth, the Holy Spirit and target certain beliefs. That means you must identify self-limiting beliefs, disassociate (disconnect, separate) yourself from them and apply the antidote (cure) of new truths. As you employ new empowering beliefs, your life will jump to a new level. To move forward in Kingdom growth, you must literally increase your capacity to receive from God. And that is often in concert with the type of person you are.

Stephen Scott in his profound book, Mentored by a Millionaire, suggests there are four kinds of people in life.[12]

1. *Drifters* are people who drift along in life. They simply go with the flow. About 50% of people comprise this category.
2. *Pursuers* are people who pursue a dream until they meet an obstacle and then back off. About 25% of people make up this category.

3. *Achievers* are people who set lofty goals and achieve some of them, but rarely achieve significant or extraordinary dreams. About 24.99% fall into this category.

4. *Super-achievers* are people who have acquired their master skills to be successful in virtually every venue of their lives. They do the extraordinary. If my math is good that leaves .01% of people who are Super-achievers.

Now notice a few things. Jesus said, "I have come that you might have life and have it more abundantly" (John 10:10). He has come that you might have a life to do the extraordinary. However, only about .01% are able to appropriate it. Remember, the term "abundance" means superabundant in quantity, superior in quality, excess, surplus, excel, superfluous or extreme. God intends for us to tap into a life of productivity if we'll simply understand and operate by His LAWS of achievement.

Noted psychologist Martin Seligman wrote a book called Learned Optimism. In the book, he introduces the idea of "learned helplessness." The idea of "learned helplessness" is that you feel helpless to change your circumstances. [13] He notes that around 80% of people have learned helplessness. Wow! 80% of people feel helpless to change their circumstances. This is what the Apostle Paul calls "strongholds" in 2 Corinthians 10:4. A stronghold is when you feel powerless to change something, though it is contrary to the will of God. It is when people hope something will change, but their past environment, experiences or thoughts indicate the opposite is more likely. A false inner personal belief system will squash any sense that things will ever change or that you can control your destiny.

The key to turn this around is the missing ingredient that is often present, but overlooked. Let's look at the missing ingredient to living a life without limits.

KEYS FOR REFLECTION

1. What does it mean to you to live a life without limits? Begin to see it in your heart.
2. Review the Six Laws to success and the process of faith. What do they mean to you?
3. Examine Steven Scott's four classifications of people – Drifters, Pursuers, Achievers, and Super-Achievers. What category do you see yourself in and why?
4. Learned helplessness or strongholds in 2 Corinthians 10:4 is when you feel powerless to change something, even though it is contrary to the Word of God. Are there areas in your life you feel that is true for you? Start the process to identify limiting beliefs, disassociate (disconnect) yourself from them and find the antidote (cure, truth) in the Word of God.

CHAPTER 2

THE MISSING INGREDIENT

THEME: DISCOVERING AND DEFINING THE MISSING INGREDIENT TO LIVING A LIFE WITHOUT LIMITS.

Lesson: The missing ingredient is heart beliefs.

Renewing the mind, establishing the heart and transforming your personal belief system = heart beliefs.
Heart beliefs is the **solution** to living a life without limits.

Sometime back I was returning home to Tulsa from an extended ministry trip. The last stop on the trip was in a great church in Austin, Texas. The ministry time was extended that morning, so when I was finished I had just enough time to gather myself and rush to the airport in my suit and tie, briefcase in hand. Now, if you fly American Airlines very much (and I do), you are going to go through the Dallas-Fort Worth Airport (DFW) at some point. Even if you're going to heaven, you've got to go through DFW. After arriving at DFW, tired and eager to get home from the long trip, I sat down to wait for my flight when this announcement came over the "P.A." system. "The flight from Dallas to Tulsa has been delayed and overbooked. Will all Tulsa passengers report to the ticket counter?" I pulled my ticket out of my suit jacket and realized I had a boarding pass for every juncture of my flight except from Dallas to Tulsa.

With some trepidation, I went to the ticket counter. The agent went into the computer and glanced at me with a sad look and stated, "I'm sorry, Mr. McIntosh." (Now I'm assuming I'm going to have to catch a later flight.) Then with a smirk she continued, "I'm going to have to put you in First Class, instead!"

Jubilantly, I responded, "I receive it in Jesus' name" (or something like that). I got onto the plane and it quickly filled up, except the last seat next to me. Just before we were to take off, the passenger who would sit in the seat next to me bounds onto the plane. I was dressed in my suit and power tie with my mega briefcase purchased in Seoul, Korea. He, however, had a mega, mega briefcase. His shoes obviously cost more than my suit did. He was obviously "successful" or at least had money.

Now I don't always like to get into conversations on airplanes, because inevitably they ask you what you do for a living. Then I have to say, "I'm an evangelist." And I had just read an article ranking fifty professions and evangelist was number 47. If I recall properly, that was just below drug dealers. I was extremely tired, and I just didn't want to get into it, so I looked out the window to avoid the conversation. There always comes that awkward lull, before conversation takes place. We're kind of looking at each other, and I didn't want him to ask me the question, so I blurted out, "What do you do for a living?"

He replied, "I'm a consultant to Fortune 500 companies." He went into his briefcase and pulled out a spreadsheet and a business plan and went into an explanation of what he does. He was explaining it in grandiose terminology that seemed very important. When he was done, I looked back out the window to avoid "the" question. Finally, the inevitable moment arrived. In almost a condescending tone in his voice he said, "What do you do for a living?"

In that moment, I gathered myself and said, "I work for the richest Jew in the world."

He said, "You what?" I repeated myself and he responded, "Well, what kind of things do you do?"

I retorted, "We take old things and make them new."

He said inquisitively, "Really!? How does that work?"

I said, "I take successful people like you, introduce them to Him and He makes them more successful than they are."

He replied, "I'd like to know more about that. Could you introduce me to Him?"

I said, "Oh, yeah!"

"Great!" he says as he is pulling his business card out of his briefcase. "Let's set it up."

I said, "I can do it right now." He asked, "Is he on the plane?" I replied, "He is pretty much everywhere!"

Straining his neck around the first-class cabin he asked, "Which one is he?"

I exclaimed, "His name is Jesus!" He laughs, "Are you an evangelist?"

I said, "Yes!"

All the way into Tulsa he told me his Oral Roberts stories, and I told him my Jesus stories. He told me his family struggles, and we talked about real success. We got off the plane and were walking down the aisle to baggage claim when he said, "I've never met anyone like you. I believe I'm going back to church." By the time he got to his rental car, he was equipped for his eternal destiny.

The world is hungry for a Christian faith that works ... that produces results. This is not the time to back up, back off, back down or back away. This is the time to press into limitless life in all arenas.

The problem is most of us have overlooked a missing ingredient. This missing ingredient is the catalytic ingredient to the next level in your life. It is virtually the key to everything. It is found in Romans 12:2, "Be not conformed to this world [system] but be transformed by the renewing of your mind, that you may prove what is the good, acceptable and perfect will of God" (emphasis added). Here is the missing ingredient . . .renewing your mind (to establish your heart and transform your personal belief system—heart beliefs). Now, before you dismiss this as something you already know, let me show you why the missing ingredient is so important.

ONE MISSING INGREDIENT

One of my favorite preachers told me this story about making chocolate chip cookies with his little children. They had done it so often they no longer needed the recipe. His little boy would get the brown sugar, butter and eggs. His even younger daughter would get the flour, baking soda and vanilla. They were very precise to put everything together in the right order. On one occasion, they were getting ready to make the cookies but ran out of baking soda. The daddy didn't want to go to the store; after all, as he rehearsed the recipe in his head, it was only one little teaspoon. After all, with two cups of flour, certainly one teaspoon of baking soda wouldn't make that much difference. However, when they took the cookies out, they were completely flat. As his son picked up the cookie to taste it, he grimaced and said, "No shape, no size, no taste." It is amazing how one missing ingredient can change everything.

The missing ingredient totally changes our perspective. How do I make a shift to limitless living to access the Kingdom of God? How do I obtain a new perspective or paradigm shift that will break self-limiting beliefs that have held me back and launch into living a life without limits?

The importance of a new perspective can be seen by a letter written by a young college girl to her parents. You might want to read this as though this is your daughter writing to you.

Dear Mom and Dad,

I haven't made many friends, but I met a boy (parents, you're already excited). He's not going to school, and he can't find a job, but he is doing better now that he has been released from prison. He didn't have a place to live so he moved in with me. After all, we're going to need a home for the baby. Dad, you'll be glad to hear it is a boy! Turn the letter over for a P.S.

You can imagine the gamut of raw emotions that must have run through her parents' minds. They must have looked at each other in bewilderment. All of their lives they only wanted what was best for their "little girl." The father had worked so hard so she could get a good education and learn a career. And now, she has married a criminal, and she is pregnant. Their hearts must have sunk, as they, trembling, turned the letter over to read the P.S.

P.S. None of this is true! None of it! But I did get a "C" in English and a "D" in Humanities and I need more money.

Now, that will change your perspective!

Biblical laws help you gain new perspective to reach new dimensions in life. It's only when we make biblical truth and God's view our main focus that we'll begin to change our perspective.

Unless you transform the blueprint of your thinking to success (the Kingdom of God), nothing you learn, nothing you know and nothing you do will make any difference. This is the missing ingredient to you living beyond limits.

I often demonstrate this by putting on a massive pair of blue-lensed sunglasses. Then, I hold up a white notecard and ask the audience members what color the card is. They usually respond sheepishly, *white*. Looking through my blue lenses, I decree it's *blue*! I usually repeat the process several times. The point is simple. Everyone seeing the card knows it is white, but I think it is blue because of my lenses. If enough people say it is white, I may even say it is white to fit in. But in my heart of hearts I still see it as blue, even though I say it is white. I will never truly see it as white until I take off my blue-lensed glasses.

It's the same way in life. I may tell you it is God's will for you to have abundance and prosperity. You may even nod your head in agreement, but until you take the glasses of your preconceived subconscious thoughts off, you'll view your life through the lenses of your self-limiting beliefs.

How do we get the glasses of self-limiting beliefs off? How do we see truth for what it really is?

Romans 12:2 reveals the missing ingredient for you to step into limitless living. It states, "Do not conform to the pattern of this world, but be transformed by the renewing of your mind. Then, you will be able to test and prove what God's will is – His good, pleasing and perfect will." (NIV).

4 Principles for Limitless Living:

1. Not conformed to this world (system)
2. Transformed
3. By renewing of your mind
4. Prove the perfect will of God

Josh Billings says it this way: "It's not what we don't know that prevents us from succeeding, it is what we know just ain't so that is our biggest obstacle."[1] Missing this ingredient has convinced us some things are really outside our grasp.

BLUEPRINT TO LIMITLESS LIVING

Let's examine these four amazing principles:

PRINCIPLE #1: Not conformed to this world (system)

Romans 12 begins with this first principle, "Do not be conformed any longer to the pattern of this world." This word "conform" is a fascinating term. It comes from two words, the prefix "con" which means with or together with[2] and "form" which means shape, way or pattern of doing something.[3] "Conformed" in this verse means we do not want to be a part of the pattern or way of doing something according to the world or this world's system.

Why does the writer give such a stern warning? He knew that when you operate according to a particular system, all you can ever produce is what is natural to that system. In other words, you can only access or attract to yourself in accordance to the system you are a part of. The world's system can only access what can be developed in the world. It's only in God's system that you can access the Kingdom of Heaven's resources as the result of the finished work of Christ. Paul wanted to show the limitation of the world's system and how to tap into God's Kingdom.

The world's system is a thought process that is alienated from God's system of thought. It is a reflection of the age we are living in and not God's supernatural provision. Greek scholar Kenneth Wuest says, "The world's system is the thoughts, opinions, speculations of people who operate outside of God's system."[4] God has implanted many of His laws in the world. Thus, the world's system does have the ability to have productivity. It cannot, however, access God's supernatural provision or find peace and fulfillment apart from circumstances going right. This is why there are people in the world's system who have success, but sometimes it is not what the scripture calls *good success* (Josh. 1:8). Good success is prosperity without sorrow (Prov. 10:22). Good success has increase, without family decimation. Good success is blessing with good character to sustain it. (The list goes on). Wittingly or unwittingly, we are all influenced in some measure by the thought process reflective of this age in which we are living that is often in opposition to Kingdom Laws (see appendix at the end of this chapter).

Conformed to this world in this passage literally means to, conform to the same pattern as, to fashion alike, to fashion in accordance, to squeeze into the mold of,[5] the world's way of doing things. Some years back during a revival outpouring the most preached verse in America was Matthew 3:2, "Repent for the Kingdom of Heaven is at hand." This verse was most often interpreted as *have godly sorrow for wrong-doing so someday you can go to Heaven.* There is certainly a key element of truth to this particular understanding of this verse. However, there is something more to its meaning. The term *repent*[6] literally means to think differently, to change our thinking, or to have another mind. In other words, change your thinking because you can't access the Kingdom thinking the way you are thinking right now.

It is crucial to understand what the concept of the Kingdom of Heaven means. God's Kingdom is certainly the rule and reign of God. However, it is also the location and resources of God (Eph. 1:3). It is important to understand that God has provided everything you need for life and godliness (2 Pet. 1:3). He purchased it through His finished work at Calvary. He did it by grace, unmerited by anything you have done, and placed it in His Kingdom for you to access by faith.

The Kingdom of God and the kingdom of this world operate in opposite manners. In the Kingdom of Heaven if you want to receive, you have to give (Mt. 6:38). If you want to increase, you have got to decrease (Jn. 3:30). If you want to become the greatest, you must become the least (Lk. 9:48). Whoever wants to be first must be last (Mk. 10:31). If you want to live, you've got to die (Gal. 2:20). If you want people to serve you, you must serve them (Mk. 10:44). The Kingdom of God operates the opposite of the kingdom of this world, and to access it we must change the way we think.

About ten years ago, while I was travelling and speaking nationally and internationally, I began asking myself some tough questions. Questions like: *If the church is the most powerful entity in the world, why aren't we more productive? If Christians have access to things unbelievers do not, then why aren't we more distinctive than we are?* God said to me, *You don't fully understand how my Kingdom operates.*

I began pouring over scripture and found Matthew 6:10, "Your Kingdom come, your will be done on earth as it is in heaven." There is little doubt God wants to manifest His Kingdom here, the way it is there. Is there sickness in heaven? Obviously, no! Is there poverty in heaven? No! Is there lack of resources in heaven? No! Is there a lack of love or joy in heaven? Again, no! Are there broken relationships in heaven? Absolutely not!

Then, I discovered Psalm 115:16, "The high heavens belong to the Lord, but the earth has been given to man." In other words, what happens on planet earth is up to man. Sometimes I hear people say that God is sovereign, but it doesn't mean He can do whatever He wants. That is not true. The word, "sovereign" means, supreme in rank or power, independent, superior.[7] Nowhere is there an indication He simply does what He wants. If He did, He sure is making a mess of things, or at worst he is a hypocrite who can do what He promised, but won't. No, the earth belongs to man, and God transforms the earth when man learns to use the keys to the Kingdom (Mt. 16:19), so He can loose heaven to manifest the Kingdom on earth.

This was God's intent from the beginning. Look at Genesis 1:26, "Then, God said, 'Let us make man in our image (nature, character, or inherent tendencies) and likeness (function) and let them take dominion ... *over all the earth*" (emphasis added). God made man to have dominion over the earth. The word "dominion" means to rule over, subjugate, dominate, govern.[8]

Captured in this verse is what I call the **4 Laws of Genesis 1:26**:

1. Legal authority to dominate the earth was given to mankind.
2. God did not include Himself in the legal authority structure over the earth (*let them*, verse 26).
3. Any influence or interference from the supernatural realm is only legal through mankind.
4. God made Himself subjugated to His laws, and He will not violate His own laws.[9]

In other words, man has to authorize and initiate God's Kingdom into manifestation by obeying Kingdom laws. Thus, man must align his thinking with Kingdom laws and obey them to release the full provision of God's Kingdom. Therefore, all

Kingdom laws are the authorization and initiation for heaven to interfere and influence earth's affairs. Thus, prayer is the authorization and initiation for heaven to interfere and influence earth's affairs. Giving is the authorization and initiation to interfere and influence earth's affairs. Faith is the authorization and initiation to interfere and influence earth's affairs. Love is the ... I think you get the picture. Obeying Kingdom Laws authorizes and initiates the Kingdom to manifest. Provision, blessing, and healing are the result of repenting (changing your thinking) to align yourself to Kingdom thinking. If you don't, He won't!

The opposite of Kingdom thinking is the "flesh." The "flesh" is a complex concept. But the essential component here is to understand that it means trying to do God's will your way. It is a mindset (Rom. 8:5, 6) that dictates our actions, in this case away from a Kingdom mentality. According to John 6:63, "The flesh profits nothing" (KJV). It doesn't take much of a business person to figure out you shouldn't invest in something that doesn't produce any ROI (return on investment) of real or lasting value. The flesh is opposite of Spirit thinking and acts according to the world's system.

If the flesh is contrary to the Spirit, what does it mean to be in the Spirit? The idea of being in the Spirit means to think **of** God, to think **like** God and to think **from** God. When a crisis or need occurs, you train yourself to immediately think **of** God. If you are in the flesh and conflict arises, instead of thinking in Kingdom principles, you try to figure out what you should do on your own. The sad thing is, so many people don't grasp the futility of the self-effort of the flesh. Instead, repent, change your thinking and think **like** God (His Word) and **from** God (His Spirit). The bottom line of the flesh (self and the world's system) is that you don't think of God, like God or from God. You are locked into the system of this world and subjugated to what that system can produce. To think **like** God means, once you think **of** God, you think according to His Kingdom Laws. Once these things are solidified in you, you think **from** God. You let the subtleties of His Word and His Voice guide you. Repentance changes your thinking to think **like** God.

The 5-fold Process of Repentance

Many times, people mistake penance for repentance. Penance suggests a self-punishment or suffering so that I can show contrition in order to earn the right to be blessed again. This has nothing to do with repentance. Real repentance is a five-fold process:

Identification – What is the shortcoming, boundary or self-limiting belief?

Antidote – What is the God mindset to break the boundary?

Revelation – Let God's Word become revelation to you to create the proper thinking to break your present limitations. Revelation is something you know, but never realized. It starts with renewing your mind (Principle #3 of Rom. 12:2).

Repetition – This is what solidifies revelation in your Personal Belief System.

Rethinking – Identification to antidote to revelation to repetition creates rethinking. Rethinking equates to expectancy, which gives way to faith.

Again, in verse 2 of this passage, Paul says, "Do not be conformed to this world." The only way to break free from the world's system and to tap into the manifestation of His Kingdom is to allow the Word of God to transform your thinking.

PRINCIPLE #2: Be Transformed

Transformation (be transformed) is the second principle of Romans 12:2. The prefix "trans" means over, above and beyond, to cross over or to transcend. Once again form means a way or pattern of doing something. Together this word means thinking over, above and beyond the world's systems. This is the Greek word metamorphose. At its root, it means radically transformed. In other words, there is a system that is radically over, above and beyond the world's system. It can't even be compared to it.

This term metamorphose is where we get our English term metamorphosis. When you think of metamorphosis, most people think of a caterpillar becoming a butterfly. A caterpillar may not look like much, but it transforms into a stunning butterfly of exquisite beauty. This is the kind of total life transformation God is offering you. Once you are transformed by His truth, you no longer resemble your former self. You leave one level of living behind and step into the abundant living God has for you. This missing ingredient of God's Kingdom is that His provision is limitless, "And He who did not spare His own Son, how will He not also along with Him graciously give us all things" (Rom. 8:32).

Someone might come to you and say, I've seen your life. It doesn't look like much. They might look at your bank account and muse, I've seen your finances; they don't look like much. You might reply, yes, but they are being transformed. Similarly, others might say the same thing about your ministry, church, or even about your spouse. Maybe they say, I know your husband. He doesn't look like much. Look at them and smile and say, Yes, but he's being transformed. Do not focus on their comments. Stay focused on what God has promised in His Word.

When my son Jonathan was eleven years old, a relative gave him a gift card to Toys 'R Us. Although he had already spent most of its value, the card had approximately $7.12 left and was burning a hole in his pocket. Jonathan encouraged me to take him shopping. After some persuasion, I agreed to take him to the toy store. As soon as we got inside, he immediately went to the PlayStation 2 section. He looked at systems and a number of the games, all of which far exceeded $7.12. I finally convinced him to look at something he could get for the value of his gift card. So we made our way to the action figure area, where he settled on a Transformer. If you have never seen these toys, they look like one thing (a person or an animal). However, by moving a few parts they suddenly transform into something altogether different (a plane, truck, or other vehicle). That is the idea of what Paul is trying to tell us in the opening verses of Romans 12. If you don't conform to the world's system, but are instead transformed, you will be changed into a person who doesn't even resemble your former self. That is why the Bible says you now are a new creation (2 Cor. 5:17).

There is a major difference between being changed and being transformed. On the surface these two terms appear virtually the same, but a careful examination reveals an important difference. The word change means to cause to go from one state to another, to alter, to make different or to cause a difference, to quit one thing and to start another or to substitute."[10]Transform, on the other hand, suggests to alter form or appearance, a metamorphosis, to conform to the will of God, a release of Divine nature, an alteration of the heart, to change in inner nature, to change one's mind or to exchange.[11] Transformation is an inward effortless change.

As you can see, change is something that comes from the outside in, while transformation comes from the inside out. Transformation is an inward, effortless alteration. The problem with much of Christianity is that we have tried to change the outside through behavior modification. No wonder so many people begin to question whether real change can happen for them. We must show them that true transformation brings alteration from the inside out through the power of Christ's life within us. The question becomes how?

PRINCIPLE #3: Renew your Mind

That leads us to the third principle, *renewing your mind*. Transformation comes by the renewing of the mind. *Renew* is another fascinating word. It means to renovate or to restore to its original state.[12] If you renovate something, you take out old things and put in new things. Recently, my wife and I renovated our house. We took out carpeting and put in wood floors. We took out old furniture and put in brand new furniture. We took out an old door and put in a new door. We got rid of the old and replaced it with the new.

The same holds true for our lives. If you don't like the output (manifestation), you have to change the input. We understand this in computer language: *Garbage in, garbage out*. Even though we know the truth of that saying, when we don't like the output, most of the time we keep focusing on the output. Remember the 6 Kingdom Laws we talked about in Chapter 1? One of the laws, the Law of Correspondence, states that your outward world directly corresponds to your inward world.[13] If you want to change your output, you must change your input.

To achieve a new level of living, you have to get rid of your old ways of thinking and replace them with new revelation thoughts. Once new dominant thoughts take root in your heart, they will bring about new actions that result in new manifestations. Proverbs 23:7 tells us, "As a man thinks in his heart so is he." The term *think* used here means doorkeeper or gatekeeper.[14] In other words, dominant thoughts are the gatekeeper to your heart. What gets in your heart is what you are going to do. This does not mean it will maybe, possibly, or probably happen—it *will* happen. You will do whatever is in your heart. The missing ingredient of heart beliefs is the answer to everything.

Proverbs 4:23 amplifies this important truth, "Above all else guard your heart, for out of it comes the issues of life" (NIV/KJV). There are several things to take note of here:

First, *above all else* means the highest priority. Sincere Believer, I can't tell you anything more important. Guard your heart, for it will produce the manifestations or outcomes of your life.

Second, guard your heart, for out of it comes the *issues* of life. This term, *issues,* means boundaries, limitations, or stagnations.[15] Boundaries you have in life are **not** the product of your background, education, or race (by themselves). They are **not** about what your mother or father said or what your friends did to you. They are about the meaning you assigned to them. Your boundaries are about one thing – what you have allowed into your heart. If you want to change the manifestations, limitations, or boundaries of your life, you must change your heart.

The question becomes how is that done? So often we say things that we don't truly know what they mean. We say, *you've got to believe from your heart*, or *do it from your heart*. Well, what does that mean? How do I do that?

Hebrews 4:12 helps put this in perspective, "For the Word of God is living and active (NIV), sharper than any two-edged sword, piercing even to the dividing asunder of soul and Spirit, and of the joints and marrow, and is a discerner of the thoughts and intents of the heart" (KJV).[16] This verse says the Word of God formulates itself as a discerner of the thoughts and intents of the heart. This verse is primarily about the Word of God, but it defines the heart as well.

Here is how it breaks down: "The Word of God is sharper than any two-edged sword." There is a reason why the author of Hebrews used this term. The common weapon of this era was a one-edged sword. The Roman Empire had just pioneered a two-edged sword, a sword that cut on both sides. The Word is *sharp-*

er than a two-edged sword. This innovation turned the Roman armies into the most powerful force on earth. The writer is using an analogy to show us that the Word of God is more powerful than any existing weapon. The writer further says God's Word is *alive and energized*. In other words, it has the energy to fulfill what it says – the will of God for your life.

The purpose of this sword (Word) is to pierce the heart[17] and to *divide asunder* the various aspects of the heart. The term *divide asunder* means to separate for the purpose of distinction. The question becomes what is it distinguishing? What is the heart?

Hebrews 4:12 tells us what the heart is:

There are two aspects of the heart that the Word penetrates and separates; the soul and the spirit.[18] The job of the heart is to mediate the soul by the spirit. When these two aspects line up, nothing is impossible with God. It is here then that the power of God is released.

Your spirit is the place where God dwells. It is the place where He speaks to you (Rom. 8:10, 16). The soul is your mind, will, emotions and imagination.[19] Your spirit man is a new creation and is perfect (2 Cor. 5:17; Heb. 12:23). The soul, however, must be renewed with God's Truth. That is the only way you will be able to make His promises work in your life. Therefore, the job of your heart is to line up the soul with the spirit. When these two forces are in agreement, this is where faith releases the energy and power of God in people's lives. The Word divides and discerns the thoughts and intents of the heart. Thoughts precede actions, and intents (moral understanding or conscience)[20] precede thoughts. Like the marrow feeds the joint so it will work, our intents (beliefs) feed our thoughts which drive our actions. God made man to operate out of his spirit, but he is often sabotaged by a soul not aligned with its intent.

The problem is that most people operate out of their soul rather than their spirit. Here is what happens. You will never rise above the image you have of yourself in your heart. Events or a set of circumstances when established create an image (imagination) in your heart. Such images solicit emotions. According to research, emotions travel 80,000 times faster than thoughts.[21] This is why you are mostly affected by your emotions rather than principles. This is why sometimes we say we believe things we don't see. In turn, your emotions affect your will, your will affects your mind, and your mind affects your actions (what you will or will not do). If we do not line up our lives to Kingdom principles, then our un-renewed soul will wreak havoc on our lives, and we miss the resources and provisions of God's Kingdom. However, the opposite is true as well. If our mind is renewed by truth that encounters us emotionally, it will affect our will, mind and actions positively. The result is provision, abundance and positive change.

Your mind is made up of two aspects: the conscious mind and the subconscious mind. The job of the conscious mind is to analyze new information, compare it with current information and determine truth in your life. The subconscious mind is like a huge data bank that records every thought, idea, emotion, or experience. It will make sure your words and actions stay in line with your self-image. Its job is to make whatever you've determined is true come to pass. This part of your mind, the subconscious mind, creates habits, comfort zones and consistency. This way, you don't have to learn things over and over. The subconscious mind creates an automatic response system and is where your personal belief system exists. Psychologists suggest that 90 to 95 percent of your daily decisions come out of your subconscious mind.

The repercussions and effects of this are obvious. As long as the conscious mind tells the subconscious mind truth that is healthy and productive, this is an incredible system. It creates healthy heart beliefs. If, however, through experiences and improper training the conscious mind has adopted "beliefs" (truths) that are contrary to the Word of God, it will produce wrong responses and actions that limit us and prevent us from growing in corresponding areas. Though we have an unlimited Gospel, many of us are leading a limited life because of our un-renewed subconscious minds.

Let me give you an example of how these two aspects of the mind work. If I taught you how to drive a car, you would first learn to drive at a conscious level. Everything would be very mechanical for you. Remembering how things work – the steering wheel, clutch, brake, accelerator, speedometer, etc. Once this process becomes a learned procedure (habit) by going from the conscious level to a subconscious level, you lose the discomfort of the rote mechanical process. In fact, many people can drive while listening to the radio, having a conversation and talking on a cell phone all at the same time. That's because the subconscious mind has created a habit and a comfort zone.

In most areas of your life the subconscious mind creates habits, personal belief systems, and comfort zones. The job of the subconscious mind is to create consistency. So, it strives to keep you in that comfort zone, so much so that if you violate it without new programming, it will work to keep you there even if it has to sabotage you.

This is what some psychologists call a "set-point." A set-point is a mindset (Rom. 8:5, 6) or a self-limiting belief. This is similar to flying an airplane and setting the automatic pilot at 30,000 feet. The automatic pilot's job is to maintain the preset altitude. If I grabbed the controls and ascended to 35,000 feet or descended to 25,000 feet, once I release the controls the plane would return to 30,000 feet.

This is exactly how the subconscious mind works. Its job is to create habits that keep you consistent with preset beliefs. If those beliefs are healthy and productive, that becomes a real benefit. However, if your habits and beliefs are unproductive or destructive, they place limitations on your life. Your subconscious mind must be renewed to the truth in order to break set-points, or those self-limiting beliefs that prevent you from experiencing what God has provided for you.

This is why studies have revealed that 80 percent of lottery winners who win millions of dollars end up back where they started or bankrupt after a relatively short period of time. It is why so many people yoyo on diets. Somewhere around 80-95% of people who lose weight on diets return to their original weight. It is why 95 percent of people earn around the same salary as their parents when adjusted by inflation. Your subconscious mind will try to keep you aligned with how your self-image perceives itself. It is also one of the key reasons why pastors or sales representatives can't break certain number barriers. The subconscious mind will actually work to keep you at the same comfort zone, or it will sabotage your efforts unless your mind is renewed. Your thinking at the subconscious level creates comfort zones that ultimately affect your destiny.

Dominant thoughts that you let in your heart determine the boundaries of your life. There is a study called Neurocardiology. Neurocardiology has discovered that the heart is a thinking organ. The philosophical or metaphorical heart and the physical heart interact. The physical heart may not have intellectual knowledge, but it does possess intuitive and emotional knowledge.[22] The heart possesses as many neurons as the brain.[23]   The neural pathway is how the body communicates. Each neuron contains memories (protein libraries). Every memory goes to every cell in your body and has the potential to change your DNA. Dominant thoughts get in your heart. What's in your heart is what you are going to do (Prov. 23:7).[24]I know it sounds like a new infomercial … another gimmick health ad from Ms. Hydroxycut or Mr. 5 Hour Energy. However, it is worth considering the latest research findings. The latest research shows that creating new dominant thoughts can change your DNA. Mr. Eric R Kandel denotes that thoughts, even imaginations, get under the skin of our DNA and can turn genes on and off.[25] Again, it sounds like an infomercial – change your mind, change your genes. However, dominant thoughts can change the structure of neurons in the brain.[26] The mind was designed to control your body. However, the heart is designed to feed the brain intuitive information from God's design.

Thoughts only have the meaning (and power) we give them. Your DNA actually changes shape according to dominant thoughts. Dr. Herbert Benson declares that positive and negative thoughts affect our body's ability to heal[27] for good or bad.

How are new dominant personal beliefs created? Consistent thoughts grow protein libraries[28] that hold memories, which, in fact, we call thoughts. Every cell in your body is connected to your heart. Thus, the mind provides knowledge, the heart provides intuitive knowledge and regulates emotions to your body. What we think about goes into every cell of our being. Renewing your mind, establishing your heart and transforming your personal belief system determines your destiny.

Let me give you a classic example from history that illustrates this point. In 1953, no runner had ever broken the four-minute mile barrier. In fact, many thought it was impossible. Some physicians and trainers of the era even believed it could not be accomplished without damaging a person's heart and possibly resulting in death. Despite the prevalent mindset of the day, one man in England, Roger Bannister, believed it could be done. He put himself through rigorous mental and physical training. In 1954, he became the first man to break the four-minute barrier. The impossible became possible.

Here is what's really amazing about the feat. Once Bannister did it, someone else broke his record within one month. Before the end of the year, six others broke the four-minute mile. Within another year, sixty people had broken the barrier. When people thought it was impossible, it was impossible. When a man believed in his heart, and changed his thinking, what was considered to be impossible became possible.

Many of us have become conditioned to think certain things are impossible for people like us. However, if you will understand what Jesus' death has already provided (Eph. 1:3; 2 Pet. 1:3), change your thinking, establish your heart and transform your personal belief system, what was impossible will become possible for you.

PRINCIPLE # 4: Prove the Will of God

Romans 12:2 admonishes us in the fourth principle, "To prove what is the good, acceptable and perfect will of God." The term *prove* means *to establish as genuine, approve, validate, discern, to recognize, revelation or by implication to manifest.*[29]

Once you are no longer conformed to this world's system (breaking free from its limitations), but instead are transformed to a higher way of thinking (by renewing your mind and establishing your heart), you will be able to recognize, validate and manifest God's will for your life. It's time to think differently and live life the way God intended.

Renewed thinking and a transformed heart result in a recognition of heaven's resources and open the doors to God's Kingdom. During a meeting with Oral Roberts one day, he told me "Miracles are coming to us all the time. People either receive them, or they pass by them." It is really a matter of whether people recognize them or not.

In your brain, there is something that causes you to filter out unimportant information and focus on what you consider to be meaningful facts or opportunities. It is called the Reticular Activating System (RAS).

There are three aspects to RAS:

1. *Positive Focusing* – An example of positive focusing might be when a party is taking place in a noisy room and down the hallway comes the faint cry of a baby. No one hears the baby except the mother. Why? Because she is focused on her baby.

2. *Negative Filtering* – An example of this is a person who has a home near an airport. You may wonder how they could sleep in a house with planes flying over frequently. The occupants of this home have no trouble because they have filtered the noise out of their thinking.

3. *Individual Perception* – This occurs when two people see the same accident but give two totally different accounts. Why? They each had a different vantage point or perception of what happened.

RAS causes you to filter unimportant information and focus on what is important for the moment according to your dominant thoughts. It immediately transmits vital information into your consciousness and causes you to recognize things you might otherwise miss.

The fundamental factor to these four renewal principles is this. Once you follow them, you will begin to see things from a different perspective. If you are not conformed to this world's system (see appendix at the end of Chapter 2), then you filter out its system and focus in on God's system. When your mind is transformed and your heart is established (your soul and spirit are lined up to truth), you will be able to perceive and receive the provision of God's limitless Kingdom, which is now at your disposal. The Holy Spirit will bring to you people, ideas and resources according to your most dominant thoughts. A renewed mind recognizes thoughts that line up with the Kingdom and finds a way to bring them to pass.

This is the dominant law in the Kingdom of God. We attract to ourselves according to our dominant images and renewed thinking. You will invariably attract from God people, ideas and resources that line up with His Kingdom.

Your renewed thinking dominates what you manifest in life more than any other Kingdom key. It is essential for you to understand that your subconscious mind (personal belief system) cannot tell the difference between what is real or imagined or what is positive or negative. It simply recognizes dominant thoughts and acts on them. Thus, it concentrates its efforts to make those things come to pass. The subconscious mind is impersonal. It does not act according to what is good or bad for you, only according to what it is told is truth. It simply manifests what you are thinking. So when people use dominant thoughts like, *I can't handle this work load, I'm not really valuable, There's not enough time, Nobody wants to hear from me, I do not want debt,* your subconscious mind begins to work to make these dominant thoughts come to pass. Thus, the Law of Attraction is working whether you know it or not. That is what Henry Ford said: "Whether you think you can or can't, either way you are right."

Now that we've established the foundational principles for living a life without limits, let's turn our attention to how we make these principles work. There are keys to what I call Productivity Theology, which is simply a practical theology that produces results in our lives.

Keys for Reflection

1. The missing ingredient to your success is renewing your mind to create new heart beliefs. Can you see how not knowing the missing ingredient could sabotage your success? Can you site some specific examples?

2. How does Romans 12:2 give you a new perspective on life?

3. Look at the 4 Principles of Romans 12:2. Give a personal reflection on how each of the 4 principles affect your productivity?

   a. Not conformed to the world's system
   b. Be transformed
   c. By renewing your mind
   d. Prove the will of God

4. Look at the 5-fold process of repentance. Does this change your mind about what repentance is? Why or why not?

APPENDIX – Chapter 2

The World's System vs. God's System		
#	World's System	God's System
1	Lust	Love
2	Drugs/alcohol	Peace
3	Pills	Joy
4	Desire to quit, not finish	Perseverance
5	Hoarding/stingy	Giving
6	Tempted to cheat	Integrity
7	Selfishness	Goodness
8	Self-effort	Self-control
9	Trying	Trusting

CHAPTER 3

PRODUCTIVITY THEOLOGY

THEME: PRACTICAL APPLICATION TO THE SOLUTION TO ROMANS 12:2.

Lesson: Learn the 4 C's application to Romans 12:2.

It is essential that we take the four Kingdom Principles found in Romans 12:2 and convert them to *Productivity Theology*—a practical theology that produces results for your life. Nobody truly wants Christianity, no matter how true it is, if they cannot get it to work. We often limit ourselves by what we think is possible. This is particularly demonstrated in the amazing story of Cliff Young.

In 1983, Cliff Young set a new record for the six hundred km race (for us Americans that is 372.8 miles) in his native country of Australia. He not only broke the record, he shattered it by thirty-six hours. What makes the feat even more amazing is that he was sixty-one years old when he did it. Astonishingly, Cliff Young was not a world-class athlete. He was a mere farmer who didn't realize that what he was doing was impossible.

All trained athletes who run this race know that the proper strategy is to run eighteen hours and then rest six hours. You run those intervals like clockwork until you complete the race. You go from race to restoration to race. The only problem was no one explained this methodology to Cliff Young. Cliff simply assumed one was supposed to run the race straight through without stopping. Unwittingly, he ran the race straight through and demolished the world record!

The biggest limitation on our lives is what we think is possible. It's like the old adage of the bumblebee who doesn't know that his wings are too small to allow him to fly. Thus, he flies anyway. Most of our limitations are self-imposed. When we learn to remove those limitations by learning who we truly are in Christ, we will soar to new heights in every part of our lives.

Paul helps us understand how to take the impossible to the possible. He shows the paramount truth to take you beyond the limitation of your current thinking. Look at this thought in Ephesians 3:20, "Now to Him who is able to do exceedingly abundantly above all that we can ask or think (imagine – Moffett; conceive – NEB[1]) according to the power that works in us." We generally approach this as a doxology to Paul's prayer in Ephesians to how infinite God is. While that is true, look what happens when you break this verse down:

- **Able** – Having the skill to, qualified, dormant ability or power not yet come to pass.[2] Notice this is potential power. It is the ability unrealized.

- **Do** – Perform, carry out, fulfill, bring to pass, produce, in exhaustive power.[3] God doesn't just intend for something to happen, He will carry it out.

- **Exceedingly** – To go beyond the limits, surpass, outdo, greater.[4] Limitless!

- **Abundantly** – Superabundant in quantity, superior in quantity, excess, surplus, superfluous (more than needed), excessive.[5] Greek scholars call this term (huperekperissou) a super superlative meaning as much as or easily more than.[6] It is beyond expression.

- **Beyond** – Farther than, outside the reach of what you think is a possibility, more than.[7]
- **Ask** – Desire or a craving one is willing to sacrifice for, inquire (not a casual inquiry).[8] The idea is I asked for a cupful, but there is an ocean left.[9]
- **Think** – To form in the mind, a belief, to expect, resolve, intend, mental concentration, reflect, meditations.[10] He is able to do what we think, then add to it.
- **Imagine (Moffett)** – Creating a picture that has never been seen, meditation (murmur, mutter, utter, ponder, muse, stretch, see beyond, remedy), creating a mentality that has never been seen before[11] (up to this point). It is important to note that the subconscious mind can't tell the difference between what is real and what is imagined. It will take a dominant thought and make it come to pass. Meditation is the key to transforming your Personal Belief System.
- **According** – Agreement, harmony, conformity, capacity,[12] in proportion to the donor.[13]
- **Power** – Miracle power of influence, ability, energy, abundance, might, enablement.[14]
- **At work in us** – Not trying to get God to do what He has already done. In other words, receive what He did by grace through faith. It is a recognition that His finished work is active in you, presently.

Before I give you the full ramification of this verse, let me uniquely outline it.

God is:

Able to do

Able to do what we ask

Able to do what we think

Able to do what we ask or think

Able to do above what we ask or think

Able to do abundantly above what we ask or think[15]

According to his power at work in us presently. (Eph. 3:20)

Please notice in all the details of this verse is the extraordinary revelation that God doesn't release all of this abundance independent of you, but through what you think, imagine and conceive in accordance with what His finished work has already accomplished in you. When your thinking is renewed to this understanding, the limits of God's provision are removed from your life. The composite of this amazing little verse begins to help us understand the scope of what God intends to unfold for our life. Living a life without limits is about coming face-to-face with barriers and busting them. God takes what you create as dominant thoughts and exceeds them.

In essence, Philemon 6 tells us the same thing, "that the communication (communion, fellowship, partnership, distribution, release)[16] of your faith" [going from things desired, to things possessed, conviction, to see what is real, though it is unseen.]

When the unseen is as real as the seen, the unseen will dominate the seen, become effectual [operative, working, efficient, effective] [17] "by acknowledging every good thing in you in Christ Jesus" (emphasis added). In other words, God has set us up for success if we can change our thinking to see what He has already done in His finished work.

How do we apply the Romans 12:2 principles to change our thinking, renew our minds, establish our hearts and transform our personal belief systems? First, let's review the four principles:

1. **Do not be conformed** to this world's system
2. **Be transformed** (to the Kingdom's system)
3. **By the renewing of your mind**
4. **And, prove** (recognize and seize) the will of God.

These principles form a pattern to help us recognize our new identity in Christ. 2 Corinthians 5:17 states, "Therefore if any man be in Christ, he is a new creation"[18] [You are given new spiritual DNA, become a new species of being. What you once were no longer exists in your spirit. Your body and makeup remain the same. If you were bald, you're still bald. If you were short, you're still short.] "Old things have passed away, the old is gone. The new is come." This verse reveals the difference in living between the old covenant and the new covenant. It is no longer people trying to live for God (alone) (Gal. 2:20; 1 Jn. 4:9), but living through Him (and His finished work). This is a real encounter with God that gives people a new spirit, a new nature and a new destiny. Once you are born again, God creates a new nature in you. You now have new inherent tendencies, new instincts and an inborn character that comes from God. Your spirit is new, but your mind and heart must be renewed to it.

You are not a person with two natures, God has given you a new one (Rom. 6:6). The problem with most believers is that after they become a new creation, they tend to operate out of their old identity. They don't see themselves as a new person. The exhortation here is to no longer think in terms of your old nature, but to see yourself in the new identity (new creation) that God has now given you (Eph. 4:20-24; Col. 3:10).

Your old nature (old self, old habits, old thought processes) is nothing more than the habit of the flesh. The flesh is man's futile attempt to try to do God's will in his own way or strength. The only real reason a person sins is to try to meet a need in their lives. Thus, a person will lust as a substitute for love and sensitivity (Eph. 4:17-19). Greed is a selfish substitute for true prosperity. It is the world's system that negates God's Kingdom. The key is to renew your mind and heart to God's system.

This dismissal of the old nature is what scripture calls crucifying the flesh, or dying to self. The scientific definition of death means *to fall out of correspondence with*[19] (Eph. 4:22-24). When I *die to self*, I fall out of correspondence with my old identity and now recognize who God made me to be. I no longer see my life out of the lens of my old perspective. My new nature gives me a new image of my life. This shift in perspective does more to change a person and allow them to see God's will than almost anything I know.

This is what Jesus is communicating to us in the Parable of the Sower (Matt. 13:1-23). He first tells us the Word of God must be sown in the heart, or it won't produce results (verses 11-15). The problem with most of us is we have substituted intellectual knowledge for heart knowledge and wonder why we can't get God's Word to work. There is a difference between mere knowledge and understanding (verse 19 – revelation). Understanding cultivates the soil of the heart. Unless there is uninterrupted cultivation it will **stunt the fruit**. Jesus puts all of this into perspective by noting, "the secrets of the Kingdom of heaven have been given to you [disciples] and not to them" [unbelievers]. "Whoever has been given more, he will have abundance. Whoever does not have, even what he has will be taken from him." (13:11-12). In other words, you get more of what you have. Thus, how do we take the 4 Principles of Romans 12:2 and get the Word in our hearts? We start by using the keys to renew our mind and establish our heart.

4 Keys to a Renewed Mind and an Established Heart

The real question becomes how do I renew my mind and establish my heart in accordance to these four transforming principles found in Romans 12:2? It is essential to understand that this process must be intentional on your part. It will not happen automatically. By learning to set our intention we can target growth and productivity on purpose. The scientific community has started catching up to the Bible and is making some startling discoveries on how to target change. The good news is, there is not only a prescribed way to do it, but they've discovered the time table it takes to accomplish it.

In the 1960s, Dr. Maxwell Maltz was a very successful reconstructive and cosmetic facial surgeon. Though he had given his patients the perfect faces they wanted, he noticed that many of them still suffered from deep personal scars of insecurity on the inside. He discovered that changing the outside of man doesn't always provide the transformation he truly desires. Maltz eventually decided to move from treating "outer scars" to trying to heal "inner scars" in the people on which he had operated. He went on to become the father of Psycho-Cybernetics, a system of thought for self-improvement. He believed that people had distorted perceptions of themselves because of wrong beliefs in their subconscious mind, so he sought to help them with his new philosophy.

During his medical studies on people who had undergone amputation, Maltz learned an interesting fact about behavioral modification. He discovered that a person who lost a limb "experienced" a phantom limb for around three weeks after the operation. In other words, even though the limb was gone, the person felt like they still possessed the limb and would often try to use it for about three weeks. The conclusion was, it takes about three weeks to change thoughts.

Maltz applied the same theory to behavioral change and found similar concurrences. It takes twenty-one days to create a new habit. No matter where you are in life, you can change the course of your life in three weeks.

Now, here is a central key to transforming your life—ideas and actions contrary to a person's core value system (spirit) will not be accepted or acted upon if they are contrary to a person's personal belief system (soul). Proverbs 4:23 tells us about how our boundaries are established: "Above all else, guard your heart, for it is the issue [boundary – in Hebrew] of life."

I may say to you, *Prayer will change your life. Prayer will change your church. Prayer will change your city.* You may nod your head in agreement with what you know to be true on the surface, but in your Personal Belief System, you prayed for someone once and they died, or you didn't get the result you anticipated. Chances are you aren't praying consistently.

A similar example might be prosperity. Someone may say to you, "Give and you shall receive" (Lk. 6:38). The Laws of Reciprocity and Attraction state, "As a man sows, so shall he also reap" (Gal. 6:7). But in your Personal Belief System, you see giving as a depletion of your resources, or you think you know someone who gives but they are still struggling. Chances are that you will not be a person who tithes even though the Scripture plainly says, "I will open the windows of heaven" (Malachi 3:10) in reference to your giving.

God has given you an innate ability to create and be productive. The real question comes down to how do you make the renewing of the mind process applicable so that you can attract the Kingdom to yourself? How do I create new thoughts and habits for productivity?

The ongoing problem is that you are giving mental ascent to truth that is contrary to what you really believe in your heart. Similarly, people try to break limitations off their lives, but they fall back into old mindsets because of certain set-points in their thinking. Psychologist Sigmund Freud writes on what he called *The Pain/Pleasure Principle*.[20] His assertion was that people will always make decisions based on what they see as pleasure and to avoid what they see as pain. Let's use pornography as an example. If a person views pornography as pleasure and God stopping him as pain, it will be virtually impossible to break the habit with any permanence. If, however, the person sees God's blessing as pleasure and pornography as pain keeping him from the blessing, breaking the habit will be much easier. The pain/pleasure principle affects a person's Personal Belief System and the time that it takes to change habits.

Most people are predisposed to making excuses for their shortcomings. George Washington Carver once said, "Ninety-nine percent of all failure comes from people who have a habit of making excuses." The moment we begin to blame someone or something else, we unwittingly disempower ourselves from being able to conquer our boundaries.

Earl Nightingale said, "Study anything for 1 hour per day for 5 years and you will become an expert on that topic." In other words, you don't have to settle for your present limitation, you can break your present barriers.

This leads us to the application of Romans 12:2. The application can be summarized using four words that begin with "C"—cognitive dissonance, confession, consistency and conation.

4 C's to Apply Romans 12:2

1. The first application is *cognitive dissonance*: This is a fancy psychological word that simply means mental discord. The first step to changing our Personal Belief System is to understand the source of our thinking. Our homes, our schools, our parents, our teachers, our churches, our friends, even something called cellular images (covered in the next chapter), etc., have all helped create mindsets, set-points and expectations in our lives. Once a very significant person in my life told me, *you will never amount to anything.* I thought to myself, *if this person loved me and this is what they saw, it must be true.* Invariably, every time I got ready to break through to a new level in my life, I would sabotage myself and remain at the same level. In the deepest part of my being, my subconscious mind believed I wouldn't amount to anything. Many people can't break certain limitations because of similar cognitive dissonance they have experienced in life.

James Allen, the author of *As a Man Thinketh*, says, a *plan consistently, persistently adhered to, good or bad, in abundance or scarcity, will produce results in a person's life.* It is Proverbs 4:23 bringing the *issues of the heart* (boundaries) to fruition.

Cognitive Dissonance simply means duality or duplicity in a person's thinking. It is what we find explained in James 1: 6-8, "But when he asks, he must believe and not doubt, because he who doubts is like a wave of the sea, blown and tossed by the wind. That man should not think he will receive anything from the Lord; he is a double-minded man, unstable in all he does."

The term used for "double-minded" here means "double souled."[21] In other words, your mind, will, emotions, and imagination are vacillating in opinion or purpose and creating doubt. Your soul is vacillating in opinion from what your spirit is saying and creating a divided heart (Hosea 10:2). The result is an unstable person, fluctuating or incongruent in his ways or his willingness to do something. A divided heart causes a person to either sabotage his own efforts or create an apprehension to step out and try. When core values and personal beliefs are in conflict, it creates immobilization, and a person remains fixed in their present state.

How does a person overcome cognitive dissonance? Psychologists encourage *Cognitive Restructuring* in order to stop "double-mindedness." *Cognitive Restructuring* has two steps:

Step 1 is **Emotional Implantation**. Emotional implantation is when someone or something "yanks your chain," and suddenly you realize you don't have to be this way anymore. Let me give you an example of this principle. Everyone knows the story of Ebenezer Scrooge. Here's the real question. What caused Scrooge to go from miser to philanthropist overnight? The answer is simple. He saw the Ghost of Christmas Past, Present and Future. He had an emotional implantation. Suddenly, he realized the course of his life was heading the wrong way, and he saw the need to change before it was too late.

For us as believers, this means we have a divine encounter with God or a revelation of truth that alters our perception. Sometimes it is a special touch from God as we are praying and reading His Word. It's our repent (change our thinking) experience. Unfortunately, most of us leave it there. We miss the critical second step.

Step 2 is **Repetition**. You simply rehearse your new thought or identity over and over again, until you create a new habit or thought process (heart belief). How long does this take? According to Maxwell Maltz, it takes 21 days. Some psychologists say it takes 30 days, and others say 42 or even 60 days. The Pain/Pleasure Principle can affect the length of time for the change, but change can be targeted and brought to resolve in a fairly short period of time.

Often in working with people I can help them get to a root self-limiting belief in a relatively short period of time. It is essential to do so. Finding the root of an emotional implantation is important; the problem, however, is that most people end their pursuit at this point. Repetition is equally important. Twenty-one days is the minimum time it takes to build a new dominant thought and neural network[22] (an ability to reach an interconnected group of neurons to communicate to the body). If this repetitive reinforcement doesn't take place repetitively over twenty-one days the neural network will decay in less than a month. If new dominant thoughts are not established it will denature (take natural qualities away and the new memory will disassemble.)[23]

This is fancy rhetoric to suggest that the new thought will not become a new dominant thought that will get into the heart. Twenty-one days is only the target time. Sometimes the process is slowed by what we refer to as the Pain/Pleasure Principle before it becomes an auto-pilot belief (subconscious or heart belief) or achieves automatization. The average person will try something for a week (7 days) or two (14 days) and feel a momentary blast of energy before returning subsequently to status quo. Again, it may take 21 days, 30 days, 42 days or 60 days. The key is to stick with it until a new dominant thought gets in your heart. You can tell this has taken place because you will see things from a different vantage point.

The real key is this—you don't see things as *they* are; you see things as *you* are in your heart. If you have a wrong image of yourself, it colors the way you see life. We'll discuss more on that in the next chapter. F. F. Bosworth once said, "It is impossible to claim by faith what you do not know is the will of God." Faith begins where the will of God is known (in the heart).

2. The second application is Confession. Joshua 1: 8, says, "Do not let this Book of the law depart from your mouth; meditate on it day and night, so that you may be careful to do everything written in it. Then you will be prosperous and then you will have good success." The next three principles come out of this verse. "Do not let this Book of the law depart from your mouth" which means let the Word continuously be on your lips ... confess it continually. There's been much written about confession in the last twenty years. It is similar to what psychologists call "self-talk" or affirmations. Some even suggest 95 percent of your emotions are determined by the way you talk to yourself.[24] Several years ago, I had the privilege of listening, via tape, to Lou Tice of the Pacific Institute. On a tape concerning "self-talk," he referred to the study of Psycho-linguistics. He said it was not only important to confess something, but how you confess it makes all the difference in the world. He said, "if you simply confess something, it goes into your Personal Belief System (PBS) about 10 percent. If you confess it with imagination, your PBS retains about 55 percent. If you confess with imagination and emotion, it will go into your Personal Belief System 100 percent."

Here is what this means. Confession or declaring the truth of God's Word by itself won't transform your Personal Belief System. Along with confession you need imagination. Imagination (Eph. 3:20) is the ability to see without limitation. It is a form of biblical meditation that allows you to see yourself according to the truth and to intentionally increase your faith. In other words, see yourself in your mind in a way that is aligned with His truth. When done repeatedly, this allows the conscious mind to give the subconscious mind new truth. Then, your subconscious mind can work with the Holy Spirit to make it come to pass. Lastly, do it with emotion. How do you do that? Two ways: One – use emotional words. Remember, an emotion travels 80,000 times faster than a thought. Two – allow yourself to have the feelings you would experience if your goal was already realized. This reinforces your subconscious mind to think of itself aligned to your goal. Feelings empower you to the fact that the truth in you is possible. Here is an example: *I am excited about* (or enjoy, love) *making* (an amount of money) *per year*. Your goal should be increase and that goal should be within what is real for you.

There is a second set of principles that govern confession. Some psychologists and motivators who promote "confession" contend that this practice should also be linked to the 3 P's:

- Personal – Make it personal, use "I."
- Positive – Make it positive. Never focus on the problem, but focus on the solution. Whatever your dominant thoughts are is what you will attract. Thinking about debt, for instance, attracts debt. For example, *I'm not going to eat as much* is focused on the problem and the future. Instead, say, *I'm excited about feeling fit and healthy at* (whatever) *weight*.
- Present Tense[25] – Also make it present tense, God lives in the eternal now. Thus, all confessions should begin with "I am."

Confess the truth of God's Word, picture yourself according to the truth and say and feel the emotion of the goal or result as a finished reality. This is calling the things that are not as though they were (Rom. 4:17).

This is why Romans 10 talks about confessing with your mouth and believing with your heart. Ancient Hebrews believed by memorizing Scripture and confessing with your mouth, the

Word went from your head to your heart. Listen to these verses, "But what does it say? The Word is near you; it is in your mouth and in your heart; that is the Word of faith we are proclaiming: That if you confess with your mouth and believe with your heart, you will be saved. For it is with the heart that you believe and are justified, and it is with your mouth you confess and are saved" (Sodzo or salvation, means to save, deliver, protect, heal, preserve, do well, make whole, rescue).[26] Your mouth affects your heart, and in turn, then your heart affects your mouth. Matthew 12:34 states, for *out of the abundance of the heart the mouth speaks*. Verse 35 even goes on to say, "The good man brings good things (good manifested) out of the good stored up in him and the evil man brings evil things (done) out of the evil stored up in him."

We store things in our heart by meditation (Ps. 1:1-2; 4:20-23; 37:4; Josh. 1: 8) and confession (Josh. 1: 8; Rom; 10: 8, 10; Mt. 12:34, 35). What is in our heart can be discerned by what comes out of our mouth. This affects what we believe, feel, and do. Ultimately, this will bring the manifestation of good success.

3. The third application is Consistency. Repetition is the key to all learning. Repetition (consistency) is the vehicle by which the subconscious mind sees a new image of you. You think something repeatedly until truth casts a new image in you.

How long does it take to create a new habit? Remember, it takes 21 days, 30 days, 42 days, 60 days … depending on the pain/pleasure principle, so be consistent. Repeatedly think the new thought until it becomes a habitual way of thinking.

4. Lastly, the fourth application is Conation. Conation is a psychology term that means *to make an effort or to pursue a thing or to act on what is known*.[27] A friend of mine who studied this term told me at its root it means, *You can't stop me unless you kill me*.[28] In other words, you must put some resolve into pursuing your dreams. If you desire something, then you must go after it with passion. Later we will talk about what the Bible means by "desire." Suffice it to say for now, according to Mark 11:22-24, the term *desire* means "wanting something for which you are willing to sacrifice."[29] a strong desire allows you to stand your ground until your Personal Belief System is established. This is what we see in Matthew 11:12, "From the days of John the Baptist until now the Kingdom has been forcefully advancing, and forceful men take hold of it."

Let me finish this amazing set of principles by giving an illustration from a personal experience. Early in my ministry, I had a leader in my church who had unsuccessfully tried to lead a local judge to the Lord. In frustration, he came to me and asked if I would visit his friend and share the Gospel. I agreed to do it. Later that day I left my pastoral office and got into my little pastoral car and took a little pastoral trip to this judge's house to do my pastoral duty. When I got to the judge's house, it was a beautiful spring day. The door was open, but a screen door shielded the entry. I knocked on the door and a hospice worker greeted me, let me in, and walked me down the corridor to his bedroom. What awaited me shocked the "pastoral" sense of duty out of me, as I came face to face with grim reality.

I had heard much about Judge Lee. I knew he was a big man, but what I witnessed as I entered his bedroom was a jolt into reality, as came face-to-face with a failing shell of humanity. His frail skeletal frame revealed a dying man.

Seeing his grim condition "rocked" me to the core of my being and stirred a deep-seated compassion in my heart. I knew I had to share the life of Jesus with this man, but I also realized I had no connection with him, no bridge to share the Gospel. So I asked this prestigious judge what he most liked in life. His answer was fishing. In all honesty, I hate fishing, but the next hour was consumed with talk of rods, lures, lines, bait, etc.

After that hour, we seemed to have a real connection. I looked at him and asked him if he had ever made Jesus the Savior and Lord of his life. He looked at me and assured me he was a good Baptist, but he had never made a personal decision for Christ. I led him in a prayer of salvation. At the conclusion of the prayer, I helped him understand his experience, and we exchanged some more pleasantries. As I got up to leave, the Holy Spirit stopped me in my tracks and said, *Tell the man he can be healed!*"

I mockingly said to myself, *But he doesn't believe in that sort of thing.* It was like I was expecting God to say, *Oh, I'm sorry, here I stopped you on the way out the door and everything.*

In the midst of my conviction, I turned to him and said, "Do you know you can be healed?"

"I've never heard of such a thing," he replied.

I told him I had a six-part series on faith I had just completed. I suggested that he listen to one tape per day until I visited him again next week.

When I arrived again the next week, it was the same scenario. It was a beautiful spring day, and I was once again greeted by a hospice worker who escorted me to his room. The scenario looked the same. It was the same disease, the same conditions, and the same frail man. When I looked at him, however, there was a little glint in his eyes. He looked at me and scowled, "Son, I didn't do what you told me. You told me to listen to one of these tapes per day for six days until we got together again. He continued, I didn't listen to one tape per day. I listened to all six tapes the first day, the second day, the third day, the fourth day, the fifth day, the sixth day, and today." He said, "Now, let me tell you what is going to happen. Next week when you come, I'll be sitting up in my bed. The next week, I'll be sitting next to my bed. The third week, I'll be sitting in my living room. After that, I'll be standing in your church telling your people about my healing."

That man prophesied his fate. The next week, he was sitting up in his bed. The week after that, he sat next to the bed. The third week, he was sitting in the living room. When I got there the fourth week, there was nobody home. The following week the judge showed up in my church, took a microphone and proclaimed that the doctors in Houston had astonishingly proclaimed him cancer free.

Now, what happened to this judge? His cognitive dissonance (doubled-mindedness) had an emotional implantation. He came to a realization that things don't always have to be a certain way. Through the repetition and meditation (implantation) of the Word of God, it brought forth a new image on the inside of him and a confession of his mouth. This process brought forth a co-nation experience, transformed him by the renewing of his mind, and broke his limitation and brought or attracted his manifestation of healing.

This is God's will for your life: to not be conformed to this world's system → but to be transformed → by the renewing of your mind → that God can bring forth His manifestation in you. Your double-mindedness will give way to a revelation. That revelation, through repetition, will change the words of your mouth and break the limitations off of your life.

Now, I want to expand on how this application can alter your image for relationships, prosperity, success and even healing and health. If you can see it, you can receive it.

Keys for Reflection

1. Explain how you view Ephesians 3:20. How does it affect your faith to reach your goals?

2. Review the material on "identity." What does that mean about who you are? Are you focused on your problems or are you focused on your identity?

3. The Parable of the Sower in Matthew 13:1-23 tells us the key to success is sowing the Word of God into our hearts to create heart beliefs. In what areas do you want to create heart beliefs?

4. What areas in your life do you have boundaries or self-limiting beliefs?

5. Look at the 4 Applications to renewing your mind from Romans 12:2. Do you have areas in your life that you have cognitive dissonance or double-mindedness (prosperity, success, feeling loved, perseverance, healing, peace, faith)? Express how this has affected you pursuing your goals.

6. You cannot have positive results without positive words. Look at the 3 P's of Confession (Personal, Present Tense, and Positive). In what areas do you find yourself violating these? Choose a set of confessions in these areas and begin to meditate on them (use Barrier Busters as a guide).

CHAPTER 4

BARRIER BUSTERS

THEME: OVERCOMING THE DEVIL'S STRATEGY

Lesson: Identifying and overcoming the devil's
4 strategies to stopping heart beliefs.

A few years ago, when I served as Campus Pastor of Oral Roberts University, I was doing some research for a book I was writing. I had traveled to one of my favorite bookstores in Broken Arrow, Oklahoma (just outside of my hometown of Tulsa), to purchase some research materials. On my way back to Tulsa, it began to snow heavily. As I was driving back, I looked up and saw a Sherman Tank, something like a 1970's Chevy, coming toward me. I later learned that the driver behind the wheel was a young teenager who had only had his license for a relatively short time. You can tell this was a bad scenario from the start. Without any warning, the young man hit an icy spot, spun out of control, slid across the dividing line and hit me head on. The impact of the collision ricocheted me off of two other vehicles and knocked me fifty feet off the street into a snow-covered field. I was knocked unconscious. When I woke up, I didn't remember anything that had happened. All I knew was there was blood and glass everywhere, and I felt extreme pain on the left side of my body.

As a testimony to God's sustaining love, a Spirit-filled nurse stopped at the scene of the accident. She waded through the snow and reached through the broken wreckage of the vehicle, praying over me while monitoring my vital signs. In a matter of moments, EMSA arrived on the scene. My car was completely demolished. They had to remove the side of the vehicle with a chainsaw to extract me. Then, they raced me to the City of Faith Hospital.

As they wheeled me on a cart through the emergency room entrance, my wife, Judy, was already there waiting. The emergency team had contacted her and apprised her about the accident. When she looked down at me in the hospital, she was "greeted" by a face that was ripped to shreds, and the blood and glass that were everywhere. Later, a plastic surgeon on call would have to suture the pieces of my face back together. In perfect supernatural control, Judy took my hand and said, "Honey, God's here … everything's going to be all right."

Shortly after arriving, they ran a set of X-rays on me in the emergency room. After a while, the doctor came back holding an X-ray in her hand and said, "Mr. McIntosh, I'm sorry to tell you that you have a broken neck. You can see the break right here on the X-ray?"

Very calmly, I asked her, "What does that mean for me?"

Standing out of my peripheral vision, the doctor mouthed the words to my wife, "It's not good."

They took me upstairs to radiology to run a full set of X-rays on me. During that time, my friends from around the city started arriving at the hospital. Oral Roberts showed up. Along with him came his son Richard Roberts, President of Oral Roberts University, and his wife Lindsay, Pastor Billy Joe Daugherty, pastor of the 15,000 member Victory Christian Church, my brother Gary McIntosh, who pastors the largest church in the north side of Tulsa, and some others. Before they took the second set of X-rays, they all gathered around me to pray. (If you're going to have somebody pray for you for healing, it might as well be Oral Roberts). I remember Oral taking my hand and declaring, "It's time to pray!" When he finished praying, I didn't feel anything. I don't think he felt anything either, but I saw a flash vision of the basketball floor at ORU. I know it sounds like a strange way to get a touch from God, but inscribed down the side of the court was my fate: *Expect a Miracle.* Somehow, when I saw it I had a feeling everything was going to be all right.

A little while later, the doctor came back in to see us. Now, it was just Judy and me. Holding both sets of X-rays in her hand, she seemed confused. She looked at me and said, "Mr. McIntosh, this is somewhat confusing. Here are your two X-rays. You can see in the first X-ray where the break is. In the second X-ray, we don't find any break whatsoever." That was a miraculous encounter that changed the course of my life forever. I had been healed!

There is a divine principle attached to this story. It is this: *If you can't see it, you can't receive it!* Faith is the product of a renewed mind that changes the way you see things. You need to see yourself according to God's truth, not simply according to fact. What you see in the natural is not how things really are. God sees from a spiritual perspective based on His truth and promises. He wants us to learn to change our perspective and focus on His Word. The fact is you might have cancer, but the truth is, you are healed by the stripes of Jesus. *Truth is stronger than fact.*

The truth is that God wants you to live a life without limits (Jn. 10:10). The fact is most of us lead limited lives, even though we have a limitless Gospel. We seem to find ourselves stuck at the same point in our lives year after year. We are at the same point in our finances as we were last year at this time. Many people seem to end up at the same level in their health, their relationships, their ministries, their jobs, etc.

Now, if this is true, and God's real provision awaits us through this process of renewed thinking and an established heart, the devil will do everything in his power to orchestrate the demolition of this process.

That is exactly what Paul addresses in 2 Corinthians 10:3-5, "For though we live in the world, we do not wage war as the world does. The weapons we fight with are not the weapons of the world. On the contrary, they have divine power to demolish strongholds. We demolish arguments and every pretension that sets itself up against the knowledge of God, and we take captive every thought to make it obedient to Christ."

This is a passage about *spiritual warfare*. When I use that phrase, I don't mean going to the highest point in the city and yelling at the devil. You can see that this passage is about the battle waged in your thinking. If the devil can deceive us in our thinking, then he keeps us from receiving God's abundant blessings and provision.

You might be thinking, *If this missing ingredient of truth is so revolutionary, why is it not more prevalent revelation among people?* This is the enemy's strategy to weaken the impact of heart beliefs. We are going to examine some important truths about this passage. The enemy has a strategy I am about to reveal, repudiate and destroy. First, Paul says, "We live in this world, but we don't wage war as the world does." The weapons or tools we use are not of this world or the world's system. On the contrary, we attack them with divine power to dismantle **4 strategies used by our enemy**:

Strategy 1: Strongholds (verse 4) – A stronghold is anything that makes you feel powerless to change, though it is contrary to the Word of God. You might remember the story of Judge Lee in Chapter 3. His lack of healing was a stronghold because of a mentality of thinking that it was not possible.

Strategy 2: Arguments (verse 5) – The definition of the term *arguments* is two contrary opinions in your life, or what we call *cognitive dissonance*. Cognitive dissonance is what James 1:8 calls double-mindedness. Self-limiting beliefs are generally contrary opinions to the truth of God's Word. These confusing arguments generally come from the 5 elements of our Personal Belief System (we will look at these elements in Chapter 6) that supplant and negate God's Word and His provision in our lives.

Strategy 3: Imaginations (verse 5) – The same word for *arguments* is also translated *imaginations*. [1] This is essential to understand. Imaginations are both the problem to our limitations and the solution to our limitations. The key is to understand that you can never rise above the image you have of yourself in your heart. Remember, the Heart Math Institute declares that the heart is not simply an organ that pumps blood. It is a *thinking* organ. It may not be cognitive, but it has intuitive knowledge. It contains the memories of every cell in your body. You will never rise above the image you have of yourself in your heart. You are who you are based on what you believe in your heart. You do what you do based on what you believe in your heart. Contrarily, you do not do certain things based on what you believe in your heart.

Memories are stored in your cells (connected to your heart) in images. Ten percent of your memories are conscious memories, and the corresponding 90% of your memories are subconscious. [2] Submerged memories in your subconscious mind are either repressed memories or cellular memories. Repressed memories are memories that you block because of trauma and/or stress. Cellular memories have been a missing piece of the puzzle. Cellular memory is a subconscious memory stored in your cells – all of your cells. In the past, many scientists felt these memories were stored in your brain, but now they know they are stored in your cells.

They first discovered this phenomenon when documenting organ transplant recipients. They found they had the thoughts, feelings, dreams and even food cravings of the donor. These cellular memories are stored in the form of images.[3] Scientists discovered that people have the cellular memories of their parents and their parent's parents. Some of these pictures have untruths if left uncorrected. These cellular memories often can be wrong beliefs or self-limiting beliefs. According to the Heart Math Institute, if you continue to think about sad memories, painful memories, or angry memories and you focus on them for an extended period of time, you will not only be depleted emotionally but literally start to send your body into the stress response.

This is why this is so important. Research expert Dr. Bruce Lipton of Stanford University notes that 95% of all disease is stress related. The other 5% of disease is related to genetics or habits. Essentially, the one source of disease and illness is stress.[4]

What is stress? Stress is a state of mental or emotional strain resulting from traumatic or demanding circumstances. Stress was a God-created release to create a flight or fight response in an emergency. However, if stress exists for a long period of time – something will break. It ultimately deters and weakens your immune system. If stress is endured for a lengthy period of time, this allows disease to manifest. Again, 95% of disease is stress-related. Remember, these subconscious memories are stored as images.

Here is the incredible importance of this revelation. Images are the language of the heart.[5] The ability to display images internally is a process called *thought*.[6] If you learn to create new dominant thoughts in your heart, you can break any self-limiting beliefs.

You cannot transform *issues of the heart* (Proverbs 4:23), or outcomes, by mere willpower. According to Dr. Bruce Lipton, the **subconscious mind** is a million times more powerful than willpower.[7] Please buckle your seatbelts and lock down your tray tables. If stress can be removed, even your genes will heal. This identified, internal healing resource is so powerful it literally has a healing effect on damaged DNA.[8]

Here is the astonishing revelation of imaginations (or meditations):

- Memories are stored images in your cells.
- Images are the language of the heart.
- If you create new dominant thoughts (images) in your heart, you can transform any self-limiting belief.
- Negative memories continued over time create illness in the body.
- Creating new images in your heart over time creates new heart beliefs.
- Such heart beliefs release the immune system, which can heal anything including genes and even transform DNA.
- Professor William Tiller of Stanford University states, if there is one source of all problems, you could simply address the one thing to solve whatever the problem is. [9]
- If you had ten problems but one source, you could heal all ten at one time.
- Memories that cause damaging stress are often the source of not being willing to do things relationally. This may cause us not to step out for success, prosperity or may block healing. Heal the one thing and you virtually heal almost everything.
- Heart beliefs are the missing ingredient. Renewing the mind, establishing the heart and transforming your Per-

sonal Belief System is the missing ingredient to take you from where you are to where you want to be.

Strategy 4: Pretension is the last strategy of the world's system listed in 2 Corinthians 10:3-6. A pretense is something based on assumption. It is a perceived truth versus a real truth. It is the difference between fact and truth. The fact is you have some diagnosis (disease, failure, lack) but the truth is you are healed (cured, successful, prospering) by the finished work of Christ (Eph. 1:2, 3; 2 Pet. 1:3).

These 4 strategies of the enemy have one primary purpose – to create double-mindedness or confusion in the minds and hearts of believers who are destined for greatness. Second Corinthians 10:5 says it clearly, "All of these things [4 strategies] set themselves up against the knowledge of God." Self-limiting beliefs negate the knowledge of God. The knowledge of God in your heart (heart beliefs) is the key to every success in your life. Then Paul exhorts in verse 5b when he says, "We take captive every thought and make it obedient to Christ." Through creating new dominant thoughts in your heart, you can control your destiny. No force can stop the will of God rightly believed in your heart. Paul concludes with verse 6, "And we will be ready to punish every act of disobedience, once your obedience is complete." This is basically the Pain/Pleasure Principle. Once you discover your self-limiting belief and make it pain, and you make your new dominant thought of God's Word your pleasure, you will go toward pleasure and away from pain. You will always make decisions where there is the most evidence. You must create evidence according to His truth in love (Eph.4:15), and your destiny will explode.

Now, that may seem like a daunting task *to take every thought captive*. The fact is we have 60,000 thoughts per day. It seems improbable to recognize every one of them. Here is how it works, at least in part. When a circumstance happens, you experience a range of emotions. We are often taught that emotions or feelings are bad. In reality, they reveal what we believe at least in the moment. Let me give you an example. If I receive a bank statement that reveals less money than my ability to handle my financial obligations, even though it is not what I thought the facts were, it may cause me to stress or fear if I'm not grounded in God's Word concerning provision. If I immediately look to God as my source, I have Kingdom mentality. If I get filled with stress, anxiety or fear about it, then I've got to make my thoughts obedient to the truth to receive God's provision or act in a way to meet my obligations.

Solutions Break Barriers

Most sincere believers stay captive to either conscious or subconscious memories and unwittingly stay stuck at similar levels for a lifetime. The key for you to break barriers is not positive thinking, behavioral modification or coping mechanisms. Those *solutions* merely cover an existing issue that remains intact, even though the pain is muted. Research from Dr. Bruce Lipton, Dr. Alex Loyd and the Heart Math Institute indicate if stress (from being double-minded) can be removed, even genes will be healed. Again, the identified internal healing resources of the heart are so powerful they literally have a healing effect on damaged DNA. Double-mindedness or confusion is the cause of virtually every issue. This double-mindedness is the result of two things:

1. Cellular memory

2. Conflict between the head and the heart or the conscious mind versus the subconscious mind.

The result of this double-mindedness is stress. Stress mutes, reduces or shuts off the rational thinking process. The body and mind are capable of doing what seems impossible. However, they are controlled by our heart beliefs. That means our problems or limitations can be summed up by one thing – wrong beliefs.

Let me give you an example. I had a significant person in my life tell me, "You'll never amount to anything." This was said to me verbally as well as being exemplified. One day in my youth, I was told by another to help this individual who was fixing a faucet. I went out and offered my assistance. As I was verbalizing my offer to help him, he broke off the faucet with a wrench. His reaction was to berate me for distracting him. He continued his berating with animated actions and vivid vocabulary. His words were explicit. He used words like, *you will never amount to anything*, *stupid*, *idiotic*, while affixing blame toward me. I remember the emotions of fear, failure and loss of self-esteem. Did this person mean these words or was it an anger-filled explosion? Likely, it was the latter rather than the former. It didn't matter, however, because I had already assumed the position and mentality of an unsuccessful failure who would never amount to anything. The results were devastating. I spent years trying to validate myself. My R.A.S. (Reticular Activating System) had me conditioned to look for reinforcing self-sabotaging behavior. Every time I would get ready for a breakthrough I would sabotage myself, remembering my feelings of stress, fear and failure. It was not until I looked into a new mirror (Jas. 1:22-24) and saw a new image that I was able to *launch* into a new level of success and productivity.

Mirror, Mirror on the Wall

The simple question is, how do we recognize self-limiting beliefs and create a different image in our hearts to break barriers in our lives? James 1:22-24 holds the answer, "Be doers of the Word, not hearers only, deceiving your own selves. For if any be a hearer only and not a doer, he is like a man who looks at his face in the mirror and after looking at himself, goes away and immediately forgets what he looks like" (Author's combination of KJV and NIV). Listen to the same verse in The Message translation: "A man who hears the Word and does not apply it is like a man who forgets the image in the mirror just cast to him from the mirror." One of the first things you do when you get up in the morning is to look in the mirror. Do you like what you see? I do not know why, but there seems to be a metamorphous of sorts that transpires at nighttime. A woman can go to bed looking like Melania Trump, but when she gets up in the morning she suddenly becomes the Bride of Dracula. A man, similarly, goes to bed looking like Brad Pitt, but when he gets up in the morning he more resembles Shrek. When I get up in the morning it looks like someone electrocuted my hair. If I were to go out in public looking like that, it would probably scare little old ladies and some little children!

So, when you look into the mirror, what do you do? You start to make adjustments, according to the new image you want. The Word of God is supposed to be a mirror that reflects back an image of who you really are. If you don't like what you see in some areas, make adjustments based on what is reflected to you from the Word.

An image is what you see. Each of us has our own self-image (how we view or see ourselves). Self-image is a predetermined belief of who we are right now and what we can become. It determines how we look to others and how others respond to us. Self-image is largely what is stored in our subconscious mind. Our lives are largely influenced by this internal **picture**. This picture controls our perception of things. It sends a message to our emotional system, physiological system and our neurological system to keep us aligned to our self-image. When the subconscious mind perceives we are not on target with our self-image, it causes a stimulus or suppression of energy, ideas and activities to keep us aligned with that image.[10] Self-image is an individual's mental and spiritual concept or picture (image) of himself, which is the real key to performance. Self-image creates boundaries for our accomplishments – good or bad. It defines what you will or will not do.

In other words, your subconscious mind's job is to keep you aligned with your image of yourself in your heart. This is why people unwittingly sabotage themselves and end up someplace they don't want to be. You can never rise above the image you have of yourself in your heart. Changing how you see yourself in your heart is where all transformation begins. Renewed thinking only works when it is consistent with your self-image. **Principles don't change a person, images do.** It is when a principle becomes an image in the heart that your life is transformed.

Changing your image engages your Reticular Activating System (RAS), or your recognition system, that we talked about earlier. Through positive focusing, negative filtering and individual perception, your RAS brings forth a recognition of people, ideas and resources in your environment that are necessary for you to reach your objective. In short, your image affects every realm of your success and productivity. The question is, what is the source of your image?

Let's look at Genesis 1:26 once again, "Let us make man in our image, according to our likeness, let them have dominion" (NKJV). God made man in His image and likeness. Remember the term *image* means reflection or resemblance. *Likeness* gives you the idea of model, shape, fashion, manner, similitude or pattern. Image is the *nature* of God, and likeness is the *function* of God. We have been given God's nature to be recognized by us and the ability to function as He does.

Now let me break this down in a way that can bring some practicality to all of this. The word *nature* means inborn character, innate disposition, inherent tendencies, instincts, essential qualities or attributes.[11] The idea behind *function* is the normal or characteristic action, performance, course of work.[12] In other words, by the very fact of creation, you have been engineered for success.

God placed His very nature in you. You have the inborn character, disposition, inherent tendencies, instincts, desires and attributes of God. If that was not enough, He gave you the ability to function or to manifest these qualities.

If all of this is true, then why don't we manifest His Kingdom accordingly? Genesis 3:1-10 talks about the *fall* of mankind. Eve submitted to the serpent's wiles and partook of the Tree of the Knowledge of Good and Evil. After Adam and Eve *fell*, they suddenly noticed they were naked. So, they hid and fashioned clothes for themselves. They saw themselves (their image) differently.

The *fall* of man distorted his view of himself. Who you are depends on what you see. When a man puts a limit on what he *can* be, he puts a limit on what he *will* be. Jesus came to restore His image in us. (See 2 Cor. 3:1-18; Jas. 1:21-24; Rom. 8:29; 1 Cor. 15:49; 2 Cor. 4:4; Col. 1:27; Col. 3:10; Heb. 1:3).

Breaking Barriers of Self-Limiting Beliefs

The enemy's strategy is simple, yet profoundly impactful. If he can create strongholds (feeling powerless), arguments (double-mindedness or confusion), imaginations (negative internal images), or pretense (false assumptions), these things can set themselves up against the knowledge of God in your life. So, how do I overcome strongholds when I have been told I will never amount to anything and I believed it? How do I take on duplicitous thoughts that cause wavering in me? How do I deal with cellular memory and repressed thoughts if 90% of them are subconscious? If I have appropriated pretense, how do I recognize and overcome them?

The simple answer is to create new heart beliefs that over-come self-limiting beliefs. Let's look at some initial steps to free-dom and productivity:

Step One: Discover self-limiting beliefs. Most of the time, self-limiting beliefs are evident by the lack of productivity or the absence of the thing desired – prosperity, provision, healing, feel-ing unloved or lack of faith (for a complete list of self-limiting beliefs, see the Barrier Busters Manual.)

Step Two: Discover emotional trails. If you find yourself readily going into similar emotions, even if circumstances do not merit it, chances are they are the result of repressed or cellular memories. There is a psychological principle called *layering*. It goes something like this: Let's suppose you have a fear issue. Fear seems to arise for no particular reason, or circumstances seem to set your fear off easily (too easily). Stop and ask yourself on a scale of 1 to 10 (10 being the highest) *How fearful do I feel?* Ask yourself, *When was the first time I felt this kind of fear?* It may (or may not) trigger a memory you haven't thought of for a long time (maybe ever). Then, ask yourself this question, *What does Jesus (the Word) say about this?* Scripture tells us that the antidote to fear is love. Now, apply the antidote scriptures to your self-limit-ing belief through prayer and by reading and meditating on key verses. Such scriptures might include 1 John 4:18, "There is no fear in love, perfect love casts out all fear." Romans 8:38, "I am convinced nothing can separate us from the love of God." Per-haps adding Ephesians 3:17-20 and 1 John 4:10 and then asking yourself on the same scale of 1 to 10, how do you feel now? Re-peat the process until it is reduced to 0.

- Here is a model in prayer: *I pray all negative images, con-scious and subconscious, particularly related to my dilemma (physical, emotional, relational, success, prosperity) be found and healed by filling my mind and heart with God's revela-*

tion of truth and love. I pray the effectiveness of my healing be made manifest more and more.

- Work this process through biblical meditation.

It is time to turn our attention to biblical mediation. This is the missing ingredient to the missing ingredient.

Keys for Reflection

1. The Kingdom principle defined in this chapter says, if you can't see it (in your heart), you can't receive it. What areas in your life are you having difficulty seeing a desired result in your heart?

2. 2 Corinthians 10:3-6 lists 4 areas (strongholds, arguments, imaginations, and pretense) that the enemy uses to defuse your destiny. Identify how any of these 4 areas may be at work to mute your destiny?

   a. Strongholds (feeling powerless; may be a family trait)

   b. Arguments (double-mindedness)

   c. Imaginations (negative internal images; stresses): See the stress test addendum at the end of this chapter. How are you doing?

   d. Pretense (false assumptions – are there things you have been taught to believe that are contrary to the Word of God?)

3. Look at James 1:22-24. What mirror are you looking into in your life, the reflections from others, from circumstances or from the Word of God? Be specific.

4. How do you see the difference between self-image and God-image?

Look at this chart of stress indicators. If you find yourself at 150 points or more, you may find yourself a candidate for sickness, disease, or nervous conditions.

SELF ADMINISTERED STRESS TEST

Place the "value" number of points in your "score" column for each event you have experienced <u>within the last 12 months</u>. Total the number of events in the "score" column and interpret your results below.

	LIFE EVENT	VALUE	SCORE
1.	Death of a spouse	100	
2.	Divorce	73	
3.	Marital separation	65	
4.	Jail term	63	
5.	Death of a close family member or friend	63	
6.	Major personal injury or illness	53	
7.	Marriage	50	
8.	Laid off from work	47	
9.	Marital reconciliation	45	
10.	Retirement	45	
11.	Change in family member's health	44	
12.	Pregnancy	40	
13.	Sexual difficulties	39	
14.	Gain of new family member	39	
15.	Business readjustment	39	
16.	Change in financial status	38	
17.	Death of a close friend	37	
18.	Change in different type of work	36	
19.	Change in number of marital arguments	35	
20.	Mortgage or loan over $20,000	31	
21.	Foreclosure of mortgage or loan	30	
22.	Change in work responsibilities	29	
23.	Son or daughter leaving home	29	
24.	Trouble with in-laws	29	
25.	Outstanding personal achievement	28	
26.	Spouse begins or stops work	26	
27.	Starting or finishing school	26	
28.	Change in living conditions	25	
29.	Revision of personal habits	24	
30.	Troubles with employer	23	
31.	Change in work hours & conditions	20	
32.	Change in residence	20	
33.	Change in schools	20	
34.	Change in recreational habits	19	
35.	Change in church activities	19	
36.	Change in social activities	18	
37.	Mortgage or loan under $20,000	17	
38.	Change in sleeping habits	16	
39.	Change in number of family gatherings	15	
40.	Change in eating habits	15	
41.	Vacation	13	
42.	Christmas season	12	
43.	Minor violation of the law	11	
		Total Score *****	

Normal: 0 - 150	Mild Stress 150- 199 33% chance of illness in next two years	Moderate Stress 200 - 299 50% chance of illness in next two years	High Stress 300+ 90% chance of illness in next two years

CHAPTER 5

THE MISSING INGREDIENT TO THE MISSING INGREDIENT

THEME: THE MISSING INGREDIENT: HEART BELIEFS. THE MISSING INGREDIENT TO THE MISSING INGREDIENT: BIBLICAL MEDITATION.

Lesson: How to practically develop
the **Manifestation** of heart beliefs.

Obviously, the missing ingredient to your breakout is establishing your heart beliefs through renewing your mind, establishing your heart and transforming your Personal Belief System. The missing ingredient to establishing heart beliefs is biblical meditation. This is not an imitation of some far Eastern country transcendental state. It is quite the opposite. Cultic and other religions have perverted what is soundly biblical.

Let me take you through a journey of medical discoveries revealing profoundly biblical concepts that are the **keys** to you stepping into your destiny.

Maxwell Maltz, in his breakthrough book *Psycho-Cybernetics*, says it this way: "Self-image is the individual's mental and spiritual concept or picture of himself, which is the real key to behavior."[1] Self-image sets boundaries for individual performance and accomplishments. It defines what you can or cannot do. If you expand your self-image, you can expand any area of your life. A positive image can imbue a person with new capabilities, talents and literally turn failure into success.[2] Renewed thinking works when it is consistent with the individual's self-image.[3] Your self-image is not transformed by knowledge, but by thinking about it and experiencing such knowledge.[4] All your actions, feelings and behaviors are always consistent with your self-image. It is really impossible to act otherwise.[5] A human being always acts in accordance to what he believes is true about himself.[6] Amazingly, your nervous system cannot tell the difference between what is real or imagined.[7] Before a person can change, they must see themselves in a new image.

Now, let's put all these thoughts in perspective. God made you in His image and likeness; He made you in His nature and function. It helps me to know I'm made in the reflection and resemblance of God. But what does that really mean to me? The term *image* is also the root for *imag-ination*. Imagination is the ability to think without limitation. As long as your imagination is based on truth, it is helpful; otherwise, it is just mere fantasy. The ability to be productive and to dominate your environment is based on your ability to break the limits off your thinking and regain your God-image. The Creator of the universe engineered you for success and achievement.

Let me give you an example. If you were to come into our church service on a Wednesday night, we periodically have prayer for the sick. Let's say we ask for people who need a touch from God, and 100 people raise their hands. After we pray, we ask all those who received a healing to come forward and testify of the results, and ten people come forward. The next week is the same scenario with the same results: 100/10. The following week, the same: 100/10. Pretty soon the image you hold in your mind about healing is about 10 percent of the people get touched. Suddenly, your touch from God becomes like the lottery. You raise your hand, hoping you'll be in the lucky 10 percent, but chances are it's not going to be you. The fact is 10 percent did get healed, but the truth in God's Word is that you are already healed by the stripes of Jesus. Truth is stronger than fact, but it takes an ability to "see" it to appropriate it.

The difference between people who are successful and productive, and those who are not, is that successful people *see* themselves bigger than their problems; unsuccessful people do not. It is a matter of perspective. For instance, use a scale of 1 to 10 (10 being the highest) and imagine you're a level 3 person. If you face a level 6 problem, it may seem devastating. If, however, you are a level 8 person, the same level 6 problem would not seem perplexing. It is truly a matter of perspective and capacity.[8] Now, the problem is no problem at all.

This is what I call the "Austin Powers" philosophy. It is the curse of "mini-me." You fail to see the true image of who you are in Christ. The problem looms bigger than it really is, and it defeats you. Successful people always focus on solutions, not problems. They don't focus on the natural realm to supply their needs. Instead, they look to that invisible realm, where God's provisions have an eternal source of supply.

Many people fail to appropriate what is rightfully theirs simply because their self-image is dwarfed. It creates set-points or self-limiting beliefs that put a ceiling on our lives. Self-image (how I *see* myself) creates self-esteem (how I *feel about* myself). When these two factors operate negatively in our lives, they create a lack of impetus to step up and try what we may know is the will of God for our lives. Self-image and self-esteem are the key factors to our success (in chapter 6 we will consider the five sources of all self-limiting beliefs).

Where do poor self-image and low self-esteem come from? Generally, they are conditioned from our childhood. A child is born with no self-image. Every idea, opinion, feeling, attitude, or value is learned from childhood experience. Everything you are today is the result of an idea or impression you accepted as true.[9] When you believe something to be true, it becomes true for you. "You are not what you *think* you are, what you *think* you *are*."[10]

If in your formative years you received 20 "no's" for every "yes," or 10 "you're wrong" for every 1 "you're doing it right," and 5 "you're stupid" for 1 "you're awesome," you're likely conditioned with low self-image and esteem.[11] These negative messages generally create comfort zones, set-points, or self-sabotaging actions that hold you back in life. For many people, the feeling of unworthiness makes them feel it is inappropriate for them to be blessed or rewarded for their efforts. They often position themselves to line up with their unworthy self-image (self-worth or the lack of it) and create the comfort zone of mediocrity or failure. It unfortunately becomes a self-perpetuating cycle that often leads to despair or self-perpetuating stagnation.

One of the stages for transforming your personal belief system is to *see* (imagine) Jesus stepping into your life. A woman I was helping once could not imagine that being true. Her religious background had thoroughly conditioned her to think she was too unworthy to have Him in her life. Once she overcame this barrier, her new image catapulted her forward in every arena in her life.

Your beliefs about yourself and your world create levels of expectation. Expectations determine attitudes, and attitudes determine behavior (what you will or will not do). If you go back to the beginning of creation in Genesis 1, you will find how God created. When He created anything, He spoke to the source, and out of the source came the thing. For instance, when He created plants, He spoke to the ground, and out of the ground came the plant. When He created the fish, He spoke to the water, and out of the water came the fish. My good friend Myles Munroe states it this way, "What happens when you remove the thing from its source? It dies!" If you remove the fish from the water, it dies. If you remove the plant from the soil, it dies. Therefore, the Genesis definition of death is separation from its source.

When God made man and woman, what source did He speak to? Genesis 1:26 tells us He spoke to Himself. What happens when a man or woman is separated from God? He or she dies! You might think, "I know a lot of people separated from God who aren't dead." Perhaps they're not dead physically, but they are dead inside. They've lost the image of God. They are spiritually dead.

If we walk according to our flesh, we *will* experience serious repercussions. Romans 8:5-6 states, "Those who live according to the (flesh) have their minds set on what that nature desires; but those who live in accordance with the Spirit have their minds set on what the Spirit desires. The mind of sinful man [flesh – doing God's will your way; for example, love versus lust] is death."

In other words, the mind of the flesh is death—separation from its source. Believers who operate in the flesh are separated from their true source, and therefore cannot receive from God whatever they need from their source. So, no matter how much you want God's provision, and no matter how much God wants to give it to you, you can't receive it because you are separated from the source of its manifestation.

Overcoming Life's Giants

We can see this in a clear example from Hebrew culture. Numbers 13:1 says, "The LORD said to Moses, 'Send some men to explore the land of Canaan, which I am giving to the Israelites.'"

It is clear from this passage that God intended to give Canaan (the Promised Land) to Israel. Moses then sent out twelve spies to explore the land. They brought back glowing reports of a land filled with milk and honey. It was bountiful and contained everything they would ever need. They brought back a cluster of grapes so large it took two men to carry them on a pole. We're talking about some significant grapes! It was a land that was beyond their wildest imagination.

Yet, when it came time to give their report on the land, here's what was said: "But, the people who live there are powerful, and the cities are fortified and very large. We saw the descendants of Anak there" (Numbers 13:28). In this country lived the Amalekites, the Hittites, the Jebusites, the Amorites, the Canaanites, the "up-tights," "out of sights" and "mosquito bites." All the "ites' lived there. There was great opposition in the land.

The ten spies gave what the writer of Numbers calls an "evil report." They spread a bad report that stirred fear among the people. They even included this phrase, "The land we explored devours those living in it." They were declaring that the people inhabiting Canaan were giants. Then, this amazing revelation came forth, "We seemed like grasshoppers *in our own eyes*, and we looked the same to them" (Numbers 13:28-33).

Now, notice the image they had of themselves. "They looked like giants, and we seemed like grasshoppers *in our own eyes*." They had spent the last 400 years in Egyptian captivity, and even though they were liberated from Egypt (slavery), they couldn't get Egypt out of their hearts. They still saw themselves as lowly slaves in their own eyes. Their image of themselves created a cognitive dissonance (double-mindedness) in them. Even though God had blessings of unparalleled proportions waiting for them in the Promised Land, their negative image prevented them from walking into the fullness of it. Suddenly, in chapter 14, they began to declare, "If we'd only died in Egypt!" "Wouldn't it be better for us to go back to Egypt?"

A low self-image will always cause people to develop a "GB" response – "Going *Back*" to an old comfort zone or set-point. People will literally sabotage themselves to stay there.

The devil's strategy is to blind the minds of people (2 Cor. 4:3, 4; 1 Cor. 2:9-16). It does not say he wants to blind the eyes of people; he works to blind their minds. Remember, you do not see things as *they* are, you see things as *you* are.

Years ago, when I worked at Oral Roberts University, we set up ministry teams that traveled all over the nation. My family and I met up with one of the teams in the Bronx in New York City. Our target was to go into locales and draw people with "upbeat" music and then minister truth to them. We really had some "hot" musicians who were playing some "hot" music. The music wasn't like "Sweet Hour of Prayer." It was more like "Devil, I'm going to rip your lips off."

The group set up in a park in the Bronx that was nothing more than a cement slab with a few swing sets. The group started playing, and soon a crowd gathered. After about twenty minutes, I took the microphone and shared how Jesus could radically change their lives, and a proportionately large number of people made decisions for transformation.

The next day we set up in the tenements. As the students were setting up the stage, I looked around and saw every excessive indulgence you can imagine. To my right they were pimping. They were selling drugs to my left, and doing drugs not far from me ... all in the eye-shot of police, and nobody seemed to care.

At the appropriate time, the team began to play a worship set. Again, people started hanging out of windows to listen and gathered around the platform. Only this time, it wasn't such a friendly crowd. The crowd began to pelt the group with glass. Fearing for their safety, I cried out, "Lord, what do you want me to do?"

In my spirit, I felt the Lord say, "If you get up and prophesy, I'll change the atmosphere of this place." Without hesitation, I bounded onto the stage, grabbed a microphone and blurted out, "Thus says the Lord, someone here is on drugs." Now, how is that for a revelation? I thought to myself, *Lord, everybody here's probably on drugs.* Then, the rest of the prophesy came, "You're on your way to commit suicide at this very moment. But I, the Lord, intercept you in your destruction right now."

The moment I said it, a young man fell to the ground and started weeping in agony. It turned out that he was a heroin and cocaine addict. His drug habit was so expensive, he had no means to pay for his "fixes." In desperation, he was on his way to the subway to throw himself in front of a subway train. People quickly gathered around to minister to him. He was marvelously set free, saved and filled with the Holy Spirit.

We later learned that not only was he an addict, but so was his father and his father's father. That low image had plagued three generations. His image of himself had been the same all his life – *It's never going to be different than it is right now.* In the middle of his desperation, God met him and set his life on a new course. At the same time, the event of that day calmed the crowd and opened the door to multiple transformations among the people in the tenements. The Lord opened this young man's mind, created a new image in his life and sent him on his way redeemed and with a new perspective about himself.

Media and television know the value of image. That is what "tele-vision" is. It is telling you a vision. That is why young girls see Lady Gaga and change their dress style. It is what car advertisers do. They let you picture yourself in their vehicle, projecting what you most want, repetitively, until you feel you have to have it.

Now, here is an amazing fact: once your subconscious mind is locked onto a "truth" (real or imagined), it tends to block out all information contrary to that belief. It is what psychologists call "Scotoma," or blind spots. There literally are beliefs that are holding you back, and you are oblivious to them. Even though God made you to be in control of your life, life seems to dictate to you. How can you turn this process around and transform your personal belief system? How can you break the frustrating ceiling of failure, mediocrity or stagnation?

The amazing process of lifting the limits off of your life is mapped out in such a way you can do it automatically.

Let me lay out a set of core principles to change what you believe, what you see, what you expect and what you will do (*remember, principles don't change a person, images do*).

Imagine the Possibilities

There is a way to intentionally increase your faith and change your image of yourself. As always, we will find the answer in Scripture. Proverbs 4:20-23 says: "My son, pay attention [or attend] to what I say [to my words]; listen closely to my words. Do not let them out of your sight, keep them within your heart; for they are life to those who find them and health to a man's whole body. Above all else, guard your heart, for out of it [your heart] is the wellspring [or boundaries] of [your] life." (Emphasis added from other translations).

Here are the core principles found in these verses:

- *Pay attention to God's words and concepts*. Literally, this means "to attend, meditate, wait upon or imagine God's Word."[12] If you don't see it, you can't receive it. For instance, if you see giving or tithing as depletion, you will never do it. You must see life through faith that has focused itself on the truth. Study all the scriptures that bring increase. (See ronmcintoshministries.com/rmmstore for the *Barrier Busters Manual* to give you all the scriptures to overcome the barriers in your life). ***Do not let them out of your sight.*** Repetition is the key to the reinforcement of truth. It takes 21 days to create a new habit or to create a new belief system. (I'll give you the application at the end of this chapter.)

- *Keep it in your heart.* Renew the soul chamber of your heart to the truth that is in your spirit. Let your conscious mind assimilate ultimate truth, and through repetition get it into your subconscious mind and set up an automatic response system that will change your present self-limiting beliefs (Again, I'll show you the direct application at the end of this chapter).

  This is primarily done through your confession. Confession by itself will get it into your belief system 10 percent. Confession with imagination brings it into your personal belief system 55 percent. Confession, imagination and emotion will get truth into your personal belief system 100%.[13]

- ***This process is life, health, and boundary-breaking in your life.*** It makes life vibrant, fresh and strong.

Jesus gives us great insight into how truth can set us free: "To the Jews who believed him, Jesus said, 'If you continue in my Word, you are truly my disciples. Then you will know the truth, and the truth will set you free'" (Jn. 8:31, 32).

Please notice: truth does not set you free. It is the truth you "know" that sets you free. This term *know* means "to know, recognize, understand, perceive"[14] This word gives you the idea to lay down with or to give birth to. The root of the word means to know experientially.[15] The implication of this word gives you the idea of getting "pregnant" by it. The point is obvious; the Word that sets you free is one that through intimacy becomes your own. In essence, you get pregnant with the truth of God's Word. It can't be Joyce Meyer's word, or James Robison's perspective or Myles Munroe's revelation. It can't be Steven Furtick's insight; it has to be the Word inside of you.

Now, exactly how does this happen to us? How do we become so intimate with truth that it transforms us into a different person? Psalm 1 holds the answer.

> "Blessed is the man who does not walk in the counsel of the wicked or stand in the way of sinners or sit in the seat of mockers. But, his delight is in the law of the LORD, and on His law does he meditate day and night. He is like a tree planted by streams of water, which yields its fruit in season and whose leaf does not wither. Whatever he does prospers." (Psalm 1:1-3)

The Psalmist begins by declaring, "Blessed is the man." The term *blessed* means *empowered to prosper, to favor, render successful, increase, advancing in growth or wealth, gain in anything good or desirable, successful progress, attainment of the object desired.*[16] One person said it this way, "Prosperity is the ability to use God's ability to meet any need."

Blessed (having the ability to use God's ability to meet my need) is the person who:

- *Does not walk in the counsel of the wicked* – who does not cultivate the world's system, because all you can ever produce is what that system can produce. That system collides with the Kingdom of God.

- *Does not walk in the way of sinners* – what is the way of sinners? It is the flesh and unbelief. Such action profits nothing, is contrary to God and the things you want to do you cannot do (Jn. 6:63; Rom. 7; Gal. 5:16, 17).

- *Does not sit in the seat of mockers* – mocking what? They are mocking the truth of God's Word. All such activity short-circuits the provisions of the Kingdom. Mockery listened to repeatedly (through all its forms – media, from authority figures or peers, etc.) brings contempt or at best confusion to the truth.

Instead, his "delight is in the law of the Lord." The term *delight* means *to have a high degree of satisfaction, to desire that which is precious or valuable, pursuit.*[17] I once had a college professor who told me it means you can't get enough of it. It's like a football "junkie" on New Year's Day. He has four large-screen TV sets going at the same time. He can't quite get enough of football. Or, like a woman at a sale in the mall, she will "shop until she drops."

The Psalmist tells us to eliminate the negatives, accentuate the positives, and delight in and pursue God's laws. What is a law? A law is a principle that tells you how a thing works best. How do you pursue these laws? By meditating on this law day and night.

The term, *meditate* means "to mutter, to utter, murmur, ponder, stretch, see beyond, muse or imagine.[18] Meditation means to mutter or utter. If we take an honest look at what we say on any given day, we already are muttering and uttering, *"I can't believe what she did to me. Can you believe it? I was minding my own business when all of a sudden ..."* Do you get the picture? If we're going to mutter, we might as well do it according to the truth.

Meditation also means *to ponder or muse*. As you dwell on God's truth, it causes you to see and stretch beyond where you are. This word also means *to imagine*. To imagine means to think without limitation. It means to see yourself according to truth (in the positive sense). Albert Einstein once said, "Imagination is more important than knowledge. Imagination is everything."[19] It is a preview of coming attractions. As you see yourself according to truth, it creates a new image on the inside of you. Your subconscious mind then works to make that image come to pass. It remedies your present situations. Biblical meditation is a way to intentionally increase your faith.

Before you start to worry that this is New Age or Transcendental Meditation, let me assure you that it is not. Remember, Satan is not a creator. All he can do is imitate and pervert truth. Don't let his deception rob you of the *missing ingredient* to transform your personal belief system. It is the Bible that encourages meditation – continual *musing* on God's Word, which is inspired by the Holy Spirit (2 Tim. 3:16).

The Psalmist says a person should meditate *day and night*. What does this mean? Quite simply, start your day and end your day in biblical meditation. Why? Because when you start your day looking into the perfect law of freedom (see Jas. 1:22-24), you begin to see yourself according to the real truth, which the enemy will contest all day long. When you end your day meditating in the Word, you will reestablish the same truth the enemy has sought to steal from you all day long. Another reason to end your day in biblical meditation is that your subconscious mind never turns off. As you feed it truth, it dwells on it all night long. That is why sometimes you go to bed thinking about a situation, and the next morning you wake up with the solution.

Now, look at these amazing results this process provides:

1. *You are like a tree planted by streams of water.* Like the vine and branches described in John 15, you are connected to the Ultimate Source of life. You are connected to the right system. When the Psalmist talks of water, the idea is water that flows in canals or is

used for irrigation. This source of sustenance (God's Word) is what causes you to flourish.

2. *You yield fruit.* When you are connected to the true Source of Life, you bring forth the desired manifestations (outcomes) in every area of your life.

3. *Your leaf does not wither.* You flourish even in times of drought or dryness.

4. *Whatever you do prospers.* You are favored, rendered successful, advanced in growth or wealth; you gain the thing desired, make successful progress and you use your ability to use God's ability to meet any need.

What an incredible picture! If we avoid living in the world's system and instead meditate on the truth of the laws that tell us how something works best, we will bring forth fruitful manifestation, attract the Kingdom of heaven, flourish, and live a life of advancement and increase. This is the Law of Attraction at work. Author James Allen said, "A man is literally what he thinks. His character is the sum total of his thoughts." This is why biblical meditation is the missing ingredient to the missing ingredient. When we allow the Word to dominate our thoughts and get into our hearts, it will create action that will break the shackles of mediocrity or stagnation.

That is the sum total of the story of the boy with epileptic seizures found in Mark 9. Whenever a seizure would occur, it would throw the boy to the ground and cause him to foam at the mouth. The boy's disgruntled father came to Jesus and said that His disciples could not cast out the demon. Jesus ultimately responded by saying, "All things are possible for those that believe." The father of the boy responded, "I do believe, help me overcome my unbelief." In essence he was saying, "I know what I hear. How do I get it to work?"

That is the heart of this book which brings us to the last set of principles (before we look at practical applications):

> "Do not let this book of the Law depart out of your mouth; meditate on it day and night, so that you may be careful to do everything written in it. Then you will be prosperous and you will have good (KJV) success." Josh. 1:8

Here Joshua amplifies 5 Keys to Manifestation:

1. *Confession* – Your confession must add to itself imagination and emotion to get into your personal belief system 100 percent.

2. *Incubation* – This is the principle of biblical meditation. There are approximately twenty-seven different terms used in the Bible for meditation and over several hundred references. Meditation is a way to intentionally increase your faith or to attract God's Kingdom.

3. *Revelation* – Incubation gives way to revelation. Revelation is something you always knew but never realized. You may know God as a healer. Suddenly, you realize He is *your* healer. You may know God as a Savior. Suddenly, you realize He is *your* Savior. You may know God as a provider. Suddenly, you realize He is *your* provider. Suddenly, you realize that what you "know" belongs to *you*.

4. *Impartation* – Your revelation gives way to impartation. What you realize becomes part of you.

5. *Manifestation* – When what is on the inside of you manifests on the outside of you, you attract the Kingdom of heaven.

The Missing Ingredient

The missing ingredient to transforming your personal belief system is biblical meditation. According to our definition of biblical meditation, there are five stages in the process. Amazingly, the first four correspond to the four major chambers of your brain. Let's consider the progression of the five stages:

Five Stages of Biblical Meditation
Stage 1
  Still Stage Psalm 46:10
  "Be still and know that I am God."

   Still in this passage means to "cease, draw toward, relax or desist."[20] The root to this term is rapha. This is the Hebrew term for "to heal, cure, repair, pardon or comfort." The still stage is what psychologists call "alpha state." Alpha state is that state between being asleep and awake. This is the state when your subconscious mind is most influenced. This is the stage of relaxation, praise and worship, healing and receptivity.

The **Medulla** regulates bodily functions.

Stage 2
  Imagination Stage Psalm 1:2,3

   This is the place where you create emotions with dominant images in your thinking. Here's where you reset set-points. In this stage the conscious mind chooses the new truth of Scripture, and through repetition this truth goes into your personal belief system in the subconscious mind. Here is where confession, imagination and emotion change your beliefs.
The **Amygdala** compares emothions with new data.

Stage 3

Strategy Stage Joshua 1:8

"Do not let this Book of the Law depart from your mouth; meditate on it day and night, so that you may be careful to do everything written in it. Then you will be prosperous and successful.

> Based on the truth that I see, what should
> I do? Write out a 5-part plan for action:
> 1. A vision (what I want to do and what I want to be)
> 2. A theme (a succinct expression of the vision_ for remembrance)
> 3. Objectives (goals to make your dreams come true)
> 4. Strategies (steps to your objectives)
> 5. Priorities (what do I focus on right now? (The act of writing goals is proven to increase the likelihood of success by 1,000 percent.)[21]

The **Cerebral Cortex** creates strategy.

Stage 4

Action or Application Stage Joshua 1:8

> The action stage is the place where I do something *every day* toward my highest priority. At the end of the chapter, there is a story about a woman on a diet that shows how this works. The difference between the strategy and the action stage is "fleshing out" the details of each strategy. On Monday I will ... etc.

The **Frontal Lobe** is the decision maker.

Stage 5
Thanksgiving Stage Philippians 4:6, 7

"Do not be anxious about anything, but in everything, by prayer and petition, with thanksgiving, present your requests to God. And the peace of God, which transcends all understanding, will guard your hearts and your minds in Christ Jesus."

Thanksgiving is the act of thanking God for your goals becoming a reality. Why? Because Thanksgiving puts a guard over your heart and mind. In other words, the act of thanksgiving protects what you place in your mind and your heart. Your feelings are a feedback mechanism to what you truly believe. Your thoughts create feelings and your feelings solidify what your thoughts say is true. Feelings give courage to your heart to try to reach your goal.

Once you discover your set-point or self-limiting beliefs, then find the antidote in God's Word. For instance, if your limitation is lack, then your antidote is prosperity. If your barrier is sickness, your antidote of truth is healing. For doubt, it's faith; for fear it's love. For guilt, fear, and inferiority, it's righteousness. (This is already done for you in our *Barrier Busters Manual*).

Once you see yourself according to the truth, then what strategy do you need to work on? Your strategy may include preparation for a new job, reading about an effective diet plan, changing your exercise regimen or learning about investments and stewardship.

The final key is to do something every day toward your highest priority. The process of manifestation is this: thoughts lead to emotions, emotions lead to solidifying your will, a solid will leads to actions and actions bring results. As much as I believe in meditation and confession, as far as I can tell, neither of them on their own brings manifestation.[22] It takes action to succeed. The bridge between the inner world and the outer world is action.[23] (Later we'll deal with the three keys that keep people from taking action.) Ultimately, it is the action that brings results.

Finally, thanksgiving puts a guard over your heart and mind. Thanksgiving helps "cement" your soul chamber to the spirit chamber of your heart, particularly the subconscious mind. The subconscious mind cannot tell the difference between what is real and what is imagined. Once it accepts what is truth, it works to bring it to pass. This thanksgiving stage is an essential part of the process. What you think about and thank about, comes about.[24] Learn how to walk through this five-fold process using *Barrier Busters*, nine biblical mediation tapes, created by ronmcintosh-ministries.com I was sharing this process in a seminar setting, and I asked if anyone had any questions. A woman stood up and said, "Yeah, I've got a question about how this works. I want to lose weight. Does this work for that?"

As she was speaking, I could see people nodding their heads like, "Yeah, does it work for that?" Unmoved, I just asked this simple question, "What is the antidote for weight loss?"

Almost indignantly the woman responded, "Eat less."

Everyone laughed, including me, but I replied, "As long as you think that, you'll never lose weight." I continued, "Let me walk you through this five-fold process for you."

You can create self-empowering beliefs through biblical meditation. Generally, the real biblical antidote is found in love, righteousness, and self-control. So, your steps are these:

1. Get **still**.
2. See (**imagine**) yourself according to the truth of the Scripture concerning love, righteousness, and self-control. First, God loves you just as you are. Second, you are in right standing with God not by your action, but based

on what Jesus did for you. Receive it by faith. Third, see yourself according to your ideal weight (I'm not talking about some phony image of when you were sixteen years old, but a realistic idea or picture of where you are heading now.) This is where your confession comes into play. "I am excited about feeling fit at (your ideal weight) pounds."

3. Create a **strategy** of how to get there. For this woman, I drew the Mediterranean Diet out for her on the board:

4. Taking **Action** looks something like this:
   a. On Monday, I'll eat… (four small meals accordingly)
   b. On Tuesday, I'll eat…on Wednesday I'll eat… etc.
5. Give **thanksgiving** to God that He is doing this (present tense) in your life.

Every person in that audience wanting to lose weight was scrambling for pen and paper to take notes. Later, I told my staff about what had transpired in the seminar. My former office manager was an attractive woman, but she was not pleased with her weight gain in recent years. She had said somewhat regularly that she wanted to lose thirty or forty pounds. Shortly after this, her husband took a job in Phoenix, and she moved away. A little over a year later they moved back to my home town of Tulsa. Shortly thereafter, she showed up at my office. When she walked through the door, I looked at her and said, "Where is the rest of you? You've lost a lot of weight."

She grinned and said, "Yeah, I lost forty pounds."

I said, "How did you do it?"

She then went through a brief description of walking out these five steps. She found her self-empowering beliefs, meditated on them, along with a visualization of her at her ideal weight. She then set out a strategy diet (remember the term *diet* means "lifestyle," not a short process of deprivation). She then redid her grocery shopping and prepared a menu for every week. Feeling empowered to do what she wanted, she followed through on her plan. The result was an amazing transformation to her ideal weight. Today, she is still thanking God.

I have seen countless people transform their lives in a number of different areas. I've seen unstable people transformed into confident, thriving individuals. I've seen people break through and overcome limitations in financial arenas, health, being at peace, feeling loved, feeling forgiven of past indiscretions, and overcoming fear, doubt and stress. The list is endless, because God's Word is limitless. (See Appendix at the end of this chapter and the *Barrier Busters Manual* for a list of self-limiting beliefs, antidotes and self-empowering beliefs).

To really understand set-points and self-limiting beliefs, we need to understand how they originate in our thinking. So, now let's dig deeper into busting the barriers of self-limiting beliefs.

Keys for Reflection

- Remember, you have got to see it to receive it. Biblical meditation allows you to see yourself according to the truth.
- Remember the devil's four strategies to keep you stagnant in self-limiting beliefs: strongholds, arguments, imaginations, pretense.
- Make sure you see yourself through the mirror of God's Word, not the mirror of experience.
- Biblical meditation is the key to transforming your personal belief system.
- Remember the five stages of biblical meditation:
    - Get **still** with some peaceful music or relaxation exercises.
    - **Imagination** – Once you've discovered your self-limiting beliefs (see Appendix at the end of this chapter), see yourself according to the antidote. If it is prosperity, how does that look to you? Remember your subconscious mind can't tell the difference between real or imagined. It simply goes to work to make it come to pass. Part of believing is "make-believing."
    - **Strategy** – You will start attracting people, ideas, and resources to your most dominant thoughts.
    Do the following exercise:
- What do I most want or want to overcome? Write clear strategy, objectives, priorities and timeline for the results you want to see in your life.

_____

_____

_____

_____

_____

_____

_____

_____

_____

_____

_____

_____

_____

- Take **Action**. What am I doing daily toward this goal? Every day do something toward your highest priority.

  Day 1. _____

  Day 2. _____

  Day 3. _____

  Day 4. _____

  Day 5. _____

  Day 6. _____

  Day 7. _____

- Now **thank** Him! Thank Him for the truth that is alive in you and is happening right now. Affirm to yourself that God's truth is acting on your behalf. Thank Him that your breakthrough is happening. Remember, you are unstoppable!

APPENDIX – Chapter 5

BARRIER BUSTERS

	Self-Limiting Beliefs	Antidotes
1	Fear, rage, anger, un-forgiveness, guilt, lust	**LOVE** (sometimes combined with righteousness and forgiveness)
2	Discouragement (dis-courage), grief	**JOY** (sometimes combined with righteousness)
3	Anxiety, worry, guilt, stress	**PEACE** (sometimes combined with righteousness)
4	Frustration, desire to quit	**PATIENCE** (sometimes combined with righteousness)
5	Doubt, unbelief, fear, faithfulness	**FAITH** (sometimes combined with righteousness)
6	Flesh (man's attempt to do God's will)	**SELF CONTROL** (sometimes combined with righteousness and grace)

BARRIER BUSTERS

	Self-Limiting Beliefs	Antidotes
7	Sickness, disease (dis-ease)	HEALING (sometimes combined with righteousness and forgiveness)
8	Resentment, anger, hatred, wronged,	FORGIVENESS (sometimes combined with righteousness and love)
9	Guilt, inferiority, fear, condemnation	RIGHTEOUSNESS
10	Lack, poverty, stagnation financially	PROSPERITY (sometimes combined with righteousness)
11	Inability to break through	GRACE (sometimes combined with righteousness)
12	Selfishness, pride, double-mindedness	GOODNESS GENTLENESS KINDNESS

CHAPTER 6

BREAKING SELF-LIMITING BELIEFS

THEME: DISCOVERING THE 5 ELEMENTS OF YOUR PERSONAL BELIEF SYSTEM.

Lesson: Learning why I believe what I believe.

Now that we have put the amazing tool of biblical meditation in your hands, you are equipped to break self-limiting beliefs off of your life and launch into the life of abundance you were ordained to live. Let me share an amazing story to get you started.

This story is about a thirty-year old woman who was married with two children ... she also suffered from amnesia. Like many people, she grew up in a home where she was criticized and unfairly treated by her parents. As a result, she developed deep-seated feelings of inferiority and low self-esteem. She was shy, negative, fearful and had no confidence. She felt unworthy and totally unvalued. She thought she had no real talent for anything.

One day while driving to the store, another car ran a red light and smashed into her vehicle. When she awoke in the hospital, she had suffered a concussion and had complete memory loss. All of her physical faculties were intact, but every memory of her former life was gone. She was a total amnesiac.

Through a series of extensive tests, the doctors determined her memory loss was complete and unrecoverable. Her husband and children visited her daily, but she had no recollection of them. The case was so unusual that doctors and specialists came from all over to visit her and examine her unusual condition.

Ultimately she went home, but her memory was a complete blank. Determined to understand what happened to her, she began to study everything she could about the subject of amnesia. She met and spoke with a number of specialists in the field. Eventually she wrote a treatise about all her findings. Sometime later, she was invited to a medical convention to address the subject of amnesia and neurological functionality.

From the time of the accident and through her recovery, something astonishing took place. She became a completely different kind of person. All of the positive attention from the hospital, the specialists and the love and support from her family made her feel valuable. The attention, acclaim and esteem from the medical community elevated her self-respect. She was transformed into a positive, confident, out-going, in-demand speaker and an authority in the medical community.

All the memory of her negative childhood had been wiped out. Along with it, her feelings of inferiority were eradicated. She became an entirely new person.[1] Usually, when I tell this story I ask the question, "How many of you know someone who needs amnesia?" It is humorous, but true. It is what Scottish philosopher David Hume called the "blank slate."[2] The idea is that every person is born into this world with no thought or idea, and everything a person becomes is a learned trait from infancy onward. The adult becomes the sum total of what they learn, feel and experience from childhood to present.[3]

The blueprint of your life is primarily the *programming* you received in your past from experiences. Your home, school, parents, friends and teachers are all influential in creating mindsets and expectations in your life. If they are positive reflections of truth, that is wonderful, but often they are incorrect distortions of truth that lead to self-limiting beliefs or set-points that can negatively impact a person for years (perhaps a lifetime). A person becomes conditioned to an automatic response that then runs their life.

The real question is, where do these limitations come from? Why do you think and act differently from the neighbor you grew up with? The storage bin of your thinking (beliefs) comes primarily from five sources: social environment, authority figures, self-image, repetitious information and experience.

There's a beautiful story of two shoe salesmen, from different companies, that were sent to Africa to explore the market for shoes. The first salesman hated the assignment and wished he didn't have to go. The second salesman loved the assignment and saw it as a great opportunity for sales and advancement.

When they each arrived at the African country, they studied the market for shoes. They both sent telegrams to their companies summarizing their results.

The first salesman, who had little use for the assignment wrote, "It is a wasted trip. There is no market in this country. No one here wears shoes!"

The second salesman, who viewed the trip as full of potential wrote, "Wonderful trip. Market is unlimited. No one wears shoes."[4]

Why two distinctly different perspectives? You see what you already believe.

Henry Ford said, "Whether you think you can or think you can't, you're right." Self-help guru, Jack Canfield notes, "Less than 10% of people who go to seminars of any kind ever apply one thing that they hear."[5] That means people who often pay *big* dollars to go to seminars with major motivational speakers rarely apply anything that they hear. One of my friends who is a leading life coach told me, "Steps of application don't really matter until you change the way you see yourself (in your heart)." One of the 6 Kingdom Laws of success and the process of faith I often quote is the **Law of Expectation**. This law says that what you expect in your heart with confidence becomes self-fulfilling prophecy. Numerous psychologists suggest that 85% of our actions are the result of our expectations. What we do or don't do are based on what we anticipate the results to be.

The question becomes, where do such beliefs and expectations come from? What you believe is the product of the 5 elements of your Personal Belief System or the Word of God, as a Believer. Let's examine the 5 elements of the Personal Belief System:

5 Elements of your Personal Belief System

Element 1: Social Environment

Environment includes the conditions, circumstances and influences surrounding and affecting a person. For instance, how many times do you see someone go to a conference or a retreat and their lives appear to be radically changed? Yet, two weeks later they're right back where they started. Why? When they got back to their environment, the conditions and influences reignited past beliefs.

Let me give you an even more pertinent example of how environment can affect your Personal Belief System. Many of you, like me, when you were kids might have asked your parents for money for some event. Many of us received a response something like this, "Do you think money grows on trees?" "Do you think there is a money tree in the backyard?" Unwittingly, our parents created a lack mindset. What they are really communicating is some people have money and some people don't. We're among the people who don't. We are back in the mindset of the blue glasses from chapter one. We're showing you a white card, but you're seeing it as blue because you have on glasses with a blue lens. So later in life, someone tells you it is God's will to prosper you. However, you have on your blue glasses and what you hear is, "Is there a money tree in the backyard?" So, your self-limiting belief causes you not to access the Kingdom for prosperity.

My dear friend, Myles Munroe, tells the story of meeting a tribal chieftain from Zimbabwe who related to him the story of a lion among sheep. The story is of a farmer who lived in a village who was a herder of sheep. One day while taking his herd to graze, he heard a strange sound that reminded him of a kitten. The old farmer decided to pursue the strange sound and found a lion cub lodged in the pasture. The lion cub was obviously separated from his family. His first inclination was the danger he would experience if the parents returned and found the cub in his possession. So, the old farmer remained at a distance to see if the mother of the pack would return to reclaim the young cub. He waited patiently, observing the cub until the sun went down. After a period of time there was still no activity, and the farmer felt that in the best interest of the safety of the cub that he should take him to the farmhouse to care for him.

Over the first few months, the shepherd hand-fed the cub fresh milk and kept him in the secure **environment** of the farmhouse. As the cub grew, the farmer began to take the young lion to graze with the sheep daily. Because the lion grew up with the sheep, he became one of them. After over a year, the cub grew and developed the strength and prowess of a fine young lion, but he acted, sounded, responded and behaved like one of the sheep. In his association with the sheep, he became like a sheep.

One day some years later, the shepherd took refuge as he watched over his flock wading into a flowing river to take a drink. The lion, who thought he was one of the sheep, followed the sheep to the river to drink. Suddenly, across the river from the brush appeared a large beast that the former lion cub had never seen. The sheep panicked and leaped out of the water and fled back to the farmhouse. They never stopped until they were huddled together shaking with fear behind the fence of the farm. Somewhat strangely, the former lion cub, now a fully grown lion, was also huddled in fear.

While the flock scrambled for the safety of the farm, the beast roared a sound that shook the foundation of the forest. When the beast lifted his head above the tall grass, the old farmer witnessed in his blood-drenched jaws the lifeless body of a lamb from the flock. The shepherd realized that a real danger had returned to the forest.

A week passed with no further incidents. Then, one day while the flock once again grazed, the young lion went down to the river to drink. As he bent over the water, he suddenly panicked and ran wildly back to the farmhouse for safety, once again. The sheep however, did not respond, and he wondered why since he had again seen the beast. After a while, the young lion returned to the herd and again began to drink. Once again, he saw the beast and froze in panic. However, what he had seen was his reflection in the water.

Attempting to understand what he saw, the young lion's contemplation was interrupted by the beast appearing again from the forest. The flock raced back to the farmhouse, but before the young lion could move, the beast stepped into the water toward him and made a deafening roar that filled the forest. In that moment the young lion felt his life was about to end. Then, in that moment, the young lion realized there were two beasts, not just one; the one he had seen in the water and the one that stood before him.

His mind was spinning with confusion as the beast approached him and growled face to face. The face-to-face encounter seemed to say to the young lion, "Try it and come follow me."

Fear gripped the young lion, but he decided to try and appease the beast by making the same sound. He opened his gaping jaws and uttered, "Baaah, baaah." It was the simple utterance of the sheep he had become. The beast persisted and seemed to communicate, "Try again!" The young lion continued to express the sounds of a sheep. After seven or eight attempts, the young lion roared with the vibrancy of the beast. He felt the stirrings and feelings rustle through his body in ways he'd never known or experienced before. It was as though he felt a **transformation** in mind, body and spirit.

Now there stood two beasts in the river, roaring toward one another. Then, the shepherd witnessed something he would never forget. As the two beasts filled the atmosphere with their sounds, the beast turned to reenter the forest. In a moment, the beast paused, turned and looked at the young lion as if to say, "Are you coming?" The young lion understood the gesture and realized a day of decision had arrived. Would he choose to continue in the safe, secure and predictable life of the sheep on the farm, or would he enter the frightening, unpredictable dangerous life of the jungle? It was a day to become his true and real self and leave the false image of his past behind. It was the invitation to a sheep to become the King of the Jungle he was ordained to be.

After looking back to the farm and then to the jungle several times, the young lion turned his back to the farm and the sheep and stepped toward his destiny. He followed the beast into the forest to become what he had always been ... a Lion King.[6]

Do you hear the voice of God in your life? It is true that most of us have elements of social environment that seem to dictate to us that we are less than what God created us to be.

Yet God created you with everything you need to be successful. However, many of us are wired for success but programmed for failure. Why is it that some people overcome obstacles while the majority of people allow life's difficulties to quench their dreams? It is often the image imprinted in their lives through their social environment. You will either believe what your environment tells you, or you will believe the Word of God.

Often people who grow up in lack remain in lack (just enough to get by) because they have received the impression their environment is speaking to them. I had a friend growing up who I will call Ernie. Ernie's dad was an alcoholic. When his dad was drunk, he became violent and would take it out on his family. Ernie would often escape his house and come over to my home to avoid abuse. Years later, after I had met Christ, I came home from college on a summer break. I heard there was a party with many of my old friends. I went to the party to reacquaint myself with people I hadn't seen in years. The party was filled with alcohol and drugs, and there was Ernie, drunk. The young boy who grew up hating alcohol became an alcoholic. Why? His environment taught him the way to escape problems was in a bottle. Often, children who come from homes where neglect is prevalent feel unworthy of attention from anybody – including God. Rejection from important people often causes people to feel rejected from God.

There are basically **6 home environments** that often affect people's Personal Belief System[7]:

A Controlling Home – People who grow up in an environment where parents are domineering or controlling are often not allowed to make choices or do anything independently. Such people tend to shirk responsibilities for the rest of their lives. You will hear these people proliferate their vocabulary with, "I can't do that" or "I don't know how," or "I'm confused."

A Fear-based Home – Children raised in an environment of fear generally lack motivation. They tend to be afraid to try anything that might end in failure. They often lack motivation to try. They have trouble making decisions because they don't want to make the wrong decision. If you are caught in this trap, you often neglect opportunities that promote your best future.

An Insecure Home – Insecurity may be the result of being in an environment of divorce, separation or tragedy. In some cases, money is a problem. In others, insecure parents will tell their children how bad they are over and over again. These children grow up with a tendency to worry about not having enough. Their whole lives are spent trying to be secure. Their framework can keep them from venturing into taking risks.

An Abusive Home – The abuse can be physical, sexual or emotional. The message received by the abused child is they have little or no value. Some of these children lean toward escapism via drugs and alcohol. There is a tendency toward rebellion against social norms.

A Performance-based home – These are homes of conditional love. Children are loved if they perform to a standard or do something well. These children tend to be people-pleasers. They rarely learn to build or take risks because of the fear of failure. They often live in fear of rejection.

A Hyper-responsible Home – These are homes where children are given too much responsibility at too early an age. They often try to recapture their youth. Sometimes overly responsible people won't take risks. They won't risk any kind of investment because that would be irresponsible. Again, this can cause someone to hesitate or miss open doors of possibility and opportunity.

I don't share these environments to say that this is your lot in life, but to suggest that you have a choice. You will either allow your social environment to affect your Personal Belief System, or you will learn to create new beliefs through the Word of God in your heart.

Sometimes neglect from key figures in your life can breed a mentality of, "I'm not worthy of attention from anyone, including God." Perhaps the opposite is true. You receive plenty of attention, but it's the wrong kind. Someone is always pointing out your mistakes or shortcomings, saying, "You're not talented enough" or "You'll never measure up." That was the issue in my life when a significant person told me, "You will never amount to anything" (Chapter 2). This false self-image kept me bound in self-sabotaging actions for years. Psychologists suggest that 85% of actions are based on our expectations. My expectation of not amounting to anything caused me to not step up and try to excel until I learned how to change how I see myself.

The impact of social environment can easily be seen when people's lives are legitimately touched and momentarily changed until environment drags them back into its clutches.

Element 2: Authority Figures

You tend to become what the most important figures in your life think you'll become. What authority figures think about themselves is often projected upon those they have influence over. This is why one of the most important things you can do is to discern who the primary sources of this programming or conditioning in your life were. For most of us, the list will include parents, teachers, friends, coaches, clergy, media and our culture. Often their training in our lives becomes the programming that creates the automatic response system that conditions how we view our world. Our ideas about our abilities, self-worth and self-image are the product of their reflection. Our attitudes about life and ourselves develop as we interact with key authority figures.

Most psychologists link feelings of low self-esteem and feel-ings of "I can't" to lifestyles of conditional love.[11] Conditional love, as opposed to unconditional love, is the idea of "love if." I love you *if* you perform in an acceptable manner. This action produces over-sensitivity for the approval of others. Ultimately, for many people, it creates inhibition to step out and try unless there's a guarantee of approval. Often a child *learns* to be inhib-ited and fearful.

Conditional love creates attitudes. An attitude is a mental conditioning that determines our interpretation and response to environment. Attitude is the integration of our self-image (how we see ourselves), self-esteem (how we feel about ourselves), self-worth (how we value ourselves) and the ideal self (the self we want to become). Attitude is the manifestation of who we think we are. *We are not what we think. What we think, we are.*

This is why the projection of what authority figures think can be so devastating. Their selfishness can leave you with a feeling of neglect, which you feel you must deserve. When they hurt you, you often feel the need to hurt. When you're abused, you often feel deserving rather than the victim, or you become an abuser yourself. Failure in your environment by authority figures can perpetuate a mentality and habits of failure in your life. That's why many psychologists will say the greatest determinant of hav-ing a good home is if you came from one. Escapism is often the product of our excuse-filled life to protect ourselves from the fear of failure. That's why George Washington Carver stated, *"Ninety-nine percent of failure comes from people who have a habit of making excuses."*

How an authority figure can have influence on someone can be seen in something I witnessed as a young boy when I tried out for baseball one year. The coach went around and asked everyone what position they played. He came to the young boy next to me, and the boy blurted out, "Batter." His answer was an immediate reflection of what he didn't know. There is no position of "batter." You play a defensive position, and batting is your offensive contribution. He simply wanted to play baseball, probably to fit in, and the one thing he knew was that batting produced the glory.

The tryout quickly revealed that this young boy had no baseball skills at all. I watched as he was humiliated and saw the devastating effects it had on his self-esteem in front of the other boys. He withdrew into the *safety* of trying to receive acceptance in any way he could until finally he simply turned and walked away, feeling dejected.

Experiences in life will show what you are good at or not good at. Everyone is not made to be good at everything. Failure at one thing is only an indication that what you're good at has been narrowed down. Will Rogers said it this way, "Everybody's ignorant, just on different topics." Anything that happens to you only has the value you place on it. Joel Osteen, in his book *Your Best Life Now,* tells another story that illustrates how we have to find our strengths as well as our weaknesses.

A little boy went out in the backyard to play with a baseball bat and ball. He declared, "I'm the best hitter in the world," as he threw the ball up into the air to swing and hit it. As the ball spiraled downward, the young boy swung and missed.

Undaunted, he tossed the ball into the air again and similarly confessed, "I'm the best hitter in the world." He swung and missed for strike two. Now, concentrating more intensely and even more determined he again declared, "I'm the best hitter in the world." *Whoosh.* Again, he swung and missed for strike three. The little boy stepped back and thought for a moment and said, "Well, what do you know, I'm the best pitcher in the world!"[8]

Now, that is what I call an attitude! The right attitude will allow you to put events and proclamations in their proper perspective. How you see yourself makes all the difference in the world.

That brings us to the *third* element of our *personal belief system*:

Element 3: Self-Image

We've already defined self-image in this book, but for the sake of emphasis, let me restate it again. Self-image is a predetermined belief of what we can become. It is how we see ourselves. You don't see things as *they* are. You see things as *you* are. This determines how we respond to others and how others will respond to us. Self-image is what is stored in our subconscious mind (Matt. 12:35-36). Our lives are predominantly determined by this internal picture. This picture controls how we perceive things. It sends a message to our emotional system, physiological system and neurological system to keep us aligned with our self-image. When the subconscious mind determines we are not on target with our self-image, it will cause a stimulus or suppression of energy, ideas, or activities.[9]

That is why you cannot change a habit until you change your image. You cannot rise above the image you have of yourself in your heart. Your convictions will regulate your thoughts about yourself and your world. Self-image is the dominant source of your actions and your response to your environment.

Some experts say the greatest psychological discovery of the twentieth century is the discovery of self-worth. The more you value yourself (and as a result, others), the more willing you are to take risks and face obstacles (even failure). According to Maxwell Maltz's breakthrough work, self-image is the key to all human personality and behavior. It is what sets the boundaries of individual accomplishments.[10] Once an idea or belief goes into this picture of yourself, it becomes "true" as far as we are personally concerned.[11] In short, we act like the person we conceive ourselves to be. Self-esteem essentially is the summation of all things.

The fourth element of our personal belief system is:

Element 4: Repetitious Information

I once heard a speaker quote Adolf Hitler as saying, "If you can tell a lie often enough, people will believe it." How true this seems to be. Recently, while watching the debates for a presidential party, I watched what appeared to be a common agenda to criticize the sitting President. Because the President had no access into the foray, his poll numbers steadily declined. Repetitious display of *fact* (right or wrong) swayed the beliefs of the public.

This is also a dominant principle for advertisers. Marketers say that a person who is about to make a purchase doesn't usually do so until they've seen three ads or commercials. Ads are a combination of information and imagination. *Principles don't change a person, images do.* Repeated exposure to *truth* is convincing people and causing them to move toward certain ends. We've all seen the TV commercials that portray a car with a certain image. The next thing you know, you see the latest model cruising down the street and heads turn to see it. Finally, you see a shot of the car going down the highway from the driver's perspective … as though you're driving the vehicle. The combination of information plus imagination plus repetition becomes a need to purchase. Repetitious information, positive or negative, can have a major influence on what we believe. That's why people who hear things over and over tend to accept them as truth. You may hear things like, "When you get older, you get arthritis." The first sign of arthritis is stiffness, so you think, "I must have arthritis." Sure enough, your subconscious mind begins to work to bring it to pass. False repetitious information can be damaging.

The *fifth* element that contributes to your *personal belief system* is:

Element 5: Experience

This area really is the largest contributor to a person's beliefs. People have a tendency to believe what they experience as being true, without realizing there were contributing factors to the experience. As I stated earlier, all children are born without fear and have spontaneous resolve. All fear is learned by discouraging experiences or conditional love. The good news is that what is learned can be unlearned. Josh Billings once said, "It's not what man knows that hurts him; it's what he knows isn't true" (or at least thinks so). Learning and unlearning both came the same way – repetitious experience. That's why Maxwell Maltz says, "To experience something, you must creatively respond to information."[12] Such action creates patterns in your brain that prompt belief and action. In fact, experience is larger than the other 4 areas combined.

The two most destructive emotions are fear and discouragement. To "dis"-courage (against courage) costs people the benefit of trying. When a person loses hope, they lose the most powerful motivator to success.[13]

All children are born with an incredible capacity for courage, hope and risk-taking. I'll never forget when my first child learned how to walk at about eleven or twelve months old. He was in our living room pulling himself up on the furniture and doing his drunken sailor imitation. While he was wobbling and trying to gain his balance, I bounded across the room, beckoning him to come to Daddy. As I said, "Come to Daddy," he looked straight at me, lifted his leg, and for some unknown reason it went sideways, and he fell. It made no difference to him; he simply got up and tried again. He had a full capacity for hope, resiliency and success.

People start out as creatures of hope and courage. Experiences, wrongly interpreted, create self-limiting beliefs and often paralyzing fears. Proverbs 13:12 states, "Hope deferred makes the heart sick." Hope unrealized causes the soul to be in conflict with the spirit and saps a person of their resolve. As a newborn child, you were completely unafraid and spontaneous. You laughed, cried, slept and ate with little or no thought whether anyone approved or disapproved. Somewhere in childhood you learned negative responses to habits, and as a result, you began to demonstrate inhibited and reserved behavior.

The biggest inhibition is fear. It is most often manifested in the fear of failure or the fear of rejection. Childhood correction without corresponding approval often results in feelings of "I can't" or "I'm not good enough." The fear of rejection is often a result of conditional love in childhood. It is acceptance based upon behavior. The result is hypersensitivity to the opinions of others. The results are often paralyzing when it comes to stepping into the destiny God has for you.

Overcoming Self-Limiting Beliefs

The key to understanding how to break the bond of mediocrity is not to *run from* self-limiting beliefs (mediocrity), but to *learn from* them.

There are the four steps that help people identify the self-limiting beliefs that hold them back from experiencing all God has for them. All of these steps are to be done within the context of the five steps to biblical meditation given in chapter 5. (See exercise at the end of this chapter to help you identify self-limiting beliefs.)

1. *Identification* – Use the exercise at the end of this chapter to identify your set-points or self-limiting beliefs.

2. *Disassociate* (disconnect) yourself from self-limiting beliefs. See yourself differently than what you are conditioned to do or be. This is part of the imagination stage

in the process of biblical meditation. See Jesus coming into the situation and changing it.

3. ***Apply the antidote of God's truth.*** Once you've identified the set-point and disassociated yourself from it, then see yourself in accordance to the truth. "Take" the antidote to your self-limitation. (See my *Barrier Buster's Manual* for a complete list of self-limiting beliefs and their antidotes. This manual also contains lists of scriptures, confessions, applications, and images of how you should see yourself in your heart.) It is here that you take the scriptures of your antidote, turn them into confessions, application and new images. Once it is done repetitively any self-limitation is easily broken.

4. ***Employ new empowering beliefs*** – Act on what you now know to be true.

God created you to dominate your environment, not to be dominated by it (Genesis 1:26-28). By correcting self-limiting beliefs with the real truth, you can automatically leap to a new level. God made you for abundance. It is now time to live in it.

Why are these five elements of your personal belief system necessary to know? It is because these beliefs formulate an automatic response system from your subconscious mind. The subconscious mind is where your personal belief system resides, and this is where 90 to 95 percent of your decisions are made daily. Perhaps you grew up with a parent who imparted ideas to you such as: "Do you think money grows on tree?" "Do you think there's a money tree in the backyard?" "We can't afford this." "There's just not enough to go around." With constant negative repetitious information, the idea that "There's really not enough" gets into your heart (subconscious mind) and formulates the beliefs of lack and decrease. Even though the Word (the truth) says, "Give and it shall be given to you" (Lk. 6:38), the idea "There's really not enough" has created an automatic response that suggests giving to God results in greater lack. This is why the latest figures of the number of tithers in the church are around 6 to 8 percent.[14]

Many people never actualize (attract) their destiny, like the Promised Land in Numbers 14, because they see the "giants" of lack, rejection, fear and anxiety waiting for them. Like the Israelites, they "seem like grasshoppers" in their own eyes. Their personal belief system (the subconscious mind chamber of the heart) has already established an automatic response to the obstacles in their path. As a result, they don't enter into God's system (Kingdom of God). Therefore, life dictates to them instead of them dictating to life.

Once you know the source of your self-limiting thinking, you can resubmit your beliefs to a new mirror (the Word of God to the conscious mind) to establish new truth. Then, through *revelation* from the Holy Spirit and *repetition*, you will recognize people, ideas and resources that are being attracted to you by the Holy Spirit from God's Kingdom. With a new self-image based on God's truth, your new expectation will allow you to step out to do things, make a plan or take a course of action (in cooperation with the Holy Spirit) to make things come to pass in God's plan for your life.

The exercise at the end of this chapter is not to reinforce negative feelings, but to show you the source of your thinking that seeks to keep barriers in your life. This is the hour to destroy your limitations. Remember, self-limiting beliefs are who you *were, not* who you *are*! Remember *who* you *are*! (2 Cor. 5:17).

Keys for Reflection

Five Elements of Your Personal Belief System – Exercise

Instructions: Find a quiet time and respond to all of the questions below on a separate piece of paper or in a journal.

Element 1: Environment

- Are there certain settings that remind you of experiences that left you with negative, limiting or discouraging feelings?

- Were there certain things in your background that made you think you were dumb, unloved, a failure or not as good as others?

- Was there an environment in your home, school, church or a prominent setting that made you feel self-defeated, worthless, limited or dumb?

- Was there an event in your life or family that scared you?

Element 2: Authority Figures

- Was there something done to you that makes you feel abused or hurt?

- Has an important figure in your life said or done something to you that would make you feel limited, worthless or willing to settle for what you've always had?

- Has there ever been an incident with your father that has changed the way you see God?

- Have there been behavioral or health problems that have become patterns in your family?

- When you think of certain people who wronged you, do you feel something wrong in the pit of your stomach?

- Are you able to receive compliments or gifts from others without feeling unworthy or guilty? If no, why?

- Are there beliefs you have that have come from people in your life that are contrary to the Word of God?

Element 3: Self-Image

- What is the thing you most dislike about yourself?
- Do you have feelings of being unworthy, unloved, discouraged, depressed, being a failure, anxiety, quitting (regularly), wavering in thought, selfishness, pride or being out of control (anger, lust)?
- Do you consistently feel stressed?
- Do you feel regular feelings of guilt, grief, worry, rage or unforgiveness?

Element 4: Repetitious Information

- What have you been taught from school, home, friends, work, media, teachers or coaches that is contrary to the Word of God?
- What things have been reinforced in you that may be construed as limiting?

Element 5: Experience

- What experience have you had that was beyond your control and left you feeling fearful, negative or alone?
- What happened to you that you would consider your biggest test in life? What is your reflection on it?
- What failure in your life looms large in your memory?
- What regret do you have in life?
- What is the one thing you wish had never happened to you?
- What experience do you wish hadn't happened in your childhood, teenage or college years?

CHAPTER 7

PREDICTING YOUR FUTURE

THEME: PREDICTING YOUR FUTURE BY LEARNING TO WRITE ON THE TABLETS OF YOUR HEART.

Lesson: Learning ways to develop specific heart beliefs.

There is a classic movie moment when Doris Day sings, "Que Será, Será." As I recall, the song goes something like this: "When I was just a little girl, I asked my mother, what will I be? Will I be pretty? Will I be rich? Here's what she said to me." "Que Será, Será. Whatever will be, will be. The future's not ours to see. Que Será, Será." What nonsense! Though that might be a memorable song in a famous musical, it is totally contrary to biblical truth on how to approach life.

This passive mentality embraces drifting along in life and taking whatever comes your way. This is hardly the intent of scripture (see Mt. 11:12). That's why business guru Peter Drucker once said in a Tulsa seminar I attended, "The best way to predict your future is to create it."

George Bernard Shaw, in Earl Nightingale's book *The Strangest Secret*, , is quoted as saying, "People are always blaming their circumstances for what they are. I don't believe in circumstances. The people who get on in this world are people who get up and look for the circumstances they want, and if they can't find them, they make them." We become what we think about.

Shaw goes on to add a profound analogy: suppose a farmer has some land and it is good, fertile soil. In essence, the land gives the farmer a choice. He is free to plant on the land whatever he chooses. The land doesn't care about what he chooses to plant. It will return what is planted.

The land doesn't care about the choice of seed. If this farmer plants two seeds – one is corn and the other is nightshade, a deadly poison, what will be the result? The land will invariably return what is deposited in it. Remember, the land doesn't care what is planted. Its job is to create an abundance of the deposit.

The human mind is far more fertile and mysterious than any land, but it works the same way. It doesn't care what we plant—success or failure—its job is to yield increase. What we plant will return to us.[1]

Jesus said "I have come to give you life and life more abundantly" (Jn. 10:10). In other words, He has come to give you life as a super-achiever, and yet those succeeding at this level seem to be few and far between. God's purpose for you is that you find the life you were born to live, fulfill your destiny, and live in success and prosperity. You need to settle this issue in you. You must discover your value, operate in the Laws of God and manifest His Kingdom wherever you go.

The Kingdom of Heaven is not simply an eternal destiny; it is a manner of rule, governance, or system.[2] It is a system based on God's laws. A law tells you how a thing works best. In this case, the "thing" is the Kingdom of God. Once these laws are mastered in connection to the Kingdom, you know how the manifestations of abundance will come into your life.

The **goal of this book** is to create a systematic plan to transform your personal belief system, not based on reflection from an improper social environment, incorrect authority figures, a poor self-image, false repetitious information, or bad experiences, but solely based on the truth of God's immutable Word.

What I think determines what I believe. What I believe determines my decisions. My decisions determine what I can accomplish. The results are a matter of choice (Deut. 30:19). Renewing my mind, establishing my heart and transforming my personal belief system is not simply memorizing scripture (truth). It is the transformation of my decision-making.

God's plan and purpose for you *is* productivity at every level. John states in 3 John 2, "Beloved, I wish above all things that you may prosper and be in health, even as your soul prospers." Notice it is an aberration in the Kingdom's system to be in sickness and poverty. The manifestation, however, is not automatic. It is dependent on a prosperous soul. What is a prosperous soul? A prosperous soul is a renewed mind, a persuaded, submitted will, positive emotions and a focused imagination (meditation). These things, in turn, produce health and prosperity.

So, why is it so many people have difficulty manifesting this promise? Paul deals with this in Ephesians 4:17ff. He states, "So I tell you this, and insist on it in the Lord, that you must no longer live as the Gentiles do [people who are out of the context with God's thinking][3] and live in the futility of their thinking." What is this? It is the world's system. This system can create a feeling of being untrustworthy, worthless or incapable of producing a desired end from God.

Paul goes on to say, "They are darkened [un-illuminated] in their understanding and separated from the life of God." The very things you want God to manifest, you cannot manifest because you're thinking according to the wrong system and are separated from the Source of your true supply.

Paul says it's because "of the ignorance that is in them due to the hardening of their hearts." The hardening of your heart is when you are more sensitive to the natural than you are to the supernatural (see Mk. 6:45-52; 8:1-21). There is no alignment or congruency in your heart.

Here's the result: "Having lost all sensitivity [to God], they have given themselves over to sensuality." Sensuality is always a substitute for sensitivity. Sensuality is an act of the flesh. Flesh is man's attempt to do God's will in his own way (See Rom. 8:5ff). Once God sees that characteristic, He backs off and lets people try to meet their needs by natural means until they come to the end of themselves. And then some, not all, turn to Him and learn to drink from the spring of living water that never runs dry.

Paul continues, "so as to indulge in every kind of impurity." What is impurity? It's not just unacceptable behavior. Impurity really means mixture. If another substance is mixed with gold, the gold is impure. Most Christians live their lives as a mixture. They mix the old man with their new identity, which hinders them from living life to the fullest. God made you a new creation with truth and grace (God's ability) to manifest His resources of His Kingdom. The mixture (allowing impurities in your life) dilutes your effectiveness and true productivity.

Paul concludes the section in Ephesians with the answer, "To be made new in the attitudes of your minds; and put on the new self, created to be like God in true righteousness and holiness" (Ephes. 4:23, 24). What a remarkable revelation. As a believer, we are to put on the new self and understand who we have become as a new creature. *See* yourself according to the truth. "Be made new in the attitude of your mind." Remember, the term *attitude* means *mental conditioning that determines our interpretation or response to our environment.* It is the integration of our self-image, self-esteem, self-worth and ideal self. Self-image is how you see yourself. Self-worth is how you value yourself. Self-esteem is how you feel about yourself. The ideal self is the person you see yourself becoming. It is the way you see yourself, and you will act according to that image. What Paul is saying is this – if you see yourself differently, then the truth will change your viewpoint to the truth. Then, you will act in accordance to truth.

It's All About Attitude

Remember, you see what you already believe.[4] You do not believe what you see; you see what you already believe. You view your life (world) through the lens of beliefs, attitudes, prejudices and preconceived notions. You are not what you think; what you *think* you *are*[5] The missing key to God's Kingdom is as much about unlearning what we perceive to be true as it is learning to see the truth of who you really are. You must recognize your present beliefs are responsible for where you are right now in life. God's secret is to break those beliefs and show you how to live by His Kingdom laws. There is a marketing principle by Henry Beckwith that says, "People hear what they see."[6] You can tell them anything, but they have a tendency to believe what they see. That's why when you tell people that God wants to prosper them, people immediately look to see if they can find any prosperity around them.

The job of the conscious mind is to determine truth. The job of the subconscious mind is to take whatever the conscious mind determines is true and create an automatic response system to carry it out. That's why perceived truth always battles new truths. Your subconscious mind will automatically make decisions in agreement with established truth – right or wrong. Your personal belief system is stronger than anything I can say to you. Knowing this is a major influence when it is in opposition to God's truth.

Your dominant thoughts get into your heart, and whatever is in your heart, that's what you are going to do. This is the *missing ingredient* to real productivity and *transformation* in your life. What is learned can be unlearned, so that new beliefs can replace the false ones that have been lodged in your heart. These new beliefs will change your personal belief system, which will now consist of a renewed mind, an established heart and increased faith. Renewed thinking done consistently creates dominant thoughts that get into your heart. When you have an established heart, it creates corresponding actions and these consistent actions increase faith. Increased faith brings increased manifestations.

Writing on the Tablets of Your Heart

Everything that happens in your life comes out of your heart. If you want to break the pattern of your present and predict your future, you must learn to write on the tablets of your heart. Look at this principle in Proverbs 7:1-3, "My son, keep my words and store up my commands within you. Keep my commands and you will live; guard my teachings as the apple of my eye. Bind them on your fingers; write them on the tablets of your heart."

The following are five principles to help you *write on your heart* God's truth and thereby predict your own future:

1. *Store commands in your inner man (within you).* This term *store* means *to put aside a supply for use when needed.*[7] Therefore, I take the truths of God's Word and store them in my heart and mind until I have future need of them. I do this by study and the five steps of meditation. Remember, meditation is a combination of information and emotion. God dwells in your spirit by salvation, but He dwells in your heart by faith (Eph. 3:16, 17). Faith is believing the truth of a renewed mind, an established heart and a new image on the inside of you (Mt. 12:34-35).

2. *Keep my commands.* The term *keep* means *to guard or protect.*[8] I protect what I store through the act of thanksgiving (see Phil. 4:6, 7). Thanksgiving puts a guard over my heart and mind. Thanksgiving is a powerful force. Emotions travel 80,000 faster than a thought. Emotions, like thanksgiving, cause your will and your mind to move into action toward a goal. That is why God's Word mixed with thanksgiving protects the truth in your heart and mind. It helps line the mind up to God's truth and, in turn, line up with your spirit. It is here that the power of God is released. Since the subconscious mind doesn't recognize positives or negatives, or real or imagined, it recognizes the emotion as an indication of the establishment of truth and rallies toward that end. That is why thanksgiving is such a powerful force.

   - The writer in Proverbs 7 says, if you do this, you will live. This doesn't mean you'll exist or that God will *snuff you out* if you don't. It means you will have the vitality (or abundance) for which you were created. The shackles of lack or mediocrity will be broken from your life.

3. *Guard my teachings as the apple of your eye.* In other words, watch over this process because this is the most important thing you can do. Your diligence in this effort indicates its value to you. Don't let new circumstances rob you of God's newly established truth. Do something daily toward your highest priority.

4. *Bind them on your fingers.* The old idea of tying a string around your finger to remind you of something is the idea here. It's like George Bailey's uncle in the movie *It's a Wonderful Life.* He was always trying to remind himself of something by tying a string on his finger. The idea

here is to remind yourself of something through repetition. It takes at least 21 days to create a new habit. Let repetition help you *see* new truths (images) in your life.

5. *Write them on the tablets of your heart.* In other words, storing (meditation), keeping (protecting), guarding (prioritizing) and binding (repetition) contribute to writing on the tablets of my heart. Once it's in my heart, it will dictate my actions.

- Writing on the tablets of our heart is primarily influencing the soul chamber and, in particular, the subconscious mind. This is the part of our heart that tries to make what we believe come to pass. This is where your personal belief system creates an automatic response system that presupposes your actions. This is why you do what you really believe. This is why writing on the tablets of your heart is far more than scripture meditation.

- To imprint new truth that you want to incorporate into your heart, you must make it personal, present tense and positive. Take the "you" of the new truth and make it personal by saying "I," or "my," or "me." For instance, if you are meditating on Psalm 35:27 (Amplified), "Let the Lord be magnified, Who takes pleasure in the prosperity of His servants," read it like this. "Lord, I thank you that you delight in my prosperity. I rejoice that you delight in and are excited about prospering me." It must also be positive. Don't think about overcoming your present lack, because focusing on lack causes you to attract lack. Instead, focus on your present prosperity. Don't look at the negative, look at the positive. Finally, make it present tense.

"I am" prospering in everything I do. Get specific about a present situation you're involved in now. Let your meditation allow you to *see* (imagine) this truth in your heart. See the benefits. Ponder the joy of your new reality. See yourself walking out the truth. Imprint it on your heart.

The writer of the Psalms reinforces this thought in Proverbs 3. Virtually every believer knows Proverbs 3:5-6, "Trust in the Lord with all your heart and lean not on your own understanding; in all your ways acknowledge him, and he will make your paths straight." It's a powerful verse. But it is preceded by verses 1-4, "My son, do not forget my teaching, but keep my commands in your heart, for they will prolong your life many years and bring you prosperity. Let love and faithfulness never leave you; bind them around your neck, write them on the tablet of your heart."

Proverbs 3 starts out saying, "Do not forget my teaching." Why? Because the five elements of your personal belief system (social environment, authority figures, self-image, repetitious information and experience) all have negative influence that is constantly challenging truth with fact.

Proverbs continues, "Keep, store, guard, bind, repeat and write on your heart, and you'll gain vitality of life and prosperity." You will be *fully alive*. Once you've mastered these principles, you find yourself not leaning to your past experience as a guide, but instead you recognize new truth, and God allows you to see people, ideas and resources according to your most dominant thoughts (direct your paths).

Recently, I was speaking at a conference in Hawaii in a beautiful setting. I had this sense that I was in this setting for a divine purpose. After several days, it still was not clear to me. I even declined my roommate's offer to go *work out* so I could pray instead. After two hours of prayer (one in my room, the other by the ocean), God spoke six things to me. The first had to do with an authority figure in my past. The person had a habit of what I call *poor mouthing*. People who *poor mouth* have a habit of always seeing and saying the negative side of things. This person not only constantly spoke this way in front of me, but they modeled this behavior. Suddenly, I realized that this self-limitation had invaded my life in certain arenas.

The moment I realized this, I began to disassociate myself from an improper image. I began to store, keep, protect, guard and write a new image on my heart of belief and expectation. In that moment, my new image became absolutely real, and six things leaped out of my heart that I was to do. One of them was to talk privately with one of the main speakers at this conference. I followed up with my friend who was the speaker to make that a reality, and we got together. I began to share some revelations God had placed on my heart. He agreed to open doors in the publishing arena and a couple of other areas. My point is not to accentuate my good fortune of a serendipitous occurrence, but to point out how breaking a set-point from my past created a new image in my heart that opened doors to my future. The result was that God directed my paths.

Paul recalls a similar idea in 2 Corinthians 3:3, "You show that you are a letter from Christ, the result of our ministry, not written with ink but with the Spirit of the living God, not on tablets of stone but on tablets of human hearts." Again, God's design is to imprint his thoughts on your heart. All of a person's faith comes out of a person's heart. We do not accomplish this process by ourselves; it is the product of the Holy Spirit's working in our lives. Paul continues by saying, 'Such confidence is ours, through Christ before God.' The result of a newly imprinted heart is a new image that fills us with true confidence. True confidence is the product of a transformed self-image. This produces righteousness by faith, which allows us to see the reflection of God's work and to be transformed from one level of glory (view and opinion of God and manifestation of His presence[9]) to another.

Ezekiel amplifies this, "I will give you a new heart and put a new spirit in you; I will remove from you your heart of stone and give you a heart of flesh. And, I will put my Spirit in you and move you to follow my decrees, and be careful to keep my laws" (Ezek. 36:26, 27). As you transform your heart to God's view and opinion, it becomes easy to keep His laws. The prophet Jeremiah declares, "I will put my laws in their minds and write it on their hearts. I will be their God, and they will be my people" (31:33). Once your heart is changed, believing new truth becomes easy.

The Yoke Is On You

Most of the time when you answer a question about life, your answer is conditioned by your experience. Experience is anything observed or lived through ... all that has happened to a person. It is the reaction to events. It is a person's personal referral system. It is your data bank of all your memories stored in your mind. You generally ask the question, *Does this jive with my experience from the past? Does this correlate with what I know to be true?* When I'm doing a conference, if I make the statement, *Parenting is easy!* I usually get a gasp. For many people, this does not correlate to their experience. They've had quite a different experience, especially if they've had to deal with a rebellious son or daughter. Or, how about this, *Crime doesn't pay.* Oh really? There are many people who have found it to be quite profitable and are living the high life hidden in this country or abroad. How you view life depends on your experience.

So if I asked the question, *Is Christianity easy?* most believers would protest vociferously. Why? There's no corroboration with their experience. Listen to what Jesus said, "Come to Me, all you who labor and are heavy laden, and I will give you rest. Take My yoke upon you and learn from Me, for I am gentle and lowly in heart, and you will find rest for your souls. For My yoke is easy and My burden is light"[10] (Matthew 11:28,29).

Jesus reveals four amazing truths in this short passage:

Truth #1: *When you are weary and weak, come to God.* Why is it so many of us are like Simba in the *Lion King*? When we are weak, weary and messed up, we want to run from God, instead of run to Him. Listen to the writer of Hebrews, "Let us approach the throne of grace with confidence, so that we may receive mercy and grace to help in time of need" (4:16).

- First, notice it's a throne of grace, not judgment. Second, notice when do we come? When we are in need. What kind of need is he referring to? When I'm weary, weak, or when I've messed up. When I've done the thing I said I'd never do. Most of us want to run from God, not to Him. And yet this verse invites us to come to a heavenly Father who longs to help just at the moment we feel weak and failing.

- Not only are we to come to Him, but look how we're to come – with confidence. How can I possibly come to God with confidence when I've messed up? We can come with confidence not because of us, but because of the righteousness we have in Jesus. Righteousness is right standing with God, not based on what I've done, but receiving by faith what He has done on my behalf. I couldn't keep the law, so Jesus did it for me. Now I receive it by faith in Him (see Rom. 3:20-26; 2 Cor. 5:20, Rom. 10:3, 4 Rom. 5:17-19, 1 Cor. 15:34, Phil. 3:7-11, Mt. 6:32, 33, Psalm 112:3, 6-8, 1 Tim. 1:9). Even when I mess up, I can run to Him, not from Him.

Truth #2: *Then I will give you rest* (rest correlates to grace; see Heb. 4:10). This second step correlates again to Hebrews 4:16. When I come to His throne of grace, He gives me mercy and grace to help in time of need. These two words do not mean the same thing. Mercy is God not giving us what we deserve. Grace is God giving us what we don't deserve (in a positive way). It is God's enablement or His ability.[11] Grace is God's ability to do what our ability cannot do. We were not made to follow the patterns of success on our own abilities. We are to get yoked up to Him. Two oxen yoked together share the burden. I can't live the super-abundant, super-achieving lifestyle apart from His infusion of grace

Truth #3: *Learn of me.* We receive the help we need by humbly submitting to God's ways. Now, what are His ways? His ways are His principles and laws of how things are to be done. Humility does not mean becoming a doormat being willfully trampled upon. It is not some weak-willed, nondescript manner of pursuing something. The word *humility* means "to submit to the view and opinion of God."[12] It is not simply some lowly mindset. Humility says, *If God says I can, I can. If God says I am, I am. If God says I have, I have.*[13] The key is learning God's laws of success. Earlier we shared about one of the laws in Physics called the Law of Entropy, which says, *Things left unattended tend toward chaos.* How true this law is for us as people. Things left unattended in our lives swing toward the chaotic. For instance, leave your grass unattended, it goes toward chaos. Leave your house unattended, it goes toward chaos. Leave your kids unattended…you get the picture. Transformation comes from intentionally going after our shortcomings and applying God's principles. All change for God is intentional, not haphazard. It comes from learning His ways.

Truth #4: *For I am ... humble of heart* means that your heart is submitted to the view and opinion of God. Your soul is submitted to your spirit in your heart by the renewing of your mind.

The result is that you will find rest or grace (God's ability on your behalf) for your heart and your soul. Obeying His ways produces a yoke that is easy and light. The Christian life becomes easy and vigorous because we are doing it in His strength and not ours.

There are two ways you can tell if a revelation is in your heart: (1) It changes your image of yourself in that area and (2) that area becomes easy.[14] Any lasting change begins by changing the image of yourself in that area. That is the biggest part of what biblical meditation does in your life. It is amazing to me how easy certain things are in my life now. For instance, I'm never tempted to do drugs. Why? That is already in my heart. My past is filled with experiences with alcohol, but today I'm never tempted with alcohol. Why? My view and opinion of my heart are submitted to God's principles. It's easy and light.

I was working with a dynamic young woman, but because of a deprecating past experience, she found herself on a roller coaster with her emotions. One day she was up, and the next she was in the depths of depression. Frankly, there was very little stability in her life, so I took her through these four truths.

First, I asked her not to ignore her past hurt, but to focus and see it clearly. I even asked her to identify the intensity of how she felt. Next, I asked her to disassociate herself from the false guilt she was experiencing from this memory. I told her to meditate on righteousness and love, while seeing Jesus healing this tragic memory. As she applied the antidote of love and righteousness to her life, I watched an amazing transformation take place. Overwhelming confidence poured into her life, and she began to walk in unbridled expectation. Daily she began to employ her new-found image and beliefs. Almost overnight she started recognizing people, ideas and resources she had been missing. Every area of her life started moving in a new direction. The transformation was as startling as the story of the woman with amnesia. Today she is a successful businesswoman fulfilled in her life.

How do you employ new empowering beliefs? Once revelation starts to get down in your heart, you've got to make them work for you. How? Every day do something to reinforce your highest priority. Find something to do that reinforces your new belief system. If you are "believing" God for new living quarters, drive by an area that is where you would like to live and just dream. If you want to lose weight, go window shopping for your new size. Begin to act in accordance to your new beliefs. Also, reinforce and reward your progress. If you want to lose fifty pounds, but you've lost twenty pounds, reward yourself (in this case, don't do it with food). Go shopping or get a massage or some activity that you enjoy.

Remember, some failure is inevitable. You may experience a set-back or two. Your attitude when you fail will make all the difference in the world. Thomas Edison is credited as being the greatest inventor of our time. He is credited with 1,093 patents. It is also true that Edison was also the greatest *failure* of our time. He failed many more times than he had breakthroughs. He would experiment and fail over and over again. His attitude was simply this, success is inevitable and failure is not an option. Don't let some minor set-back deter you from your destiny. Remember, failure is merely an opportunity to start again more intelligently.

Once you master renewing your mind, establishing your heart and transforming your personal belief system, you will be positioned to learn the laws that make success inevitable. Once biblical meditation secures new empowering beliefs, the momentum to do God's will is like a wind in your sails. Now, it's time to examine how all of this applies to faith productivity in every area of your life.

Keys for Reflection

Remember the *five keys to writing on the tablets of your heart:*

1. Store the truth of God's Word in you.
    a. Study until you have revelation
    b. Meditate
    c. Let God's truth create a new image in you

2. Keep, guard and protect the truth you have received with thanksgiving. Thanksgiving reinforces to the subconscious mind the truth associated with it as something it needs to pursue until what you desire becomes true.

3. Guard your new truth (*as the apple of your eye*) as the most important pursuit of your life. Don't let new current circumstances rob you of the truth.

4. Bind the truth on your finger, which means make their repetition a priority. It takes at least 21 days to create a new habit.

5. Write the truth on your heart. Remember, your boundaries in life come out of your heart. By confessing God's truth as personal, present tense and positive, new truth becomes imprinted on your heart.

In summary:

- Identify self-limiting beliefs.
- Disassociate yourself from the image of these self-limiting beliefs through the imagination stage of biblical meditation.
- Apply the antidote of the truth from the perspective of God's Word.
- Employ new empowering beliefs by confessing and applying God's Word.

CHAPTER 8

THE DEFINITION OF FAITH

THEME: THE END PRODUCT OF HEART BELIEFS IS THE DEVELOPMENT OF UNWAVERING FAITH.

Lesson: To get what we say we believe to manifest itself

All of this renewing the mind, establishing your heart and transforming your personal belief system stuff has an end in mind. That end is **faith**. Faith is the principle that taps into the creative power of God, whereby man can transform conditions, circumstances and situations in the natural realm. Most principles are easy to learn and difficult to apply. It's easy to do; it's easy not to do. Renewing your mind and establishing your heart is the substructure of faith. Faith is that quality that allows a person to tap into the unseen resources of the Kingdom of God. Again, the Kingdom of God is more than the rule and reign of God. It is also the location and resources of God. It is everything Christ's finished work (Jn. 19:30) has provided for your salvation. Now this term "salvation" in its original language means to save, heal, deliver, protect, preserve, to do well, to make whole, rescue, keep safe, defend, to prosper.[1] Salvation is both here and now and there and then. Jesus' finished work has given us "everything we need for life and godliness" (2 Pet. 1:3). What God provided by grace (unmerited by our efforts) we receive by faith (Eph. 2:8, 9).

Let me give you an example. A few years ago, I was ministering in a large church on a Sunday night with a crowd of 1,500 to 2,000 people. I ministered on faith, and when I gave the altar call, a minimum of 1,000 to 1,200 people came forward to receive a touch in their lives. There were people everywhere. They filled the altar area and were stacked up every aisle. A little overwhelmed, I stepped off the platform and waded into the sea of people. I walked up to the first person and asked, "What do you need from God?"

The person leaned into me and whispered, "I have AIDS." Without hesitation I ministered to him and God manifested Himself. (By the way, about a month later he showed me a doctor's report that he had been healed of AIDS).

I went to the next person and inquired, "What is your need?"

This man answered, "I have a congenital heart disease, and I've been given a few months to live." Without hesitation I spoke over him and God manifested Himself again.

I went to the third person and inquired of her need. She said, "I've been diagnosed with a terminal disease!" I again ministered to her and God appeared on her behalf.

Wow! The first three people came with big problems and God showed up. Personally, I would have preferred to start with headaches and worked my way up (☺). After ministering to these three people, further ministry went on for some time until the service concluded.

After the service was over, I was standing in the auditorium conversing with people when a young man came up to me and asked, "Can you 'lay' your hands on me, so I can get what you've got?"

Without any sense of false humility I replied, "You've already got what I've got!" He continued on, "I don't think you understand. I need you to 'lay' hands on me so I can get what you've got." I once again replied, "No, I don't think you understand. You've got what I've got!" This happened a couple of more times until he grabbed my hand and dramatically placed it on his forehead and barked, "Would you just pray for me?" I did, realizing he was quite missing the point that we have all been given the *same* measure of faith (Rom. 12:3).

A young man overhearing all of this quipped, "You must be a great man of faith." I responded, "Not really! My faith is not in my faith. My faith is in His grace." This is not all about me or you; it is all about Him. He has provided everything we need for abundant life (Jn. 10:10; 2 Pet. 1:3). We must simply learn to establish our hearts for unwavering, doubtless, effortless faith. It is easy to learn and hard to apply.

In a leadership class I teach to future pastors, I often reflect on the foibles of what I call *ought to* preaching. You ought to pray more (witness more, be more holy, etc.). I am very sensitive to this type of preaching. After I came home from my first year of college after being born again, I was hired to do an internship at a church in a particular city. The pastor of this church was an *ought to* preacher. I was constantly asking him, "How does that work or what does that look like?" I don't want simply to be told what I ought to do, but how do I apply this stuff?

I want to take faith out of the ethereal and bring it into the practical. Writing on the tablets of your heart builds the substructure to effortless faith to manifest the Kingdom of God. What you struggle with can become easy with some simple understandings.

The Definition of Faith

It is essential that we define faith. A wrong definition can cause misapplication and misappropriation of God's Kingdom (and often does for believers). So, let's first examine **what faith is not**:

- Faith is not what I do to get God to respond to me or for me to move God. God moved 2,000 years ago. I am not waiting on God; God is waiting on me. The problem for many believers is they are New Covenant believers living in an Old Covenant mentality. Unwittingly, some well-meaning theologians have dispelled the idea of adhering to the Old Testament. They conjecture all we need to do is adhere to the New Testament (beginning after the cross in the Book of Acts). Nonsense! The Old Testament is merely a testimony of that time as the New Testament is for its time. We understand the Old Covenant is a substructure to the New Testament. However, the two covenants are not equal (Heb. 8:6, 7, 13). In the Old Covenant, we live in a way to beseech Him to do something in the future. In the New Covenant, the work is already done through Jesus Christ, so I simply reinforce what He has already provided for us.

- Faith is **not i**ntellectual agreement of facts. Faith is a heart thing. You manifest what is in your heart.

So then, what is faith? Faith is primarily trust.[2] Faith trusts the character and motive of God.

- The Character of God – Character is based on the mental characteristics that distinguish a person or personality. For example: God cannot lie (Numbers 23:19). He has integrity (Proverbs 11:3). He is truthful (Jn. 17:17), and He is faithful (Heb. 10:23).

- The Motive of God – His motive is love. God's motive toward His people is love (1 Jn. 4:16, 17). Thus, God always has our best at heart and our best interest on His mind.

Once we settle the issue of God's character and motive, faith becomes easy. Once we convince ourselves that God cannot lie to us and He always has our best interests on His mind, faith becomes easy.

Faith is belief in your heart. You might ask the question, *how do I know if a belief is in my heart?* You know if two things happen: (1) It changes how you see yourself and (2) Change in that area becomes easy (Mt. 11:28-30). You will manifest what you believe in your heart. How does this apply to faith? Let's see how this works in God's definition of faith.

God's Definition of Faith

Hebrews chapter 11 is God's definition of faith. In this passage, He lays out the definition and function of faith: "Now faith is the **substance** of **things hoped** for, the **evidence** of things **unseen.**" Let's break this definition down.

Faith – Trust in the character and motive of God. God's motive for me is always in love and for my good. Love is not just a characteristic of God. God is love. Everything He does is out of a motive of love. His character is he **cannot** lie (Titus 1:2; Hebrews 6:18; Numbers 23:19).

Substance – Tangible, reality, foundation, substructure, title deed, substance, substantiates, confidence, assurance, inventory.[3]

- Faith is not ethereal, it is **substantive.**
- Faith is an **undergirding** of the finished work of Christ for you.
- It is a **title deed**. I may not be able to see it presently, but it is proof of what I possess. If I have a title deed for land in Florida, and I am in Oklahoma, it is proof of what I own.
- Faith is **inventory**. Inventory is a detailed listing of one's possessions. It has been estimated that the Word of God contains over 7,000 promises that are our possessions

by grace. It is this inventory that creates an expectation in us. Expectation creates a corresponding action (Jas. 2:14) to appropriate what is ours.

- Faith **substantiates**. The idea of *substantiates* means *to establish as evidence, to prove, verify, assurance, to give substantial form, to make real.*[4]

Of **things** – The term *things* used here in Greek is the word *pragma.*" *It means a thing already done or previously accomplished.*[5] There is an inventory with my name written on it of what God has already appropriated for me by grace. Wow! A thing (pragma) has to do with what the finished work has provided. This is revealed in Ephesians 1:2-3, "Grace and peace be to you, from God the Father and the Lord Jesus Christ" (v.2). Grace is really four things biblically:

- **Unmerited favor**[6] – God has given us something incredible that we could never earn.
- **The finished work of Christ** – What He has given us by unmerited favor is the finished work of Jesus Christ. Everything for life and godliness is at our disposal (2 Pet. 1:3; Jn. 19:30).
- **A Divine influence upon the heart**[7] – Grace allows us to live from the inside (heart) out, not the outside in.
- **Empowerment or ability**[8] – I like to say it like this: it's my ability to use God's ability to meet any need in Ephesians 1:2-3. After grace, the verse notes, "and peace." I define peace like this: the ability to not be influenced by circumstances and surroundings. In other words, what grace gives, peace keeps. Verse 3 adds, "Who has [past-tense – already done] blessed [empowered to prosper] us [you and me] in the heavenly realm [Kingdom of heaven] with every spiritual [given word

for supernatural] blessing in Christ [His finished work] (emphasis added).

Let's go back to a verse I used in the introduction of this book. Matthew 16:19 says, "I will give you the keys of the Kingdom of heaven and whatever you bind [that is declare to be improper and unlawful] on earth, must already be bound in heaven; and whatever you loose on earth [declare to be lawful] must already be loosed in heaven" (AMP). In other words, I can **assess** whatever is not in keeping with the Kingdom of God and **align** myself with the finished work of God already completed, so I can **access** it for my life.

Look at this incredible passage from 1 Corinthians 1:20, "For no matter how many promises God has made, they are **yes** in Christ. And, so through Him the **amen** is spoken by us to the glory of God. Now it is God who makes both us and you **stand firm** in Christ ... guaranteeing what is to come." The word *promise* used here carries the idea of declaring assurance that He will do what He has said. In this case, God will keep His Word. His promises are yes and amen (so be it). God never says "No" to a product of His finished work, if we fulfill the requirements. He may say "Wait," but not, "No!" This term *stand firm* in the NIV or *established* in the KJV carries the idea of *to confirm*." His promises are confirmed in Christ's finished work. It is a deposit guaranteeing what is to come in our future. Wow! There is much attached to this word "*things*".

Hoped for – Obviously, hope means *anticipated or expected (anxious anticipation, earnest expectation)*.[9] There is in scripture what I call the Law of Expectation. The Law of Expectation is that which you believe in your heart with expectation becomes self-fulfilling prophecy. Many psychologists suggest 85% of our actions are the result of our expectations. What we are willing to do, or not to do, is based on our expectations. Faith is an in-

ventory of things already done (by grace in Jesus' finished work
– Eph. 1:2-3) that creates earnest expectation, which results in a
corresponding action. For instance, if you are expecting company,
you clean up the house. If you are expecting a baby, you create a
nursery. If you are expecting money, you think about what you
can buy, or where you can give. Expectation gives way to preparation, which gives way to corresponding action.

Evidence – This word evidence means *confident of being evident, proof, making, easy to see, clear, obvious, to persuade.*[10] The key
element to faith is to gather evidence to persuade your heart of
the truth. Abraham, in Romans 4, is described as a man who did
not *waver* through unbelief regarding the promises of God, but
was fully persuaded that God had the power to do what He had
promised. He had unwavering, doubtless, effortless faith! Really?! You mean the Abraham whom God told to leave his country,
his people and his father's household behind and go to the land
promised to him, but took Lot (his nephew) with him (Gen.
12:1-3)? You mean Abraham who lied to the king of Gerar that
his wife was his sister to save his neck from the king who wanted
his wife (Gen. 20:1-2)? You mean Abraham who when God told
him at 100 years old and Sarah was 90 years old, they would have
a child who would be their heir? Romans tells us they were well
past the time of childbearing (Rom. 4:19) and when Sarah, his
wife, heard it she laughed. I am not sure how the conversation
went, but I imagine it went something like this, "Abe, I'm old, I'm
tired, I've got a headache, and you better not touch me." After
some years go by, she suggests, "Why don't you try my maidser-
vant, Hagar?" Abraham responds, "Yeah, that'll work!" I am not
the sharpest saw in the shed, but even I know better than to do
that. Does all of that sound fully persuaded to you? Of course
not! However, in time Abraham grew to be fully persuaded, immoveable and unwavering in God. How? God helped him gather

evidence until the truth got in his heart. Trust me, this was a process for him. Every time God's Word would fade, He would take Abraham to a visual answer. In Genesis 15, He showed him the stars and exhorted him to count them. Can you **imagine** a starry night and trying to process the huge number of celestial beings? This was to be how his offspring would be. On another occasion He [God} said, "Count the sand on the seashore so shall your offspring be" (Genesis 22:17). Just try it with a handful of sand sometime. Try to count the number of grains. God had him use his imagination (meditation) to persuade his heart. It was not automatic, and it took quite a process. Then, Abraham was asked to sacrifice his only son Isaac (born when he was 100 years old – Genesis 22). Abraham defied the illogic of sacrificing the heir to God's promise, rationalizing if his son was sacrificed God would raise him again to life (Genesis 22:5; Heb. 11:17-19). I would call that fully persuaded and unwavering in faith. He called the place Jehovah Jireh or *the Lord will provide.*

God used His imagination to focus Abraham's heart with a confident expectation to see the end product. The question becomes, what is the **focus**? Do you focus on the circumstances or upon the evidence? Our job is to gather evidence. How? Meditate on the unseen evidence of the finished work of Calvary (Isa. 53:1-6) until it supersedes all other truth. When what you see in the unseen is greater than what you see in the seen, the unseen will dominate the seen. Put feelings to new thoughts. That is how we create new dominant thoughts.

Often in the Body of Christ, we are taught that feelings are negative things. We are exhorted not to live by feelings. However, I venture to say we do. Remember, feeling travels 80,000 times faster than a thought.[11] Thoughts with feelings are what create heart beliefs.

My good friend, Dr. James Richards, believes that feelings and emotions are two different things. He says that emotions follow thoughts, and feelings follow the heart. Emotions are often the result of circumstances. To change emotions, you simply change your focus. Focus on the evidence, rather than your surroundings. You can only focus or think about one thing at a time. Change your focus and you change your direction. This is what Paul is referring to in 2 Corinthians 10:5-6, "We take captive every thought." We choose our focus. I have often said the difference between omnipresence and manifested presence is focus or recognition. He is always here, but sometimes we don't recognize it. It is why scripture says, "Magnify the Lord" (Psalm 34:3, Lk. 1:46). Magnify means to make greater or bigger.[12] When we magnify the Lord we see Him larger than our circumstances or problems. The ability to see yourself (in the Lord) bigger than your problem is often what separates great people from ordinary people.

Focus creates neural pathways, which make it more natural for you to be more capable to experience what you focus upon. For instance, if you focus on fear, you are more likely to experience it. You can focus on the problem, or you can focus on the promise (evidence). Either way, the likelihood of experiencing what you focus on increases. Focus is the key to gathering evidence. Fear focus is the expectation of bad. Faith focus is the expectation of good.

Remember the story of the twelve spies in Numbers 13 (from Chapter 2)? The ten spies who produced the evil report were focused on the giants in the land. The two spies who eventually took the land were focused on the promise of God (Num. 13:1, 30). Continued focus (21 days, 30 days or 60 days) creates an established or steadfast heart (Ps. 57:7). This will in turn create an identity in keeping with God's view of you.

The principle of *evidence* is essential to faith. For instance, if you focus on a negative doctor's report (evidence), you will most likely promote fear. If you focus on the promise (of healing), it creates faith. Faith is based on evidence. What is true to you is based on where there is the most evidence. Please note that other people's evidence may affect you momentarily, but you must gather your own evidence to be persuaded. Focus on God's evidence in such a way that you cannot believe anything else (when what you see in the unseen is more real than what you see in the seen, the unseen will dominate the seen). Persuade your heart through imagination and meditation.

Evidence in what?

Notice, the end of verse one tells us where we gather evidence *of things not seen*. The evidence for the manifestation of God comes from the unseen finished work of Christ placed in the Kingdom of God by grace to be accessed by faith. Therefore, the evidence of the seen is in competition with the unseen. That is why it is essential to *practice the unseen evidence daily*. Wherever there is the most evidence is what you will believe. Therefore, meditate on the benefits of the finished work of Christ (the over 7,000 promises of God) so that when crisis comes you are ready for the unseen to dominate the seen.

Evidence is data on which a conclusion is based. In a court of law, a lawyer produces evidence before the jury. We all understand about evidence today. Television shows like *C.S.I.* have made us all the more aware of the importance of true evidence. You can say to me, "I haven't been in your living room." Yet, when I examine my living room, I find your fingerprints on my coffee table. Even though I have never seen you in my house, I know you were there based on the evidence. Evidence causes you to believe and even reevaluate what you thought you believed to be true previously. The evidence points to the fact of what God has already done for me.

The author of Hebrews goes on to explain this further in 11:3, "By faith, we understand that the universe was formed at God's command, so that what was seen was not made out of what is visible." Now, notice it does not say these things were made from things that do not exist, but from things (already done) from the invisible.

Andy Andrews illustrates this from his book *The Traveler's Gift*. In this book, the chief character, David Ponder, is an Executive at a Fortune 500 company. Another company buys out the company, and David's job is eliminated. His life begins to spiral downward. At fifty years old, he has difficulty finding a job. Since he cannot find work, he eventually loses his house, car, money and everything materially important to him. The crisis reaches a zenith when his daughter becomes sick and needs an operation that he cannot afford. Realizing he is losing all that is important to him, he contemplates suicide. He tries to call out to God, but in desperation he thinks, *I can't even pray*. He contemplates further options and ponders the fact that he no longer has a purpose. Ultimately, he rationalizes to himself that *everyone would be better off without me*. Without further conscious thought, he accelerates his car toward a tree and his ultimate demise. Gripping his steering wheel and racing toward his doom, he is somehow mysteriously transported back in time. In the past, he meets six or seven different people who expose the real secrets to success in life. He meets President Truman, King Solomon, Christopher Columbus, and others. The last person he meets is the archangel Gabriel. Gabriel gives him a tour of heaven. There he sees rooms filled with money, some with inventions not yet experienced, even some with cures for diseases. There were rooms with photographs of children and stacks of food.

Dazed by what he was seeing and confused by its meaning, he looks at the angel and asks, "Why am I here?"

Finally, the angel answers his question by asking another question, "In despair, why does one person take his life, while another is moved to greatness?"[13]

Reeling in confusion, David responds, "I don't know."

The angel responds, "Circumstances are rulers of the weak. . .but they are weapons of the wise. Circumstances do not push or pull. They are daily lessons to be studied and gleaned for new knowledge and wisdom."[14]Struggling to understand the panorama before him, he cries out, "What is this place?" Gabriel responds, "This, my friend, is the place that never was. This is the place where we keep all the things about to be delivered just as the people stopped working and praying for them. The contents of this place are 'filled with the dreams and goals of the less courageous.'"[15]

This dramatic scene captures the essence of Hebrews 11:3. God has an invisible Kingdom filled with the provisions necessary for fulfilling your destiny if you will have faith and courage to receive them.

Here is a main key from this passage in Hebrews. The parent force of the *seen realm* is the *unseen realm*.[16] Faith is not *fake it until you can make it*. Faith is seeing what is real even though it is unseen. Paul says, "We call the things that are not as though they were" (Rom. 4:17). Therefore, when Peter says, "By his stripes you *were* healed," it exists in the unseen realm. The problem is that most of us cannot believe until, or if, we see it manifested in our body or in our situation. That is why Paul says, "We walk by faith and not by sight" (2 Cor. 5:7). Faith = Belief + Expectation + Corresponding Action. Faith is the ability to *see what is real,* though it is *unseen.*

I heard my Pastor Billy Joe Daugherty give this example in a message based on Hebrews 11:3. He said, "Presently, there are radio and television waves in this room. We cannot see them, but they are here. The reason we know they exist is because when we plug in a television and properly receive its signal, we can get a picture on the screen. The signals were here all the time. We just had to learn to receive what was being transmitted." God's provisions are available to us if we learn to attract them to us (receive what is transmitted).

We do not have to deny the physical realm to recognize the spiritual realm. That is what Metaphysics and Christian Science does. As believers, we acknowledge that the physical realm is dominated by the spiritual realm. We do not have to deny cancer exists, but decree that, "By His stripes, we are healed" (1 Pet. 2:24). This is why understanding a hardened heart is so important. We must get rid of the unbelief in our lives that causes a hardened heart. Then, when what you see in the spiritual world is more real than what you see in the physical world, the spiritual world will dominate your natural world.[17] This is the point of the story of Elisha and his servant in 2 Kings 6. The king of Syria is at war with Israel. Every time he sets a trap for them, God speaks to Elisha, who warns Israel, and they continually avert the *best laid plans of mice and men*. Not understanding the spiritual dynamics of these events, the Syrian king can only assume he is being betrayed by a spy in his camp.

Finally, the king of Syria successfully surrounds the prophet at Dothan. The servant of the prophet arises the next morning to discover the dilemma. In panic, he races to the prophet and exclaims, "We're surrounded."

Unmoved, Elisha responds in 2 Kings 6:16, "Don't be afraid. Those who are with us are more than those who are with them."

You can almost see the stunned look on his servant's face. Obviously, the product of a higher education math program, the servant sets out to do some addition. As he pokes his head out the door, he begins counting. . .50, 100, 200, 300, 500. He looks back inside and looks at Elisha and counts. . .1, 2. He must have thought, *I don't know where you got your education, but your math leaves something to be desired.*

Then, this unforgettable scene unfolds. Elisha says, "O LORD, open his eyes so he may see. Then the LORD opened his eyes, and he looked and saw the hills full of horses and chariots of fire [angelic hosts] all around Elisha" (2 Kings 6:17).

God's forces then strike the enemy with blindness and ultimately deliver them over to Israel's forces in Samaria. In like manner, the issue for most of us is we only see the physical realm. The chariots of fire didn't just arrive when Elisha's servant's eyes were opened. God's provision existed all the time. The reason we can attract God's Kingdom unto ourselves is because God's provision already exists. Calvary's sacrifice set in motion the New Covenant provisions we are to claim as our own.

The key is we need to learn to see with the *eyes of our heart* (Eph. 1:18). When our soul lines up with our spirit (Heb. 4:12), we will recognize people, ideas and resources we have missed up to that time.

The Application of Faith

Now that we have an accurate definition of faith, we can take a look at the application of faith. An improper definition will promote a misapplication of faith – and often does. The best place to look to apply this definition is Mark 11:22-24. "'Have faith in God,' answered Jesus, 'I tell you the truth, if anyone says to this mountain, "go throw yourself into the sea," and does not doubt in his heart, but believes what he says will happen, it will be done for them. Therefore, I tell you, whatever you ask for in prayer, believe that you have received it, and it will be yours.'"

There are five applications to the definition to faith. Jesus begins by saying have the God kind of faith. Operate in **the** measure of faith God deposited in you through salvation. He then gives us four vital applications of faith.

Have faith in God – The Greek term for faith (pistos) means trust or trustworthiness.[17] Faith is the abandonment to the trustworthiness of God. It is trusting in the character and motive of God. I believe God doesn't lie and his motive is always love. He always has my best interest in mind . It is, therefore, easy to believe what He says. By grace (unmerited by me) He has already accomplished *things* (pragma)[18] in the unseen Kingdom for my success and benefit. This creates expectation in me as I reinforce (focus, imagine, meditate) the evidence of His finished work for my life. The end of faith is not obedience, but relationship. Relationship is the product and obedience is the bi-product. Here is why this is imminently important. If the end product of your faith is obedience, in difficult times you will ask the question, *What did I do wrong?* However, if the end product of your faith is relationship, in those same difficult times you ask, *Lord, what should we do about this?* The latter produces faith, the former promotes doubts. Therefore, I take action by doing the following:

- **Speak to your mountain.** It is time to stop telling God about your mountain and start telling your mountain about your God. This is the principle of **confession.** This is your pronouncement of faith. Stop confessing your circumstance and confess the truth. There is a difference between fact and truth. The fact may be that I have a diagnosis of cancer, but the truth is I have been healed by the stripes of Jesus (1 Pet. 2:24) (See the *Barrier Buster's Manual* for a complete listing of self-limiting beliefs and the antidotes of truth with a complete list of scriptures to confess). Confess it personal, present tense and positive. Confess it, imagine it (see it) and feel the emotion of it being true. Speak the Word into your situation.

- Do not **doubt** in your **heart**. The Greek word for *doubt* here is *diakrino*. This word means *to decide between two*.[19] It gives you the idea of a judge discerning truth based on the evidence. It is resolving double-mindedness. It is submitting to the view and opinion of God and His Word. It is also important to note that one is not to doubt in their **heart**. Psalm 57:7 tells us to have a steadfast or established heart. Confession, meditation and imagination can establish your heart. Talk back to the A.N.T.S. – automatic negative thoughts (subconscious, self-limiting beliefs). An established heart creates an **identity** in Christ. This is a call to fully persuade the heart with the evidence of God's character and motive. It is your understanding to be immoveable and unstoppable.

There's a difference between healing and a miracle. A miracle is an instantaneous touch from God. Healing comes from the Greek term "therapeuo." It is where we derive our English term 'therapy.' Therapy describes a touch that takes place over a period of time. It is here that confession becomes so important. Let me give you an example.

- Whatever you ask for in **prayer** – There is a Hebrew word for prayer called *palai*. This word means *to judge or assess*.[20] In the New Covenant we **assess** what is not like the Kingdom, then we **align** ourselves to the Kingdom (the finished work of Christ in Eph. 1:2-3), to **access** the Kingdom. New Covenant prayers operate in Divine authority.

- **Believe you have received**. We operate by faith, not by sight (2 Cor. 5:7), based on the *evidence* we receive. Gather the evidence, meditate, confess the Word and stand until it manifests. How can I say I am healed or prosperous if the evidence of a doctor's report or a bank account is contrary? Let truth overrule fact. Practice this daily. When crisis comes, your heart will be steadfast.

As my good friend, Dr. Jim Richards, says, "You've been wired for success but programmed for failure." God equipped you for success, but the five elements of your personal belief system have set you up for failure.

Faith brings the spiritual world into the physical world. Everything you receive and attract from God comes from heaven to earth. We walk by faith and not by sight. The God kind of faith establishes your heart. A steadfast heart creates a true identity.

The Truth Sets You Free

Some time back, my pastor asked me to share with our college age ministry. That night I addressed around 600 college age students with the principles that are woven throughout this book. After I finished teaching and then praying for a multitude of students, I interacted with an Oral Roberts University student by the name of Omar. He told me some astonishing happenings in his life. He related to me that in 2010 he noticed the first symptoms of negativity in his body. From that point on, the symptoms became progressively worse. He explained to me that because he had a class that ended at 10:00pm on Wednesday, he was unable to attend his regular church service, so he began attending our college service on Tuesday nights. During this time, his bodily symptoms were progressively getting worse. The doctors were unable to give him any answers, and he began to have great anxiety and stress over physical symptoms. Shortly thereafter, he was diagnosed with cancer. After that diagnosis, he found himself attending the college service where I was speaking. After the service, he said he felt compelled to talk with me because he was intrigued by the principle of renewing the mind and establishing heart beliefs for his healing.

I remember praying for Omar and told him I had a set of *Barrier Busters* Meditation CD's that included a Healing CD that could help him solidify healing in his heart. He came the next day and picked up the CD. Omar told me later he was so touched by the CD that he purchased the entire set of *Barrier Busters* CD's. He told me he loved how it was based on scripture. Omar said he loaded the CD's on his iPod and used his headphones to meditate day and night. Initially, sitting still was difficult for him, because he had developed so much anxiety due to worry about his health. He forced himself to complete the meditations several times a day, and eventually it became a routine. Soon the anxiety left, and he became peaceful. He told me the most important thing for him were the meditation CD's that took him to his secret place (Psalm 91:1).

This process allowed him to visualize several times a day God's promise to heal him. Part of the teaching was to see Jesus healing him and actually driving all the sickness from his body. Once he saw it, he could believe it and receive it. In the letter (email) he sent me that I am taking this testimony from he further related, "My faith grew by hearing and seeing; my knowledge increased, and with the meditation CD, my healing was engrained in the inner most part of my heart. Shortly after my body followed. I believed I was healed by the stripes of Jesus, and I saw myself healthy daily because of meditating. As I am typing now, I am healed and cancer free. God is so faithful."

This young man meditated on the truth and overcame the facts. His worry, stress and anxiety gave way to peace. Truth got into his heart, and he was able to appropriate what God had already provided for him. The God-kind of faith activated the Kingdom of God on his behalf.

Faith brings the spiritual world into the physical world. Everything you attract and receive from God comes from heaven to earth. We walk by faith not by sight.

The God-kind of faith establishes our heart, and a steadfast heart creates our true identity. Let's turn our attention to identity.

Keys for Reflection

- The definition of faith is trust in the character and the motive of God. The simple adherence to this definition makes faith easy, doubtless and effortless.
- The wrong definition of faith always ends up in the mis-application of faith.
- Faith is not about faith in my faith, but faith in His grace.
- Faith doesn't believe God will, but faith believes God has.
- Hebrews 11 tells us faith believes in "things" already done.
- A key is to gather evidence of the unseen.
- Faith speaks to the mountain.
- Faith is established in your heart through confession, meditation and imagination.
- The Hebrew word "palai" means to **assess** what is not like the Kingdom, **align** to the Kingdom and **access** the Kingdom.
- Trust → Confess → Establish your heart → Align and pray → Receive.

CHAPTER 9

THE ANSWER TO EVERYTHING

THEME: IDENTITY IS THE ANSWER TO EVERYTHING.

Lesson: Establishing your heart shows you
who God is, what He has already done and
who He has made you to be.

In the last chapter, we solidified that an established (steadfast or fixed – Ps. 57:7) heart sets your identity. I often say identity is the answer to everything. Your understanding of who you are positions you for success or failure, perhaps more than any other thing.

For many years, our church participated in the National Day of Healing. Throughout the day, we would position key staff members to speak and pray for people in one-hour sessions. I did this for many years. One year, I got ready to start my segment when I saw three people carry a woman into the meeting room. It turned out this woman had the worst case of fibromyalgia I personally had ever seen. She had not been out of bed in over a year. Everything she did caused pain, and she was in complete fatigue. It hurt for her to wear clothes. In desperation, her friends brought her for prayer. After a short message to build faith, I asked them to bring the woman forward for a touch from God.

We "spoke to the mountain" in her life, and she felt some immediate relief. However, she still had pain. I offered to give her my biblical meditation CD on healing. Before I could do that, one of her friends bought a copy of the *Healing* CD the next day. Unfortunately, I lost contact with Janine for about six months. One day at our Bible College we were starting a new quarter, and while I was opening my class I looked out and to my shock Janine was sitting in the front row. I stopped the proceedings and asked what happened to her. She stood up in class and shared she had taken the *Barrier Busters* CD on Healing and followed the directions and listened to it every morning and every night for about three months. She said one day while listening to the healing CD she suddenly saw herself differently. Then, she proclaimed, "I saw myself functioning in my destiny." At that moment, every symptom of her fibromyalgia was gone. Then, she proudly announced, "I'm enrolled here in Bible College!"

Please note, when she understood her identity in her heart, she was healed. You will never rise above the image you have of yourself in your heart. True identity allows you to see yourself bigger than your problem.

Every speaker or writer has favorite phrases they use more often than others do. For the Apostle Paul, it is the phrase *in Him* or *in Christ*. Paul uses this phrase and its derivations approximately 165 times in his 13 Epistles (or 48% of the New Testament books he penned.) It is used over 300 times in the entire New Testament. *In Him* for Paul describes the experience for not only him but for every believer. *In Christ* is how God views you, not on your merit but on His merit. It is you learning to operate through His finished work. It is your co-inclusion in His death and resurrection. It is your identity.

Second Corinthians 5:16 states, "From now on we regard no one from a worldly point of view." In other words, we do not assess people by their appearance, circumstances or perceived capabilities. We look past their exterior situations and recognize their potential in Christ. Verse 17 continues, "Therefore, if anyone is in Christ, he is a new creation; the old is gone, the new is come!" The idea of a new creation in Greek means new species of being or having a new spiritual DNA. Your past does not dictate to your future. Your old man is gone (dead – Rom. 6:6). You are completely new. Look at how the Mirror Bible translates this verse, "Now, in light of your co-inclusion in His death and resurrection." Whoever you thought you were before, *in Christ* you are a brand-new person! The old ways of seeing yourself and everyone else are over. Acquaint yourself with this new assessment of your life in the Gospel.

Once I was ministering in a Midwestern city. I was helping a throng of people at the conclusion of my message, when I noticed in my peripheral vision a woman patiently waiting to speak with me. When the crowd dissipated, I looked over at this seemingly despairing woman and asked, "Can I help you?"

This woman looked at me quizzically and said, "Don't know."

I responded, "Obviously something happened tonight that put enough hope in you to wait a long time to talk with me. So, let's give it a shot."

Her eyes glanced immediately downward to avoid eye contact with me as she stammered to get some words to come out of her mouth. She finally muttered a small litany of inadequacies and problems. Her list of insufficiencies included everything from being overweight to not enjoying life to some specific failures to criticisms from her husband and finally to family problems.

Trying to get her attention, I asked. "On a scale of 1 to 10, 10 being the most acceptable, how accepted do you feel?" She pondered for a long time before answering. Finally, she stuttered, "I'm not sure, but no higher than a 3."

I followed up with a second question, "On the same scale, how accepted do you feel by God?"

Her eyes rolled with the agony of her response, "Less than 2." She could not even say 1, so she said, "Less than 2." Then, tears streamed down her face.

I gently caught the glance of her eyes as I responded, "It's hard to feel intimate with someone that you don't feel accepts you."

She began nodding with the agony of her revelation. Again, grabbing her attention, I reflected, "I don't think you've grasped how much God loves you, and nothing can separate you from His love (Rom. 8:39)." In the ensuing moments, I elaborated on God's love, grace, righteousness and identity. I was privileged to witness a transformation of countenance that would rival the metamorphous of a caterpillar becoming a butterfly. Assuredly, this was the beginning stages of a radical transformation.

This story illustrates a key principle: how you see God and how you see yourself determine how you experience God. If God is someone who slaps you down at every misstep, that is how you are going to experience Him. If you see him as someone you can never measure up to, that is how you will experience Him. If you see Him through the eyes of your true identity, that is how you are going to experience Him.

So what is your identity in Christ? I like to define it this way. One of the definitions of identity is knowing who God is, what He has already done and who He has made you to be. All three aspects are essential:

Know who God is – Most Christians know *about* Him, but they do not *know* Him. I do not want you to simply know about the Book, but to know the author of the Book. This is a call to intimacy with God. That is why it is essential to know God's grace and righteousness (see my book, *Organic Christianity*) to help you find your identity.

Know what He has already done – Stop trying to get God to do what He has already done and receive what He did by grace through faith.

Know who He has made you to be – You are not what the 5 elements of your Personal Belief System tell you. You are who the Word of God says you are!

Identity is also the condition or fact of being the same in quality, sameness, oneness or identical.[1] Wow! My identity in Christ means God has positioned me to be the same in quality as Christ. "As He is, so are we in this world" (1 Jn. 4:17). You are created to be a perfect representation of Christ to this world.

Remember, leading Psychologist Martin Seligman in his book, *Learned Optimism* says that 80% of people have what he calls *learned helplessness*.[2] These are people who feel helpless to change their circumstances. If 80% of people who have learned helplessness, it is apparent that most people feel like victims, rather than victors. It is true for most believers as well, unless they discover their identity.

Let's examine what God tells us about our identity in the Bible.

- **Colossians 1:27** – "Christ in you the hope of glory." Christ in me gives me anticipation of His glory. The term glory is a comprehensive word. Its meaning is widespread. *Glory* means weight, copious (abundance, profuse, plentiful).[3] It is visible manifestation, splendor, pre-eminence (above all others), and submit to the view and opinion of.[4] One of these best definitions is the view and opinion of God. When you understand that your function and operation comes from Christ being in you, you tend to operate out of the view and opinion of God. Submitting to the view and opinion of God releases the copious, plentiful, manifested presence of God. Daily I ask the Holy Spirit to remind me of this incredible revelation.

- **2 Corinthians 5:17** – "Therefore if any man be in Christ, he is a new creation. Old things are passed away; behold all things become new." The idea in this passage is that we are a new species of being. We have a new spiritual DNA. Being born again does not mean we are a better *us* – it means we are a new and distinct kind of variety. It means our past does not dictate to our future.

- **Galatians 2:20** – "I am crucified with Christ; nevertheless I live, yet not I, but Christ lives in me. And the life I live in the flesh I live by the faith of the Son of God." This is the exchanged life, not just the changed life. I live my life through Him. Death to self is simply repenting or submitting my will and opinion to His will and opinion. It is what empowers me.

- **1 John 4:9** – "This is how God showed His love among us: He sent His one and only Son into the world that we might live through Him." It is far more important that we live through Him rather than for Him. How do I live through Him? By operating in faith in His finished work.

- **Ephesians 1:2, 3** – "**Grace** and **peace** to you from God the Father and the Lord Jesus Christ who **has blessed us** in the **heavenly realm** with **every special blessing in Christ**." God has given us grace (unmerited favor, the finished work of Christ, Divine influence on the heart, empowerment or ability) and peace (to be unmoved by my circumstances). What grace gives, peace keeps. In verse 3, we answer four questions: (1) When? This verse is written in the past tense. These are things that are already done – one Greek scholar calls it the eternal past. (2) With what? God gave us every spiritual blessing. This term spiritual means supernatural.[5] The term blessing here means benefit, bounty or empowerment.[6] God has already provided for us every supernatural provision for our success. We are **wired for success**, but often **programmed for failure.** Overcome your self-limiting beliefs and God will launch you to great success. (3) Where? In the heavenly realm. That is simply Paul's words for the Kingdom of God. Everything you need to succeed is already been placed in the Kingdom by grace, unmerited by you, to access by faith. (4) How? In Christ. It has been accomplished at Calvary in the finished work of Christ. This work has provided every aspect of salvation. The term salvation in Greek is a comprehensive definition: to save, rescue, safety, deliver, heal, health, prosper, to do well, to make whole, preserve.[7] You already have access to every supernatural benefit for success through Christ's finished work.

- **Philemon 6** – "That the communication of your faith may become effectual by acknowledging every good thing that is in you, in Christ Jesus." Again, note, every good thing we need is already in us, in Christ Jesus.

- **2 Peter 1:3** – "His divine power has given us everything we need for life and godliness." God's power has already granted us everything to succeed in life and to live like Him.

- **Romans 5:17b** – "Those who receive the abundance of grace and the gift of righteousness" [right standing with the Father, not based on what I've done, but what He has done, and it is received by faith]. Therefore, I can come to God without guilt, fear, inferiority or condemnation. "Therefore I am qualified in Him" (Col. 1:12) [(to be blessed and used] "To reign in life **through** the one man, Jesus Christ." I was made to dominate life, not be dominated by it.

- **Colossians 2:10** – "And you are complete in Him." The term complete means whole, entire, finished, lacking in nothing.[8] I must understand I am positioned to lack nothing.

- **1 John 4:17** – "As He is, so are we in this world." We function on planet Earth just as Jesus did, so we can produce what He did (and does).

- **Romans 4:13** – "His offspring [us] would be an heir of the world." Our inheritance is planet Earth. It is time we accessed it and acted like it.

- **Colossians 1:12** – "Thanks to the Father who has qualified you to share in the inheritance of the saints in the Kingdom of light." In Christ, I am qualified to be blessed and used.

- **1 Corinthians 1:30** – "It is because of Him, that you are in Christ Jesus, who has become for us wisdom from God – that is our righteousness, holiness and redemption. All of these things are mine because I'm in Him."

- **Colossians 1:27** – "This mystery which is Christ in us the hope of glory!" Because we recognize Christ is in us we anticipate His glory. *Glory* is a comprehensive word that has many meanings, one of which is the view and opinion of God.[9] When we embody the view and opinion of God, nothing is impossible to us.

- **Philippians 4:19** – "And my God shall supply all your needs according to His riches in glory by Christ Jesus." Christ's finished work has provided a supply in this Kingdom for every need to be met in our lives.

- **John 14:10-12** – "Don't you believe that I am in the Father and that the Father is in me? The words I say to you are not just my own. Rather it is the Father living in me who is doing the work. Believe me when I say that I am in the Father and the Father is in me; or at least believe on the evidence of the miracles themselves. I tell you the truth, anyone who has faith in me will do what I have been doing. He will do even greater things than these because I am going to the Father." It is evident from those verses that Jesus performed His miracles because He was in the Father and the Father was in Him. Who does these miraculous things? Obviously, it is the Father in Him. Then, He adds this bombshell of a verse. "The very works I do, you will do and greater." Wow! How? Look at verse 20. The same way Jesus is in the Father and the Father is in Him, we are in Jesus and He is in us. The way we do the works He did and greater is by recognizing our identity in the Father.

- **John 15:7** – "If ye abide in me, and my words abide in you, you shall ask what you will, and it shall be done unto you." If you remain in consistency in your identity and God's Word, it remains in you consistently. Then, you can ask anything in regards to the finished work of Christ, and it will be done for you. Wow!

Therefore, "abide" really means to put Kingdom principles into practice from the heart.

So you will either believe what the Word says about you, or you will believe what the 5 elements of your Personal Belief System tell you. The key is to not let your environment, authority figures, your self-image, repetitious information or your circumstances and experiences dissuade you of your identity.

This is what James is trying to tell us when he says, "But be doers of the Word and not hearers only, deceiving yourselves. For if anyone is a hearer of the Word and not a doer, he is like a man observing his natural face in the mirror, for he observes himself, goes away and immediately forgets what kind of man he was" (Jas. 1:22-24 NKJV). The Greek in this verse gives you this idea. The problem is not that you've never been a doer. It is the idea that you're not a doer now.[10] Look at the Parable of the Sower (Matthew 13:1-23). In this parable, the seed equals the Word, and the soil is the heart. If we do not allow the Word to get into our hearts (*hearers only*), we are like the man looking into a mirror who forgets what he looks like. He forgets who he is. He loses sight of his identity. The pleasures of life and established self-limiting beliefs in our hearts rob us of our true identity.

In 2 Peter 1:2-9, Peter starts by saying, "Grace and peace be yours in abundance." This is more than just a greeting. Peter uses this opening to communicate his heart over and over again (see the beginning of many of his epistles).

He is saying *grace* to you. Grace is the finished work of Christ. Grace is unmerited favor. Grace is a divine influence upon the heart. Grace is God's empowerment or ability on your behalf. Grace to you in its fullness.

Then he adds, "and peace." Peace is the ability to be unaffected by your circumstances. What grace provides, peace is the ability to keep.

This comes in *abundance*, "through the knowledge of God and our Lord Jesus Christ." The term *knowledge*" is not the word for facts or understanding, but means personal, intimate, experiential knowledge.[11] Grace and peace are the result of intimacy with God. This knowledge is not just facts, but knowledge of Him (verse 3-6). This kind of knowledge is a reflection of our spiritual identity (knowing who He is).

Now, verse 3 begins this amazing revelation, "His divine power has given us [past tense] everything we need for life and godliness through our knowledge of Him, who called us by His own glory and goodness. "Through these ..." (verse 4). What *these* is he referring to? *These* refers to *His glory, His goodness, His knowledge, His grace and His peace.* This is a call to understanding our identity.

This thought is reinforced by the rest of the verse, "He has given us His very great and precious promises, so that through them you may participate in divine nature and escape the corruption of the world, caused by evil desires." Watch this amazing progression of this passage in verses 2-4: "Grace [unmerited favor, the finished work of Christ, divine influence upon the heart and God's ability] gives way to peace [the ability to keep what grace has given to us], gives way to like precious faith [the same faith Peter used to raise Dorcas from the dead is the same faith in us], gives way to knowledge [intimate, experiential knowledge of God], gives way to God's divine power [supernatural power], which gives us everything we need for life [vitality or the God kind of life][12] and godliness [ability to be God-like]. This in turn allows us to receive knowledge [experiential, intimate knowledge], which promotes His own glory [the view and opinion of God]".[13] This is how we are led to repentance or rethinking – Rom. 2:4. This in turn opens the promises of God to us (the laws of how the Kingdom of God operates) that allows us to participate in divine nature (Christ in you – Gal. 2:20), that causes us to conquer the world (world's system). What a mouthful that is!

In other words, we understand our spiritual identity through our knowledge of Him (verse 3) – who God is, what He has already done and who He has made us to be. Now comes the amazing part of this revelation in verse 8, "For if you possess these qualities in increasing measure, they will keep you from being ineffective and unproductive in your knowledge of our Lord Jesus Christ. But if anyone does not have them, he is nearsighted and blind and has forgotten that he has been cleansed from his past sins." Tighten your seat belts and lock down your tray tables, this is essential to grasp. Anyone who does not grasp their spiritual identity lives in myopia, blindness or amnesia. In other words, the best-case scenario is Christians who do not know their spiritual identity live seeing just in front of themselves. The worst-case scenario is a believer completely blind and in the dark to what God is doing. We live like someone who does not understand (remember) the meaning of their past sins (amnesia). Our spiritual identity solidifies our qualification to receive the blessing to be effective and productive.

Can you imagine waking up and suddenly having lost all of your memory? You cannot remember your name, your address, your mate, your children or your family. You cannot remember your occupation or the skills you used to become successful. You would feel lost to proceed with any kind of security or competence. If you become insecure enough, you might cast off restraint and act like someone you are not. This is what Peter is describing in this passage. Believers who lose their sense of identity act as if they have forgotten that their sins have been forgiven. Your spiritual identity is perhaps the most important aspect to live victoriously and successfully.

The Rest of the Story

Once we understand how we see ourselves and how God operates (His Kingdom) it changes everything about how we approach God. Look at how the writer of Hebrews tells us, as Paul Harvey would say, *the rest of the story*.

"Therefore, since the promise of entering His rest still stands, let us be careful that none of us be found to have fallen short of it. . .but the message they heard was of no value to them because those who heard it did not combine it with faith. Now we who have believed enter that rest. . .and yet His work has been finished since the creation of the world. . .for anyone who enters God's rest also rests from his own work, just as God did from His. Let us therefore, make every effort to enter His rest" (Heb. 4:1-3; 10, 11).

Understanding the New Covenant causes us to live a life of rest. The concept of rest is not always what we think of in the American culture. For instance, in Genesis 2 when it tells us that God created the world, it says God worked for six days, and on the seventh day He rested. Let me tell you what this is *not* saying. This does not mean that God extended Himself for six days, and He was exhausted so He took a *siesta*. The term *rest* gives you the idea of calm or tranquil.[14] The concept of biblical rest is more like the concept of a lawyer who when his argument is finished says, "I rest my case." Rest here means it is finished. As **believers** we can rest (take ease) in the finished work of Christ. It is not something I produce; it is something I acquire, that is already done for me. It is not about **achieving;** it is about **receiving**. It is not about living **for** God as much as it is about living **through** Him. It is not as much about the **do** as it is about the **done**. It is not as much about the **changed** life as it is about the **exchanged** life.

Scripturally, the concept of rest is equated to God's inheritance for his people (Deut. 3:18-20; 12:9-11). For Israel, it was the Promised Land. In the same way, the writer of Hebrews is suggesting that New Covenant believers *rest* in the inheritance of Christ's finished work at Calvary. The blessings of God are not *achieved* (earned); they are *received.*

However, it is worthy to note that, "He that entered into His rest has also ceased from His own works, as God did from His (4:10). We must also labor therefore to enter into His rest" *(Heb.* 4:11 KJV). Now, there is an oxymoron to ponder. In other words, what God did by grace, unmerited by us, we have to receive by faith. God's grace is His finished work (Eph. 1:2-3) that He did without *meritocracy* (merit), so I can by faith (with corresponding action) take dominion (dominance) over my environment. The reason I can rest is because it is not faith in my faith, but faith in His grace. *I am qualified* (Col. 1:12) in Him to access His Kingdom. That is why He tells me *I'm complete* in Him (Col. 2:10). The word *complete* means to fill up, to cram, to be replete, to furnish, to finish, to cause, to abound, accomplish, render perfect, lacking in nothing.[15]

Identity: The Answer to Everything

Knowing our identity is having an understanding of who we are in Christ in our hearts. Heart beliefs create identity. Information + Emotions + Consistency = Heart Beliefs. When significant information is coupled with emotions consistently, this causes belief in your heart. Unfortunately, much (perhaps most) of the input into our hearts is done by default. It is rare that we set ourselves apart for the express purpose to seek God in our hearts.[16]

No thought has meaning until you attach significance to it. Significance is only appropriated when information is combined with how we see ourselves. Our self-worth is the determining factor of how we respond to any input. This significance is the beginning process that influences the subconscious mind and has the ability to influence our hearts and to transform our lives. Our experience is not based on what happens to us; it is based on our interpretation of what happens to us (attitude) and how it causes us to see ourselves. Thus, steps to application do not really matter until you change the way you see yourself (in your heart).

The problem is most of us influence our hearts by default, allowing information and emotions to come from facts rather than truth. Thus, we often negate the process of faith-filled intentions. When the Bible talks about "guarding our heart," it is all about our ability to see ourselves according to our biblical identity. Remember, the study of neuro-cardiology shows us that there are more neurons in the heart than there are in the brain. The heart is using neural pathways to communicate to the rest of the body. Every neuron contains memory experiences. Every cell has the memory of your heart. Ultimately, it has the potential to affect our DNA makeup. Your experiential memories often seek to compete with your identity. Emotions can be the result of thought. To change our emotion, we simply have to change our thoughts—think about something else. It is the result of where we put our focus.[17] Therefore we can consciously change our image by changing our focus. The key is to connect as much emotion as possible with new God-given thoughts. This, in turn, creates new neural pathways and reprograms your sub-conscious.[18]

Unless you create positive emotions with new thinking, it is nearly impossible to overcome negative feelings. In other words, old habitual thinking comes back. It is why so many well-intentioned believers lose sight of who they really are.

This is a call to create what I have called for years *the new normal*. It is a call to break the reign of self-limiting beliefs and awaken to your God-given identity. God-given identity allows you to see yourself bigger than your problem.

Again, review Colossians 2:10, "And you are complete in Him." The question is if you are complete in Him, what do you lack? Nothing! People who feel lack have a tendency to try to make up for what they lack—by the flesh. Flesh is simply trying to do God's will your way. Those who are complete in Him know they have access to whatever they need and are confident it belongs to them. The solution is to affect yourself at the subconscious (heart/cellular) level.[19] Colossians 1:27 reveals this to us when it says, "Which is Christ in you the hope of glory." The revelation that Christ in us is the anticipation of glory. Glory is one of the most comprehensive words in scripture. It means splendor, magnificence, excellence, personal excellence of Christ, glorious in condition, manifested presence.[20] Remember, identity also means the view and opinion of God.[21] My identity allows me to anticipate that His view and opinion will prevail. Paul finishes this thought in Colossians 3:1-3 by noting, "Since then, you have been raised with Christ, set your hearts on things above, where Christ is seated at the right hand of God. For you died, and your life is now hidden with Christ in God."

This verse is pregnant with truth. The word *set* used in this passage means *to have understanding, to feel, to think, to have an opinion of one's self, think of one's self, to set one's opinion, to cherish the same view, to be harmonious, and to look.*[22] To *set* your heart means to have understanding in your heart in a way that it affects how you see yourself because you are harmonious with God's point of view. Then, add to that, it causes you to *die* to self. This is a key concept we will unlock more in the next chapter. However, death to self in its simplest form means take every thought not like God's thoughts and submit them to His mindset. Submit to His view and opinion. Humility is not being a doormat. It means if God says it, it is so, and I receive it. Now then, Paul continues, "Your life is hidden, concealed with Christ in God." In other words, God sees your life through Christ. It is the exchange of His perfection that allows me to have intimacy with the Father. The result is our lives are not about the life of God – He *is* our life, the Divine exchange.

Let me summarize this in a practical way:

1. **Set your hearts** – Have understanding of who you are and what His Kingdom provides in your heart. Take the new information of God's truth about what He has done and who you are, create a joyous emotion in you until it is established in your heart.

2. **Set your mind on things above, not on things on the earth** – Renew and set your minds not on circumstances and experience (facts) but set your minds on the unseen truths of the Kingdom of God. 1 Corinthians 4:15 says it this way, "So we fix our eyes [eyes of our heart – Eph. 1:18] not on what is seen, but what is unseen. For what is seen is temporary, but what is unseen is eternal." When what you see in the unseen is more evident to you (in your heart), then what you see in the seen the unseen will dominate the seen. Practice, meditate the unseen finished work of Christ until it dominates your heart, and the unseen will manifest itself in the seen.

3. **Die to self** – Submit everything in your view and opinion that doesn't line up to His Word, to His view and opinion.

4. **Understand, you are hidden in Christ** – Therefore, you can come to God with boldness and confidence to receive in time of need.

5. **Christ is your life** – The Divine exchange (Gal. 2:20) allows you to see His life flow through your life (1 Jn. 4:9).

Overcoming Side-Effects

Life can be like the commercials you see on TV for a drug to help your symptoms. The drug is usually some unpronounceable

name followed by a name in parenthesis you can at least recognize. It is usually pictured by a sweet girl frolicking through
a field while the voiceover tells you everything is going to be
alright if you take our wonder drug, which is followed by a list
of side-effects. If after taking this drug you begin bleeding from
your eyeballs and one or more eyeballs explode, see your physi-
cian!? If excess bloating takes place that leads to the exploding
of your intestines, remember your earache is gone—because it is
a good drug. Listen to the side-effects. A person not solidified
in their identity often tries to do things or take things not in
keeping with Kingdom laws, and this results in side-effects. Solidifying your identity in your heart positions you for the manifestation of God's Kingdom.

Tim Tebow (former Heisman trophy winner from the University of Florida and former NFL quarterback) is an outspo-
ken Christian. When asked why he unashamedly proclaimed his
faith he responded, "When your identity is in Christ, your identity never changes."[23] Your identity in Christ always positions
you for God's provision.

Let me close this chapter with a keen example from Jesus'
life. In John 6, Jesus faces an impossible situation. He is preaching on a mountainside to 5,000 men, which means when you
add women and children it could be as many as 20,000 people.
Verse 5 tells us, "When Jesus looked and saw a great crowd coming toward Him, He said to Philip, 'Where shall we buy bread
for these people to eat?' He asked this only to test him, for He
already had in mind what He was going to do. Philip answered,
'Eight months wages would not buy enough bread for each one
to have a bite!'

Another of the disciples, Andrew, Simon Peter's brother
spoke up, 'Here is a boy with five small barley loaves and two
small fish, but how far will they go among so many?'"

Then, Jesus prayed and multiplied the loaves and fishes until they had fed the up to 20,000 people and had twelve baskets left over.

Here are a couple of points I want to make. First, what His disciples saw as lack, Jesus saw as an opportunity for God's supply. Notice that Jesus did not respond to the meager five loaves and two fish with, "What are you expecting me to do with so little provision?" Instead, He responded in faith. Again! Faith is trusting in the character and motive of God. Jesus knew God was a provider, and He loved these people. That brings me to my second observation and the key to this miracle! Mark's account of this story reveals the answer to this situation. . .and to everything else for that matter. Listen to how Jesus prayed, "Taking the five loaves and the two fish and looking up to heaven, he gave thanks and broke the loaves" (Mk. 6:41). This phrase *and looking up to heaven* is pivotal to understand what really happened. This phrase in the original language means *recovery of sight*.[24] This was beyond Jesus' human capability and He had to recover His sight. He had to recover His identity. He had to remember who He was in His heart. Identity is the answer to everything!

Perhaps the greatest battle fought among men is the battle for their identity. Identity theft is not a modern day phenomena. It has been going on from the foundation of time. The enemy is passionately seeking to cause you to lose sight of who you are. He uses the 5 elements of your Personal Belief System to distort who you really are. You end up looking into the mirror of the Word (Jas. 1:22-24), but when you walk away you forget what you look like. When God's Word is established in your heart, He creates an identity that makes you unstoppable. You realize you that as an heir of this world (Rom. 4:13), you are to dominate your environment.

Now, let's look at the Law of Capacity, which is a critical key to unlocking God's abundance in your life. You can only receive from God in direct correlation to your **capacity** to receive from God.

Keys for Reflection

- An established, steadfast, fixed heart sets your identity.
- We judge no one after the flesh (2 Cor. 5:16). We don't assess a person by perceived capabilities, appearance, circumstances or exterior stiuations.
- *Dying to self* is not a religious concept. It simply means to submit your view and opinion to God's view and opinion. This positions you for the manifestation of God's Kingdom.
- How you see God and how you see yourself determine how you experience God.
- Identity: Knowing who God is, what He has already done and knowing who you are.
- Meditate on your identity scriptures to establish them in your heart (for a full list of self-limiting beliefs and their biblical antidotes, go to ronmcintoshministries.com to order the *Barrier Busters Manual* and *Barrier Busters Meditation* CD's).
- A loss of identity creates spiritual myopia (near sightedness), spiritual blindness and spiritual amnesia (2 Pet. 1:2-9).
- Once you understand your identity, you will enter into rest. Biblical rest means to trust Jesus' finished work.
- Heart identity is created by coupling new information with focused, positive emotion—repeatedly.
- Don't simply influence your heart by default but be intentional (meditate day and night).
- You can change your emotion by changing your focus.
- You are complete in Christ (Col. 2:10). People who see lack are limited to their own effort. People who see themselves complete trust God's character and mo-

tive. They open themselves to the manifestations of God's Kingdom.

• Intentionally set your heart by setting your mind on things above (the unseen provision of His Kingdom). Die to self (submit your view and opinion to His view and opinion). See yourself in Christ. Live through the exchanged life.

CHAPTER 10

THE LAW OF CAPACITY

THEME: YOU CAN ONLY RECEIVE FROM GOD IN DIRECT CORRELATION TO YOUR CAPACITY TO RECEIVE FROM GOD.

Lesson: Discover the 4 keys to increase your capacity.

Many laws for success have been propogated over the years. One of those laws is the "80/20 Rule." This rule states that 20% of your efforts produce 80% of your results; 20% of your people produce 80% of your money; 20% of your people produce 80% of your results. The "80/20 Rule" is an observation, not necessarily a biblical law.

Most of you know or have heard of the "80/20 Rule." But how many of you have heard of the "16/40/60 Rule"? The rule says that, "At sixteen yers old, you're worried about what everybody thinks about you. At forty years old, you don't care what anybody thinks about you. And, at sixty years old, you realize there is nobody thinking about you." However, today I want you to think about you.

Here is an unequivical maxim. There is a difference between being committed to your success and being interested in your success. If you're only interested in success, you will do what is convenient. If you are committed to success, you'll do what is necessary. The fact is, most people are only interested in being successful.

There is an ancient story of a wealthy father who summoned his twin sons to his death bed. In that moment in time, the father gave to his sons three gifts from his life, all wrapped around his philosophy of life. He imparted the understanding of a gift that is easy to give and never runs out. It is the philosophy of love. The second gift is easy to give, but not easy to have. He imparted his philosophy of money (1 Tim. 6:9-11; 17). Lastly, he showed them the importance of the philosophy of choice.

He promptly put his last philosophy to the test. He told his sons he was going to give them a choice of their inheritance. He said, "You have a chioce. You may have one million dollars in cash today or receive one penny doubled for a month (31 days). I will instruct my accountant to act according to your choice."

The first son chose the million dollars almost before the father finished his sentence. The second son asked for 24 hours to think over his choice.

The first son took his million dollars and immediately assembled a consultant and manager to counsel him. Within a few days they had hired a staff of the best financial advisors anywhere. They began around-the-clock brainstorming sessions. They concocted and contrived an investment plan for the first son's money. They ran the ideas through a variety of experts. After the first week they began to implement a glorious investment scheme.

Meanwhile, to his shock, he heard his brother had chosen the second offer. They met together to get an account of each other's activities. The second son took his father's offer of one penny and left for a relaxing day. On day 2 he had two pennies. On day 3 he had four cents. By the end of the week he had amassed sixty-four cents. By week 2, around the half-way mark, he had amassed $81.92.

During this period, the first son's investment began paying off. His investments were succeeding. He once again checked on his brother. By the end of day seventeen he had the sum total of $655.36. He thought to himself how foolish his twin was. Soon his investment began to turn into great profit. His brother seemed unperturbed by his paltry progress.

By week 4, the first son saw the market take a sharp turn downward, and he ended up with something slightly lower than where he began minus the personnel expenses. He decided he would see how his brother had fared. He had last contacted his brother at day 17 with $655.36. To his great shock, by day 28 the one penny doubled turned out to be $1,342,177.28. By day 30, it had compounded to over $5 million dollars. And, on day 31 he had accumulated $10,737,418.23. The choice of the second son was wisdom.[1]

The application to this old parable are many, but perhaps paramount is this: doing the little things daily increases your capacity. Most people have a profound interest in being successful, but once things become inconvenient or they don't see immediate results, they stop doing the little things that create compound growth. They try that *meditation thing* for a couple of weeks, but nothing seems different, so they quit. What they don't realize is that 21 days is the minimum time to build a new neural pathway (could be 30, 42, 60 or 90 days). If you quit too soon you denature (undo) your progress. Doing the little things every day for at least 21 days makes the difference. The result is an almost unwitting multiplication in your capacity. You seem to have a multiplication of growth that is supernatural for its time framework. What seemed too big for you becomes a natural happenstance. God's will for you is abundance.

Look at the following scriptures:

- **John 10:10** – "I have come that you might have life and have it more abundantly" (KJV). The term *abundant* here means *superabundant in quantity, superior in quality, excess, surplus, superfluous, excessive.*[2] God wants you to have life that is too much.

- **Job 36:11** – "If they obey and serve Him, they will spend their days in prosperity and their years in pleasure."

- **Joshua 1:8** – "Don't let this Book of the Law depart out of your mouth; but you shall meditate in it day and night. Be careful to do all that is written therein. Then will I make your way prosperous, then you will have good success."

- **Psalm 1:2, 3** – "But his delight is in the law of the Lord; and in His law does he meditate therein day and night. He is like the tree planted by streams of water which yields fruit in season and whose leaves do not wither. Whatever he does prospers."

- **Psalm 35:27** – "Let the Lord be magnified who delights in the prosperity of His servant."

- **Psalm 84:11** – "No good thing does He withold from him who walks uprightly."

- **Proverbs 8:21** – "That I may cause those who love me to inherit wealth, and I will make their treasuries full."

- **Proverbs 11:24, 25** – "One man gives freely, yet gains even more, another witholds unduly but comes to poverty. A generous man will prosper. He who refreshes others will himself be refreshed."

- **Psalm 115:14** – "May the Lord make you increase, both you and your children."

- **2 Corinthians 8:7, 8** – "But just as you excel in every-thing—in faith, in speech, in knowledge, in complete earnestness...see to it you excel in this grace of giving. ..for you know the grace of the Lord Jesus Christ that though He was rich, yet for our sakes became poor, so that you, through His poverty might become rich."

- **2 Corinthians 9:6-10** – "Remember this: whoever sows sparingly, will also reap sparingly, and whoever sows generously will reap generously. Each man should give what he has decided in his heart to give, not reluctantly or under compulsion, for God loves a cheerful giver. And God is able to make all grace abound to you so that in all things at all times having all you need, you will abound in every good work . . . now He who supplies seed to the sower and bread for food will also supply and increase your source of seed and enlarge the harvest of your righteousness. You'll be made right in every way— so you can be generous on every occasion, and through us your generosity will result in thanksgiving."

- **Philippians 4:19** – "And my God shall supply all your needs according to His riches in glory in Christ Jesus."

This list of scriptures could go on and on (for a more complete list check out the *Barrier Busters Manual*). Here is the question: Is this how you see yourself and how does it make you feel? Do you see yourself in lack or in complete access to the Kingdom (Eph. 1:2-3)?

Now, here is one of the biggest problems in the Body of Christ. Believers are asking for God to give them things they don't have the capacity to receive. They have not done the simple things daily that increase their capacity. That is what people of abundance do: simple things that are easy to do.[3] Because they're all also easy not to do, and while anyone could do them, most don't.[4] Here is the problem: Every action that is easy to do is also easy not to do.[5]

Let's review the **6 Biblical Laws of Success and the Process of Faith**.

1. **The Law of Capacity** – A person can only receive from God in direct correlation to their capacity to receive from God.

2. **The Law of Control** – A person is happy in life to the dimension they are in control of their life (authority of the believer).

3. **The Law of Belief** – What you believe in your heart with confidence becomes your reality. Everyone manifests what they believe in their heart.

4. **The Law of Expectation** – What you expect in your heart with conviction becomes self-fulling prophecy. Your steps are ordered by your expectation. Eighty-five percent of your actions are the result of your expectations.

5. **The Law of Attraction** – You attract to yourself people, ideas and resources according to your most dominant thoughts. You recognize open doors and opportunities according to your dominant thoughts.

6. **The Law of Correspondence** – Your outside world corresponds directly to your inward world. In other words, what is without is what is within.

These six laws work in unison to manifest God's Kingdom. However, the Law of Capacity forms the foundation.

The Law of Capacity

If our problem is that we can only receive from God in direct correlation to our capability to receive from God, how do we increase our capacity? Let's begin by defining capacity. *Capacity is the ability to contain, hold, absorb or to receive; it is the maximum amount of something contained or the ability to contain.*[6] It is also *aptitude. Aptitude is the ability to learn.* It is the ability of the mind (and heart) to receive ideas or knowledge.[7] It is in essence, *how you see yourself.*

I've been in various situations where I've heard speakers say, "How many of you want to experience the overflow?" The obvious idea is that you would experience more than enough or excess, that there is abundance. However, that is not even the main question. The real question is, "What is the capacity from which you receive of the abundance?"

One of the major obstacles in many people's lives is that they ask God for things that are beyond their capacity to receive or maintain. They may ask, "Lord, I need a million dollars," but they don't have the capacity to receive or maintain it. Remember, 80% of lottery winners who have received millions of dollars unwittingly sabotage themselves and end up right where they were in the beginning.[8] Ninety-five percent of dieters regain all the weight they have lost. I've also heard it said that 95 percent of people earn within five percent of their parents income when adjusted for inflation. You can only contain what you have the capacity to receive.

The **Law of Capacity** states, "A person can only receive from God in direct correlation to their capacity to receive from God." God's supply may be limitless, but your capacity may have a *cap* on what you receive.

When I speak live I often give this illustration. I take a very large pitcher of water and three cups. The pitcher of water, in essence, represents a limitless supply of water. The 6, 8 and 16 ounce cups represent our capacity. I can pour as much water into each cup as it has the capacity to hold it. After that it overflows. My key to receiving from God is not just overflow but my capacity to receive. If I take those same cups and poke a hole in them, then my capacity is further limited to the level of the hole. No matter how much I pour into the cup, it will always drain to the level of the hole. The hole represents your self-limiting beliefs. The key to receiving more in your life is not simply getting God to send more in your direction, but to also increase your capacity to receive what He is pouring out from His abundance (by eliminating self-limiting beliefs and unbelief).

There is a classic story that is told about a man catching fish. Not only were the bugs biting that day, but the big fish were biting as well. One fisherman kept reeling in fish that were a foot long, but he kept throwing them back. A nearby fisherman kept watching with an alternating mixture of disgust and amusement. Finally, he couldn't resist the prodding of his curiosity any longer and called out to his fellow fisherman, "Why are you throwing all those big fish back into the lake?" His answer was more disturbing than the fact he didn't keep them. He yelled back, "I've only got an eight inch pan."

So often we are just like this fisherman. We ask God in acordance to what we think we can do, rather than what He can do. We come to God with an eight inch pan and say, "Fill it up," when God's abudance is much greater. When we consider the power and scope of God, sometimes our perspective and prayers do not correspond to His ability. Remember Jeremiah's words, "Call unto me and I will answer you and show you great and mighty things, which you know not" (Jeremiah 33:3, rephrased).

How then do I increase my capacity? Look at this amazing formula in Matthew 25:14-30.

> 14 "Again, it will be like a man going on a journey, who called his servants and entrusted his property to them. 15To one he gave five talents of money, to another two talents, and to another one talent, each according to his

ability. Then he went on his journey. ¹⁶The man who had received the five talents went at once and put his money to work and gained five more. ¹⁷So also, the one with the two talents gained two more. ¹⁸But the man who had received the one talent went off, dug a hole in the ground and hid his master's money.

¹⁹After a long time the master of those servants returned and settled accounts with them. ²⁰The man who had received the five talents brought the other five. 'Master,' he said, 'you entrusted me with five talents. See, I have gained five more.'

²¹His master replied, 'Well done, good and faithful servant! You have been faithful with a few things; I will put you in charge of many things. Come and share your master's happiness.'

²² "The man with the two talents also came. 'Master,' he said, 'you entrusted me with two talents; see I have gained two more.'

²³ "His master replied, 'Well done, good and faithful servant! You have been faithful with a few things; I will put you in charge of many things. Come and share your master's happiness.'

²⁴Then the man who had received the one talent came. 'Master,' he said, "I knew that you are a hard man, harvesting where you have not sown and gathering where you have not scattered seed. ²⁵So I was afraid and went out and hid your talent in the ground. See, here is what belongs to you.'

²⁶His master replied, 'You wicked, lazy servant! So you knew that I harvest where I have not sown and gather where I have not scattered seed? ²⁷Well then, you should have put my money on deposit with the bankers,

so that when I returned I would have received it back with interest.'

²⁸'Take the talent from him and give it to the one who has the ten talents. ²⁹For everyone who has will be given more, and he will have an abundance. Whoever does not have, even what he has will be taken from him. And throw that worthless servant outside, into the darkness, where there will be weeping and gnashing of teeth.'"

Jesus used this parable to teach His disciples the importance of placing value in whatever the Lord gives you. Within these verses in Matthew, the Lord has given us the **formula** to increase our capacity.

Defining the Keys

1. **Ability** (v. 15) – the power to do something, skill, power to perform or capacity.[9]

   2. **Resources** (v. 16) – something to take care of a need, or something to use for advantage, a means to resort to, or supply.[10]

3. **Attitude** (v. 16) – a mental conditioning that determines interpretation and response to your environment. It is the integration of self-image, self-worth, self-esteem and the ideal self. Attitude determines altitude, how high you will go with your goals.

4. **Stewardship** (vv. 28, 29) – is the concept of management or the dispensing of provision. In other words, it is not only about how much you receive, but how much you keep. There's a major mentality difference between the poor and wealthy. It is not just how much comes in, but keeping the increase.[11] This is why Proverbs 11:16 (KJV) states, "A strong man retains wealth."

KEY #1 – Ability

Ability is the power to do something, skill, the power to perform or capacity. So if you want to increase your capacity, ask yourself, "What abilities do I need to increase to grow in this area? What resources do I need to appropriate in my area of increase? What kind of mental conditioning do I need to develop? And, how should I learn to manage the increase that comes my way?"

Before we look at some specific applications, let me lay out the concept behind this key that we find in Matthew 25:14ff in the Parable of the Talents:

"It will be like a man going on a journey, who called his servants and entrusted his property to them. To one he gave five talents of money, to another two talents and to another one talent, each according to his ability" (vv. 14, 15).

This passage used to really irritate me. Why would God show favoritism to some by giving them more than others? If you notice, however, he didn't just pass out more talents to his favorites. He gave each one according to their abilities. In fact, the Spanish Bible uses the word *capacidad* which means capacity. Each person received supply according to their capacity to perform. In other words, the more abilities you add or develop in your life, the greater entrustment from the One who supplies all good gifts (Jas. 1:7).

One of the main ways to increase my capacity is to increase my abilities. A person's abilities includes a better understanding of one's gifting, personality, talents and needed skills. Ability is a God-given skill, talent or capability to perform a specific task. If you force someone to excel in an area they have no ability in, you unwittingly set them up for failure. You also limit their capacity to receive in that area. We must allow people to discover their unique gifts and then surround them with an atmosphere of encouragement and freedom. The Spirit of God has given gifts to all so we must help free them from their bondages and self-limiting beliefs so they can use their gifts for the **Kingdom**.

The **Key of Ability** works on two levels: (1.) *finding your "genius" level* and, (2.) *finding your productivity level*. I believe everyone has a *genius* level. It is what I call "Finding the Life You Were Born to Live." Your genius level is made up of a combination of *passion + talent + values + destiny = genius*.[12] If you devote your time and energy to discover your passion, talent and value, you will step into your destiny.

First, look at your *passion*. What is it you love to do? Ask yourself what excites you in life? What do you do when you have free time (hobbies)? What gives you a sense of fulfillment? What strong interests do you have? This reveals your passion or your compelling motivation; the things you will naturally pursue with earnestness.[13]

Then, look at your *talents* or *skills*. What are you naturally good at? For what kind of things do you get compliments? For what achievements have you been recognized? How have you excelled in your past? What do people in your life say are your strengths?

Now look at your *values*. What is really important to you? Ask yourself, "If I could do anything and not fail what would I do? What do I stand for? Is there something for which I'd risk my life?"

Lastly, consider your *destiny* or *purpose*? What were you born to do? Where do you seem to make a difference? What are your unique qualities to offer in life?

If you list three or four answers in each category, it will help you discover your genius or gifting. (Take a moment with pencil and paper and do it right now). This is where you'll find your highest levels of success…by doing your best at what you do best.

The ability aspect of capacity, however, also has a productivity side. This is where you develop capacities in areas of interest or need. Abilities include not only skills and talents but knowledge. It has often been said, "Knowledge is power." The fact is, however, *applied* knowledge is power. The real fact is: *valuable* knowledge *applied* is power. Many people are filled with knowledge, but it is of no value to anyone. Knowledge used to benefit yourself or others is what creates true value or makes you valuable. Many people spend years acquiring college degrees, but many are filled with knowledge that has no value. To be successful there's certain knowledge you must appropriate to equip yourself for meaningful productivity. *Valuable knowledge applied is power*. Your *ability increases your capacity* to do your desires.

KEY #2 – Resources

Next we must examine the **Key of Resources** to increase your capacity. In the Parable of the Talents, God gives resources according to one's ability (v. 15). Ability will begin to attract people, ideas, and resources according to your most dominant thoughts. *Resources are something we use to take care of a need, use for advantage, or as a means of supply.*

They are something to use for advantage, a means to supply what is necessary. In other words, what do I need to accomplish the task?

Capacity is partially dependent on the assimilation of resources, the materials necessary to succeed. If you want to lose weight, you have to have some expertise beyond *eat less.* Once you find a lifestyle that fits you, you need a plan and the resources to carry out that plan. You may have to empty your kitchen cabinets and fill them up with healthier foods. You need a plan to implement your resources properly: a daily or weekly eating schedule for success.

If you want to increase your prosperity, you need to do and accumulate things that increase your *value.* I've heard it said that 90 percent of all fortunes are still made selling familiar products in local markets to regular customers.[14] All you need to start building a fortune is a new idea, 10 percent new operating capital, a source of information, a new bent or insight and the ability to apply it in your *niche* market. Your ability to apply ideas is what separates you from anyone else. You must make your ideas worth something.

I have said for years, "Leaders are readers." The highest paid professionals read on average two to three hours per day.[15] Yet, 80 percent of American families didn't buy a book last year. Remember, Earl Nightingale says that if you study any subject one hour per day for five years, you can become an expert on that topic. In other words, it doesn't matter where you are right now, you can develop the resources that make you valuable.

Stop dismissing all the reasons why you *can't* do something and begin to take actions to put the resources in your hands to advance to the next level. James Allen once said, "A plan consistently, persistently adhered to— good or bad, abundance or scarcity— will produce results in a person's life." In other words, if you increase your ideas (good ideas come from several ideas), learn to apply them consistently, persistently (repetitiously), you will create value, and value creates abundance.

So, read books and magazines, listen to teaching CDs, attend seminars and trade shows. Increase your resources, and in so doing, increase your value. It is important to understand that God will provide all the resources you need to accomplish your dream. Once you renew and focus your mind on God's truth, your subconscious mind, in cooperation with the Holy Spirit, will go to work on generating ideas and actions to accomplish your goals. Next, you'll begin to notice resources you could use to make the dream a reality. You will notice people who could help you that you passed by before. You suddenly become aware of people, information, seminars, books or a variety of things you missed up until now. Your internal radar will zone in on everything you need to make your goal come to pass. You'll find yourself motivated to act and to activate your vision. As you begin to imagine how good this will be, persistence will strengthen on the inside of you. You will rally all the internal qualities you need to make your dreams come true.

The greatest resource at your disposal is knowledge. In the first chapter of his second epistle, Peter reveals the momentum this resource grants. He tells us in verse 2, "Grace [unmerited favor, the finished work of Christ, a Divine influence on the heart, empowerment or ability] and peace [the ability to be unmoved by my circumstances] be yours in abundance through the knowledge of God." In verse 3 he reveals "everything we need for life and godliness comes through our knowledge of Him." The knowledge referred to here is not mere information. The Greek word for *knowledge* used here means *personal, intimate, perceived, fully discerned knowledge.*[16] It is knowledge of the heart. It is one of our greatest increasers of capacity.

KEY #3 –Attitude

Attitude is the third determinant of increasing your capacity found in Matthew 25. ***Attitude is a mental conditioning that determines your interpretation and response to your environment.*** That is why two people can have the same experience and one person is devastated while the other is motivated. The difference is attitude, and attitude does determine altitude.

Ephesians 4:22-24 reveals the attitude that is the solution to everything. It says, "You were called to put off the former way of life which is being corrupted by its deceitful desires, to be made new in attitude of your mind and put on the new in the attitude of your mind and put on the new self, created to be like God in true righteousness and holiness." The Mirror Bible says it this way, "Be renewed in your innermost mind. This will cause you to be completely re-programmed in the way you think about yourself. Immerse yourself into the God-shaped new man from above. . .this is what true righteousness and true holiness is all about."

In this passage, Paul unfolds what one author calls the solution to everything.[17] He outlines an incredible progression that literally is the solution to everything. Paul says:

Step 1 – *Put off* the old man.

Step 2 – *Be made new in the attitude of your mind.*

Step 3 – How? *Put on* the new man.

How do I put on/put off to create a new attitude that creates a mental conditioning that interprets and responds to circumstances from God's perspective? Our ultimate goal is to respond to circumstances with faith to experience the Kingdom of God and the life of God (Jn. 10:10).

Put off refers to ridding ourselves of the old man. It is important to note that we don't have two natures, an old man and a new man. The old man (old self) was crucified with Christ (Rom. 6:4, 6; Col. 3:9, 10; 2 Cor. 5:17; Gal. 2:20). You have a new nature. However, we are made new in our spirit, but our thinking must be renewed (Rom. 12:2). We still have a tendency to think according to the 5 elements of our Personal Belief System (Social Environment, Authority Figures, Self-image, Repetitious Information, Experiences). To *put off* the old man, you have to repent. Again, the term *repent* is not primarily a religious word. It simply means to change your thinking.[18] Sometimes, there is compunction or emotion attached to it, but that is far from the end-result. This is not penance (paying for your sin) in order to regain favor with God. I am the righteousness of God in Christ Jesus (Rom. 5:21). There are 5 basic steps to real repentance:

1. Identity – Identify self-limiting beliefs
2. Antidote – Find the antidote to self-limiting beliefs; a remedy to counteract the self-limiting belief; create a scriptural antidote.
3. Repetition – Repeat the antidote by biblical meditation until it lodges in the heart.
    a. Meditation is most effective when it has:
        i. Frequency (day and night)
        ii. Duration (several seconds to several minutes)
        iii. Vividness (how clear you see it)
        iv. Intensity (the emotion you feel. Allow yourself to feel the emotion as though it were an accomplished fact – because it is in the spirit realm).

4. Revelation – Repeat it until it becomes a heart belief (21, 30, 60, 90 days).

5. Rethinking – The end-result is rethinking.

The latter part of the *put off* experience is the beginning of the *put on* experience. *Put on* is renewing your mind, establishing your heart and transforming your Personal Belief System.

The result is, you are being renewed in the *attitude* of your mind. The word *spirit* in verse 23 of Ephesians means *mental disposition.*[19] *Putting off* the old man and *putting on* the new man creates a mental disposition to interpret and respond to your environment according to God's perspective. It is why you can remain positive, while others let their environment dictate to them. I've watched countless people use the key of attitude to multiply their capacity and launch forward with new resolve to fulfill destiny. The applications are endless. Whether it is reconciling relationships, stepping into prosperity, changing their outlook, receiving provision or seeing open doors missed up to that point. They see what others miss.

Attitude is thinking, then feeling and then acting accordingly. Attitude is the integration of self-image (how I see myself), self-worth (how I value myself), self-esteem (how I feel about myself) and the ideal self (how God sees me). We live our lives based on who we think we are. It is also a reflection of what you believe about God. You will never rise above the level of what you believe about God and what you believe about yourself in your heart. The problem is that we often view God through the portals of our own experience. And quite often, that view does not line up with the truth of God's Kingdom. We try to make God in our image rather than being made in His image. If we change our attitude to view life from God's perspective about ourselves and our world, our life would dramatically change.

Noted Harvard psychologist William James said, "The greatest revolution of my generation is the discovery that by changing the attitude of your mind you can change all other aspects of your life." Earl Nightingale suggested, "Attitude is the most important word in the English language." Attitude does determine altitude. In essence, attitude is a mental conditioning of how you see yourself in reference to your environment. How you feel about yourself determines your impact on those around you more than any other factor.

If your attitude is one of *I'm unworthy or undeserving of blessing or benefit* (by the way you're qualified in Christ – Col. 1:12) you will find a way to make that happen. Why has it been said that the average number of times people try before quitting is less than one? It's attitude! Your outer world is always a reflection of your inner world. If you live in blame, anger, bitterness, self-pity or irresponsibility, your attitude is one of disempowering self-limitation. How you see yourself (your image) determines what you will or will not try. It determines what you will or will not receive. It determines whether you see yourself in control (authority) or a victim.

Let me give you an example of an attitude that stands between you and success. It is courage. Courage is a mental attitude of facing what is difficult or dangerous (pain) and not withdrawing. Pain is the difference between where you are and where you want to be. Winston Churchill rightly called courage the foremost virtue upon which all others depend.[20]

The simple insertion of a prefix changes the entire meaning of a word. For instance, the prefix *dis* means *separation, negation, reversal or opposite*.[21] When circumstances or environment *dis-courage* us, it separates us from courage, and we tend to withdraw or retreat from trying.

The prefix *en* means *to put into or on, to make or make into.* Thus, when we are *en-couraged* by someone or something we put courage into ourselves and we take the steps to succeed.

Here's an example from King David's life. First Samuel 22:1, 2 states, "David left Gath and escaped to the cave Adullam. When his brothers and his father's household heard about it, they went down to him there. All those who were in distress or in debt or discontented gathered around him, and he became their leader. About four hundred men were with him."

Now, there's a good way to start an enterprise of any kind. Let's start our business with all our relatives who are distressed, who owe money and are generally discontented. "Hi! I'd like to introduce you to my new Board of Directors. They've got no money, no success and they are generally stressed out and dis-couraged about everything. They're going to share with you how to be encouraged about our endeavors." Right!

However, something amazing happens. By the time we get to 2 Samuel 23:8ff, it says, "These are the names of David's mighty men." What happened to the distressed, in debt and discontent-ed? Listen to their exploits:

1. Josheb-Bassahebbeth – "Raised his spear against eight hundred men, whom he killed in one encounter" (v. 8).

2. Eleazar, son of Dodo, (I always feel better knowing that if the son of Dodo can do it, I can do it)—"Stood his ground and struck down the Philistines till his hand grew tired and froze to the sword. The LORD brought about a great victory that day. The troops returned to Eleazar, but only to strip the dead" (vv. 9, 10).

3. Shammah stood his ground when the enemy banded together in his lentil field. He stood in the mid-

dle of his bean patch, struck down the enemy and won a great victory (vv. 11, 12).

4. Some of David's men at Adullam heard he wanted a drink from the well at Bethlehem. So thirty men broke through the enemy line, drew water from the well of Bethlehem and carried it back to David (vv. 13-16).

What transformed the distressed, in debt and discontented men who stood their ground for a bean patch or risked their lives for a cup of water? What gave a group of malfunctioning individuals the bravery and temerity to stand against all odds without flinching? It was simply an attitude adjustment. Something they saw in David adjusted their mental conditioning (perspective) to their environment. What was it?

In between these two events were some astonishing moments. First Samuel 30 records one such occurrence. At one moment, David is sleeping in the palace on satin sheets: he was in training to be the next king. Saul, the present king, who was going insane, one day in jealousy hurls a spear at David causing him to run for his life. The next thing we know, David is sharing a rock with a coyote. He is surrounded by what most people would call losers. He must feign insanity and live among his enemies. One day while he was out on an expedition, his enemies ransack his city, burn it and take captive the wives and children of all his men. This is what you call a bad day. About the time you think it can't get any worse, his men become further distraught and decide to take up stones to stone him.

Yet, in the midst of these difficult circumstances, an amazing twist takes place in the story. David, greatly distressed by the events of the moment, does something astounding. It says, "He encouraged himself in the LORD" (1 Sam. 30:5 KJV). In the midst of one of the most debilitating times in his life, David looked unto the Lord and drew courage (an attitude that doesn't withdraw out of difficult or discouraging circumstances) into his life to press through the difficult moment to success.

How did David encourage himself in the Lord? The passage doesn't say, but I imagine David rehearsed for himself past moments of former successes in his life. He remembered the times when looming failures were converted to successes. He recalled the time when he slew the lion and the bear that threatened his livelihood and even his life. He remembered how he slew a seemingly invincible foe named Goliath.

David's nation, Israel, was embattled against the Philistines, whose army was led by a seemingly unconquerable champion named Goliath. Goliath stood over nine foot tall. He was a combination of Andre the Giant, The Rock and Shaquille O'Neal. His battle gear weighed almost as much as young David, who was about to challenge him. Every day Goliath stood at the forefront of his army and taunted his seemingly insipid foe. He intimidated the entire army of Israel. They were all dismayed and terrified. After all, they had a good grasp on height, and no one had the courage to take on this giant.

Like a WWE wrestling event, every day Goliath barked out a verbal barrage targeted to strike fear in their ranks. Saul's army shuddered at the prospects of being humiliated and vanquished. In the midst of this humiliation, David, a young teenage boy, comes on the scene and declares, "Who is this uncircumcised Philistine that he should defy the armies of the living God?" (1 Samuel 17:26)

This may seem like an odd assertion for David to make. In fact, I can see some of the troops puzzled and asking, "You want us to kill this guy because he hasn't seen a Urologist?" However, circumcision was a sign of covenant with God. Covenant, in essence, meant God saying, "If you give me all you have, I'll give you all I have." What David was saying was, "As I stand before this Behemoth, I am keenly aware I have a covenant with God, and this Philistine does not. Therefore, why should I be afraid?" What separated David from everyone else? It was how he saw himself and his relationship with God. He knew that in his own strength he was no match for Goliath, but he had learned long ago to depend upon his God.

For years this young man tended sheep on the backside of the desert ministering to God in worship and meditating on His laws. It was this same young man who wrote, "Blessed is the man who does not walk in the counsel of the wicked or stand in the way of sinners or sit in the seat of mockers. But his delight is in the law [principles that tell you how a thing works best] of the LORD, and on his law he meditates day and night. He is like a tree planted by streams of living water, which yields fruit in season and whose leaf does not wither. Whatever he does prospers" (Psalm 1:2, 3).

David sat in the desert for hours imagining himself according to God's truth and not just the facts. It created an attitude in him that only saw the possibility of prosperity and success. Remember, prosperity is really the ability to use God's ability to meet any need. This process had forged in David an irrevocable attitude of invincibility (taking you beyond the possibility of defeat). A person who changes their thinking in this manner only sees darkness as an opportunity, not a probability for the worst-case scenario. Successful people not only see more opportunities, they seize them. And, seize it David did.

Goliath bellowed out to the ruddy-faced teenage boy with a slingshot in his hands, "Am I a dog that you come to me with sticks? Come here and I will give your flesh to the birds of the air and the beasts of the field."

Undaunted because he had *en-couraged* himself, David replied, "You come against me with sword and spear and javelin, but I come against you in the name of the LORD Almighty, the God of the armies of Israel, whom you have defied" (1 Samuel 17:45).

Why was David able to respond in courage when everyone else had cowered in fear? It is because David had already seen truth ahead of time. It is what I call the "Principle of the Prequel." Prequel is now common nomenclature. The original Star Wars movie trilogy was followed by three films that were prequels. A prequel is something that precedes an event. The "Principle of the Prequel" allows you to see truth before facts ahead of time. It goes beyond being proactive to being *pre-active*. This is the key to helping people become *principle* based and not *emotion* based. This is why you tell a child, "It is okay to turn out the lights; there are no monsters in the room. See, look under the bed and look in the closet. There are no monsters." You tell them what is true. They are not in danger. As true as it might be, they still want the lights on. Why? Fear dominates logic. Emotion dominates truth until real truth becomes a part of your personal belief system (subconscious mind).

That is why David wasn't intimidated. He had seen his life in truth ahead of time. Meditation is a way to intentionally increase our faith. David now knew how to get ahead ("a head"). David ran toward his *undefeatable* enemy, armed with only a sling shot, smote the giant in the head, then took hold of Goliath's sword from his scabbard and cut off his head. It was the result of courage that came from being *pre-active*.

Courage is not the absence of fear. Think of how many things you would never have done if you had to wait for fear to disappear. You would never have jumped from the high dive, ridden that bike, slept with the lights off, had a date or gotten your driver's license.[22] Sometimes you *do it afraid*, because you know that truth is bigger than facts.

We've got to learn to overcome *psychosclerosis,*[23] *the hardening of the attitudes.* Nothing is more powerful than a positive mental attitude. Attitude is the perspective by which you view life. Winston Churchill once said, "Courage is rightly considered the foremost attitude upon which all others depend. A positive mental attitude is the key that expands the capacity to all the other laws of success. The ability to see truth expands your capacity to receive it."

Now, David had encouraged himself in the Lord. An *en-couraged* man can stand the onslaught of all the doubt around him. David then rallied his men. They pursued his enemy, and they recovered all that the Amalekites had taken (30:18). Attitude causes you to get all that is coming to you. It increases your capacity.

The King of Attitude

There is a beautiful story of attitude captured in the animated classic *Lion King.* Herein is the story of a young lion son, Simba, born to a king. Sound familiar? His uncle, Scar, is upset that he has lost his succession to the throne. He plots to kill the king, Mufasa, Simba's father. He not only succeeds, but through lies and deception he also convinces Simba to feel responsible for his father's death. Remorseful and humiliated, Simba flees to escape the overwhelming guilt of his seeming misdeed. For a while he hides in obscurity and from responsibility with his new friends Timon and Pumba.

In time, he grows up carefree, trying to forget his past. Years later, his childhood sweetheart Nala, looking for help in her troubled homeland, stumbles into Simba. With romance rekindling, Nala ultimately asks, "Simba, where have you been all these years? We've really needed you."

Simba's response is startling and typical. "No one needs me."

Nala responds, "You're the king!"

Simba protests, "No, I'm not." Then he shouts, "Haku-na Matata!"

This is a Swahili phrase that depicts a carefree lifestyle and means "There are no worries here" (just excuses).

Then Simba continues, "Sometimes bad things happen, and you can't do anything about them."

Isn't that how most of us feel? Bad things have happened to us in our past, and there's nothing we can do about them. Unfortunately, for many people the past also seems to rob them of the resolve to do something about their present.

At this point Nala is confused and responds, "You're not the Simba I remember."

Often our past creates images of fears, guilt, and worries that begin to dictate what we will or will not try in the future.

Simba, dejected and facing the confusing emotions of his past, responds, "You're right, I'm not."

How often have we learned fears crippled us from the willingness to step out into our destiny? How many times have we allowed past shortcomings to cause us to forget who we are in Jesus?

Reflecting in anger, Simba says to Nala, "You're starting to sound like my father."

She responds, "Good, somebody needs to."

Now, reinforcing his guilt and conviction, Simba says, "I can't go back (and face his fears while trying to help the people of his homeland). It wouldn't change anything anyway. You can't change the past."

All of us can relate to that to some degree. We feel we can't change our past, but our simple acquiescing to it robs us of our future and limits our lives.

Simba turns and runs from Nala and his destiny. Crossing over a body of water, he sees his reflection, but he doesn't like what he sees. As he continues on his pilgrimage, he runs into Rafiki, the High Priest of the jungle. His eccentric ways irritate Simba, but ultimately Simba asks, "Who are you?"

Rafiki responds, "The real question is, 'Who are *you*?'"

Simba comes to a poignant moment in his life as he states, "I thought I knew. Now, I'm not so sure."

Further dialogue with Rafiki causes Simba to state, "I think you're a little confused."

Rafiki responds, "I'm not the one who is confused. You don't even know who you are. You're Mufasa's boy (in essence, you are the son of a king).

One of the greatest deterrents to breaking the shackles of mediocrity is our failure to realize that God has transformed us into a new creation. Instead, we try to live our lives out of an old identity. You are a completely new creation, but you try to express it through what the apostle Paul calls the "old man."

In his breakthrough book *Wild at Heart,* John Eldredge uses a profound quote from Irenaeus, "The glory of God is man fully alive." The truth is, most of us do not feel fully alive. We hate the fact there seems to be a significant gap between what we know is God's abundant life and the limitations we are experiencing.

Now comes the impacting moment of this encounter for Simba. Rafiki says, "Your father, the king, is still alive." Dazed, confused, but inquisitive, Simba chases after him in pursuit of truth. He comes to the edge of his new adopted country, glances back at it, and turns to continue his pursuit.

The fact for every one of us is that we must decide between the safe, secure, predictable comfort zone we have chosen or to step into the frightening, wild, untamed world of our destiny.

As the chase continues, Rafiki leads Simba to a body of water and exhorts him to look into it. Hesitatingly, Simba gazes into it and steps back, shaking his head. Disappointed, he says, "That's just my reflection (image)."

Insistent, Rafiki chides, "Look harder … you see, he (the father king) lives in you."

How easy it is to forget who it is that lives in us. It is impossible to fail in His will.

As Simba looks the second time, he sees Mufasa's image mingled with his own. Suddenly, a heavenly vision of Mufasa appears and speaks the words of Simba's destiny, and yours.

"Simba, you have forgotten me."

Simba responds, "No, Father, I have not forgotten …"

How easy does it seem that you forget who God is and who we are in Him?

Mufasa continues, "You have forgotten who you are (so you've forgotten me). You are more than you have become."

Simba protests, "I'm not what I used to be."

Finally, Mufasa echoes, "Remember who you are. Remember who you are."

Isn't it amazing as believers how often we forget who we really are?

We allow our past to rob us of our future. Our past disappointments, rejections, bad habits, comfort zones and attitudes dictate what we will or will not go after. So often they create self-sabotaging behaviors that keep us in line with a depleted self-image.

Finally, Simba emerges from the vision and says to Rafiki, "Looks like the winds are changing. I'm going back to face my past. I've been running from it so long."

In a moment's notice, *whack*, Rafiki hits him in the head with his staff. "What's that for?" Simba cries out.

Rafiki says, "It doesn't matter; it's in the past."

If we could only get that revelation in our hearts. It doesn't really matter; it's in the past. Your past is not a determinant of your future ... unless you allow it to be (Phil. 3:12).

Finally, Simba says, "Yeah, but the past still hurts."

The past only has significance according to the value you put on it. The way to change your future is to put a new value on it.

Rafiki says, "There are two things you can do with your past. You can run from it, or learn from it."

Suddenly, Rafiki swings his staff at Simba's head but Simba ducks and he misses ... Simba had learned from his past. The scene ends with Simba returning to his home in Pride Rock to take his rightful position, no longer fearing his past. While much of the story has New Age implications, the lesson of self-image (God-image) is undeniable.

Attitude is everything. Look! There are 15 theological lessons from Lion King (I bet you never thought you'd hear that)!

1. Simba was born son of a king (So are you!)
2. He lost sight of his identity through the self-limiting beliefs of guilt, fear, remorse and regret.
3. In leaving his home in fear he learned a new philosophy: "Hakuna Mattata" – no worries, no responsibility, just excuses.
4. His childhood love, Nala, arrives and love kindles a new perspective. (God's unlimited love does the same for you. See 1 Jn. 4:19. It is more important for you to let God love you than for you to try and love Him. Once you experience His love, you can't help but love Him).
5. When he encounters the monkey prophet, Rafiki, he discovers his self-limiting belief and set-point, "No one needs me." He has no self-worth.

6. Then he declares, "Sometimes bad things happen and you can't do anything about them." That is true, but attitude determines whether you quit and retreat or press on.

7. Nala says to Simba, "You're not the same Simba I remember." Self-limiting beliefs make us less than we are.

8. Simba responds, "You're starting to sound like my father." There is always something trying to get us to remember the voice of the Father. Nala responds, "Good, somebody needs to." Simba says, "But I can't go back" (and face my fears). Not only should we go back and face our fears, but we must. Finally, Simba relents, "It wouldn't change anything, anyway. You can't change the past." The key is you can't change the past, but you can't let the past change you.

9. Crossing over a bridge, he sees his reflection in a body of water, but he doesn't like what he sees. Self-image is crucial!

10. Simba asks Rafiki, "Who are you?" Rafiki responds, "The real question is, 'Who are you?'" Identity is the answer to everything. Simba reflects, "I thought I knew; now I'm not so sure." This is the dilemma we all face, the search for our true identity. You are more than you imagine. Then Simba reacts, "I think you're confused." (This is because of the fact that Rafiki called him the son of a king). Rafiki notes, "I'm not the one confused." He could see that Simba had a blind spot to seeing who he really was.

11. Then Rafiki, shouts out, "You are Mufasa's boy." In essence, remember, you are the son of a king. So are you!! We often miss the understanding of our true identity!

12. Then Rafiki states, "Your father the king is still alive." In agony, Simba tries to deny what Rafiki is stating. Rafi-

ki says, "Follow me!" Simba bounds after Rafiki that by chance it might somehow be true. He comes to the edge of an entangled forest. He stops, looks back, then leaps forward in pursuit of the truth. Before he does, he glances back to his safe, secure territory. He has to choose between the safe, secure, predictable comfort zone or the wild, untamed, frightening world of his destiny. And, so will you!

13. Rafiki leads him to a body of water and tells him to look into it and he will see his father. He looks in and sees only his reflection. Rafiki implores him, pointing again to the lake. "Look harder. You see the king lives in you." Wow! What a revelation. Suddenly, his father's voice rings loud and true and he says 3 things:

> One: "You have forgotten me." Spiritual amnesia can be critical.

> Two: "You have forgotten who you are." Identity loss is far less important with your credit card than it is with God's **Kingdom**.

> Three: "You are more than you've become." Wow! We can allow our past to rob us of our future. Then, he echoes the key words, "Remember who you are!" Discover your true identity! Then, allow this mindset and attitude to redefine your future.

14. The revelation of truth causes you to change your perspective.

15. When the revelation strikes home, Simba declares, "I'm going to face my past. Rafiki hits him on the head with a stick. Whack!! Simba says, "What is that for?" Rafiki responds, "It doesn't matter, it's in the past." Simba states, "Yeah, but the past still hurts!" Once again, Rafiki swings his stick at Simba's head, but this time Simba

dodges it. Rafiki exclaims, "See, you can run from it or learn from it."

Wow! How can so much insight come from an animated film? See, attitude determines altitude. Attitude expands your capacity to see from a new (higher) perspective.

KEY #4 – **Stewardship**

The last aspect of the Law of Capacity is *stewardship* (Ability + Resources + Attitude + Stewardship = Capacity). ***Stewardship is defined as the management and dispensing of provisions.***[24] There is a major difference in the way wealthy people think and the way people experiencing lack think. A person who is experiencing lack asks, "How much money can I make?" A wealthy person asks, "How much money can I keep?" A person who has a mentality of lack sometimes will make money, but they will find a way to lose it or spend it until nothing is left. The stewardship aspect of the Law of Capacity not only wants to see increase, it wants to keep increase. *Increase can only occur when we position ourselves to receive abundance.*

Let me give you an example of what I mean. A recent headline read, "American Airlines Eliminates One Olive from Salads." You might think, *"What difference can one olive less on first class salads make toward profitability of the world's largest airline?"* Well, in the case of American Airlines, it came out to around $50,000 per year. Sometimes little things can make a big difference.

Now $50,000 may not seem like much money to the profitability of a major airline. However, coupled together with its other cost cutting efforts (stewardship) the results are amazing:

- Reducing reserve fuel from 99 minutes to 90 minutes (twice the legal amount), lowered the weight of each flight by 100 pounds. The result was—are you ready for this?—$100 million dollars per year.

- Removing kitchens from the cabin class because they no longer serve hot meals in coach, along with adding six new seats in its place raised income $34 million dollars.
- Taxiing to the gate with one engine, instead of two, saves $4 million dollars per year.

It's not simply how much you can make, but how much you can keep.[25]

Abundance takes place when you find a way to invest surplus, not just spend it. It has been said, "A fool and his money are soon separated." *Stewardship* is a real key in *capacity*.

Proverbs 3:1-2 says it this way, "My son [daughter], do not forget my teaching [truth], but keep my commands [truth] in your heart [by meditation into the soul chamber of the subconscious mind], for they will prolong your life many years and bring you prosperity."

What this means is, "Let the meditation [implantation] of God's truth create an image in your heart. Once you see God differently and see yourself according to His truth, God's Word will provide health and prosperity." (emphasis added).

Abundance is always the result of value. If you have something of value, people will remunerate you for it. If many people share a value, it decreases its worth, because it is accessible from many sources. If few people have your value, it increases its worth. Abundance is always created out of value.

Prosperity is the result of increasing your value in some way. If you create a solution, increase your knowledge, show people a better or faster way, reveal benefit for a clientele or demonstrate a way to access resources, then abundance will follow. Do it faster, improve quality, make things easier, improve service, make something less expensive and people will bless you with increase.

Abundance usually follows doing what you love. When you do what you love, it creates a momentum or an impetus in your heart to pursue a thing to completion. Once I was training people in a seminar, and a woman protested, "Oh, that's great for sales people, but I'm a teacher."

"It's true," I replied, "Public teachers don't make much money, but I can show you a number of people who teach and train who make a lot of money. You must find the right clientele in the right format with the right value."

There are really three aspects of *Stewardship*:
- *Setting your intention*
- *Giving and receiving*
- *Managing your increase*

In order to be prosperous, I must believe it is God's will, see myself in line with that truth and act as if it is true. Every day you must see yourself in accordance to the truth of Scripture.

The first aspect of stewardship is **setting your intention**. I met one day with a "productivity expert." This man meets with corporations to help them increase sales, customer service, etc. So I asked him, "What is the main thing you teach to help people become more productive?" He then gave me this formula: $I + M = R$. The formula stands for **Intention + Mechanism = Results**. As I thought about it, I said, "Is that anything like **Faith + Corresponding Action = Results**?"

He said, "Exactly!"

Then, with a gleam in his eye, he asked this question, "What percentage of the formula do you think is intention, and what percentage do you think is mechanism?"

Wanting to sound intelligent, I thought to myself, "*It's 50 percent intention and 50 percent mechanism. Then, I waivered, maybe it's 80/20.*" Finally, I settled on 80 percent intention and 20 percent mechanism because it sounded more intelligent, and blurted out my answer.

Smiling broader now, the productivity expert looked at me and said, "No! You're exactly wrong. It's 100 percent intention and 0 percent mechanism."

I immediately protested by arguing how could it be a formula if the second entity doesn't really exist?

This productivity expert explained to me that in their seminars they give people an assignment during a lunch break to show this principle. During the break, the participants are to interact with one another about their main goal (personal or corporate) for the next six months.

After reconvening, the leader of the seminar asks for a volunteer to demonstrate $I + M = R$. A willing participant is to stand before his peers and yell, with conviction, his goal to the group. Then he is to travel past a "barrier" as a sign of the mechanism.

So the first participant stands and proclaims, "I want to double my sales in six months." He then proceeds to *walk* past the barrier as a sign of his mechanism to the cheering of his peers and the prompting of the leader.

The next volunteer cries out, "I want to lose twenty-five pounds in six months." Before they can engage in walking out their mechanism, the leader says, "You've got to do something different than your predecessor for your mechanism!"

Somewhat confused, the second volunteer says, "What do you mean?"

The leader responds and says, "They *walked* past the barrier as a sign of their mechanism. You can do anything but *walk*."

Momentary confusion disappears as that moment of *revelation* appears in their eyes, and the second volunteer *runs* past the barrier. Suddenly, it dawns on the group that they are all going to have to come up with an alternative mechanism to everyone in front of them. Mild panic begins to hit the person who is number seventy in line. So people began to *skip, hop, somersault, etc.* through seventy mechanisms.

A subtle groan of relief hits the last participant as they squawk like a chicken for their mechanism. Without warning, the leader announces everyone has to go back the other way and do new mechanisms all over again. The mechanisms get more and more innovative (creative) as they reach one hundred forty. Subsequently now, the leader prompts a third try at mechanism displays. Now, they have totaled two hundred ten various mechanisms.

At the conclusion, the application is obvious. There are infinite amounts of mechanisms. If your *intention is set*, you will find the mechanism to put into action what you desire.

How do I bring more increase? Intend it! Find God's will for your life and set your faith in agreement with it, and your subconscious mind along with the Holy Spirit will find a way to bring it to pass (Mk. 11:24). Your solution must be believable to you. Intend it (believe it), and it will be yours. One woman told me how God led her to raise money for a new truck for their Christian school's football coach. She met obstacle after obstacle and was ready to quit. Suddenly, she remembered **I + M = R (F + CA = R)**. She went to the car dealer and put down a down payment of $1,500. She said, "If I don't have the remaining money in thirty days, you can keep my $1,500. All of a sudden, new strategies came to her. What she hadn't able to do in several months was completed in fifteen days.

Negative feelings block ideas from coming to you. Faith in God's provision opens the windows of heaven.

The second aspect of stewardship is **giving and receiving**. The Scripture says, "Give, and it shall be given to you. A good measure, pressed down, and shaken together and running over (overflow), will be poured in your lap. For the measure [capacity] you use, it will be measured to you" (Lk. 6:38). Galatians 6:7 says, "For whatever a man sows, that he will also reap" (NKJV). 2 Corinthians 9:6 states, "He who sows sparingly will also reap sparingly, and he who sows bountifully will also reap bountifully."

Giving is a powerful action that brings increase into your life. It is a **Kingdom Law** that you have to see in your heart. When you are giving you are saying, "I possess excess."[26] It is why the wealthiest people on the planet are the greatest philanthropists.[27]

If you focus on getting out of debt, it will cause you to create dominant thoughts of debt. What you focus on you tend to create. When you focus on lack and scarcity and what you don't have (and fuss about it with family and friends), this is what you tend to create. You attract it because you are looking for it. If you are looking at what you can't afford, you'll perpetuate it.[28] Charles Filmore said, "The spiritual substance from which comes all visible wealth is never depleted. It is right with you all the time and responds to your faith— and your demands on it."

The real reason *giving* works can be seen in the four Laws of Genesis 1:26 (see chapter 1). It is the initiation and authorization of man on earth to attract God's provision from the **Kingdom** of heaven. This is a **Kingdom Law** that when believed and acted on draws the resources of the Kingdom. For some of us it is a huge paradigm shift to think that giving is increase for us, not depletion. Proverbs 11:24 says, "One man gives freely, yet gains even more; another withholds unduly, but comes to poverty." In the natural, it doesn't make sense, but in God's system this Kingdom Law brings increase.

The third aspect of stewardship is *managing your increase*. For years, multiple books have given simplistic strategies for wealth:
- Tithe (pay God 10 percent)
  - Managing your increase allows God to protect your funds or storehouse (Malachi 3:6-12).

- Save 10 percent (pay yourself 10 percent)
- Invest 10 percent
- Live off of 70 percent and don't spend more than this.

This may seem obvious, but not when you consider over 70 percent of people live from paycheck to paycheck. Only 56 percent are saving for retirement at all.[29] One financial expert suggests 90 percent of your problems can be fixed with finances. Spend less, invest more and abundance will follow.

People have a tendency to spend emotionally. Two-thirds of Americans have credit card debt of at least $5,000 or more.[30]

If you were to save $25.00 per week at _10 percent_ interest the result would be:

5 years	10 years	20 years	30 years	40 years
$7,808	$20,655	$76,570	$227,933	$637,628

At **_12 percent_ interest:**

5 years	10 years	20 years	30 years	40 years
$8,249	$23,234	$99,195	$352,999	$1,188,242

Similarly, if you were to start saving $3,000 per year at 10% interest rate starting at age 15 for 5 years, your total investment of $15,000 with compounding interest would be $1,600,363.40 by age 65.[31]

The **Law of Capacity** is the real key to abundance:

Abilities acquired + resources assimilated + positive attitudes achieved + stewardship that promotes proper management and investment = increased capacity.

This formula creates a systemic approach to a guaranteed increase. This is how you overcome the kind of self-sabotaging actions that limit how much you can receive. It is time to *take the limits off.*

If you are not living up to your full potential, it is likely that life is affording you more than you have the ability to receive. All of life is the result of a proper belief system aligned with proper principles.

Using the four keys to **The Law of Capacity** unlocks momentum in your life: *Ability + Resources + Attitude + Stewardship = Capacity.* The ability to go from where you are to where you want to be demands that you increase your capacity.

My intent in writing this work to give you viable principles and keys that bring transformation to your life. So, let's turn our attention to putting it all together.

Keys for Reflection

- Ask yourself, are you committed to your success or merely interested in your success? The way you can tell is if you do what is convenient or you do what is necessary.

- Review and meditate on the scriptures listed on prosperity. How do you see yourself in reference to these verses? Imagine what it would look like (including how you could bless others).

- Go to pages 181-182 and take the Genius Test. What does it show you about your life and ministry?

- Remember, abundance comes out of value. What resources are you using to increase your value?

- Review the definition of attitude. What attitudes are moving you forward and what attitudes are holding you back? Fan the attitudes moving you forward and find antidotes to the attitudes holding you back.

- Based on your reading, what act(s) of stewardship do you need to work on?

- How does I + M = R apply to you? How are you setting your intention?

CHAPTER 11

PUTTING IT ALL TOGETHER

THEME: HOW TO APPLY EVERYTHING YOU READ AND STUDIED.

Lesson:
1) How to diagnose self-limiting beliefs.

2) Find the antidote to your self-limiting beliefs.

3) Mediate on the antidote to experience heart beliefs.

4) Experience transformation in your heart.

5) Enjoy the results.

I had just finished a leadership seminar in a church located in a southern state. I was milling around and conversing with some of the people who had participated in the event. In the midst of exchanging pleasantries with many of the people, the participating lead pastor interrupted the process and asked if he could talk with me. "Ron," he began, "This is without a doubt the best leadership seminar I have ever participated in or been a part of." He paused a moment and then in an almost embarrassed tone continued, "Now, we are not going to do any of it, but it was great!"

I was not the least bit offended, but I responded in a puzzled manner, "Why not?"

The pastor continued, "I really mean it was great, but it is just too hard. It takes too much effort."

I began to protest, "It does take effort on the front side, but it will build momentum on the backside."

His astonishing response continued, "Yeah, I know, but I'm so busy I can't. . ." His voice began to fade out of my conscious mind as I listened to an obvious litany of reasons I knew could not be resolved in his mind.

I have little interest in penning a work that will be praised without transforming lives. I am not interested in you being enamored with material you do not apply. I am not concerned with writing a bestseller (not that I am against that) as much as helping people find the life they were born to live. This book is about giving you the missing keys to help you to step into your destiny. You have digested a lot of information. Now, what do you do with it?

Let's imagine you walk into my office for some personal coaching. You've read the material and want to know how to put it all together. Let's take a look at how to begin:

Step 1 – Diagnose your self-limiting belief.

Self-limiting beliefs are often evident, but not always identified or able to be named. These beliefs usually show through a form of lack (financial struggle, health or sickness, stagnations, excess worry or frustration, discouragement, doubts, inferiorities, double-mindedness, etc.), or sometimes a self-limiting belief is a blind spot (scotoma) that others see but you are blind to see. With blind spots, a good counselor or coach can help you find them. Most of you can identify a self-limiting belief without help. However, if you are having difficulties identifying your frustrations, ask yourself a few questions:

1. What area(s) am I having trouble getting a desired breakthrough?

2. What area of character (fruit of the spirit) seems to be a shortcoming in my life? Alternatively, what character deficiencies do others constantly reflect to me? This thought process is not intended to discourage you, but it is an honest evaluation for growth.

3. Look at the most common areas of self-limiting beliefs listed in the *Barrier Busters Manual* and honestly evaluate what seems to be holding back your breakthrough.

4. Perhaps your self-limiting belief is attached to an ongoing shortcoming or area of sin. Remember the Greek word for *sin* means to miss the mark of the prize. *The prize is the life of God or the manifestation of His Kingdom.* I am righteous in Him. The more I believe it, the more I'll act like it. (See my book *Organic Christianity* for a more detailed explanation). Your self-limiting belief may cause you to act in the flesh. Flesh is my attempt to do God's will, my way. That often leads to a lifestyle of sin that causes me to miss the abundance of God's life. (See Keys for Reflection at the end of Chapter 6 for a thorough examination for self-limiting beliefs).

Step 2 – Find a biblical antidote to your self-limiting belief.

An antidote is something to counteract something, in this case, a shortcoming or shortfall. It is anything that counteracts your misdirection.

1. You may instinctively know the antidote to your self-limiting belief. Many are obvious. If you are struggling with lack or poverty, prosperity is the obvious antidote.

2. If you are struggling to identify the antidote, use the *Barrier Busters Manual* as a guide to find it. For instance, the antidote for fear is love. 1 John 4:18 tells us, "Perfect love casts out all fear." Sometimes using the love scriptures with righteousness (right standing with God through faith in His finished work) is a great combination. Agape love or unmerited love with righteousness (I am qualified through Christ to receive) can be a liberating combination.

3. For this session let us assume your self-limiting belief is lack.

Step 3 – Meditate on your antidote.

1. The antidote for lack is prosperity.

2. Find God's Word (Kingdom principles) on prosperity. If you can find them on your own, great! If you want or need an accumulation of scriptures, the *Barrier Busters Manual* contains scripture listings.

3. Commit to meditate on the prosperity scriptures every morning and every evening before you retire. You will need to set aside about 20 to 25 minutes for each meditation period.

4. Remember that biblical meditation to renew your mind, establish your heart and transform your Personal Belief system takes a minimum of 21 days. It could be 30 days, 60 days or even 90 days (depending on the Pain/Pleasure

Principle—see Chapter 3). Meditating regularly will create new neural pathways in the brain (dominant thoughts that will affect the heart). Interrupting the process prematurely causes you to denature (stop) the progress, before it is established.

5. How do I meditate on prosperity?

    1. Still Stage

        • Start by being still. Remember the alpha state—the state your brain moves into just before you go to sleep. If you have trouble coming to a relaxed state try the *Barrier Busters Meditation* series. It provides relaxation exercises before rehearsing scriptures.

    2. Imagination Stage

        • See yourself according to the evidence of (unseen) truth, not facts. Create new dominant images. Reset your set-points.

        • Remember effective imagination should include:

            • Frequency— Meditate day and night.

            • Duration— Focus on the image several seconds to several minutes.

            • Vividness—How clear is the image?

            • Intensity—See the emotion as though your vision is accomplished.

- Practice the 4 steps to reconditioning your subconscious mind

  - See it! Create a new vision.

  - Say it! Create power confessions.

  - Feel it! Create emotional anchors.

  - Do it! Have a consistent day and night routine.

- Confession—confess your truth.

  Make it:

  - Personal

  - Present Tense

  - Positive

  - Confess it, imagine it, feel it!

3. Strategy Stage

   - Based on what I see, what action should I take?

   - Revelation leads to action.

4. Action Stage

   - Every day do something toward your highest priority.

5. Thanksgiving Stage

   - Thanksgiving solidifies my heart and changes my attitude.

   - Thank Him for what He has done.

Step 4 – Experience the transformation in your heart.

1. How do I know if something is in my heart?

   - According to Matthew 11:28,29:

     - It changes how I see myself.

     - It becomes easy to do.

Step 5 – Enjoy the results.

1. Heart belief = Identity

2. It changes my momentum and capacity.

Now that I have walked you through the 5-fold process, let me give you an example. I was teaching a seminar on how to break self-limiting beliefs and a friend of mine in the group was fascinated by the teaching.

One day after the study, he approached me and asked, "Could this apply to my prosperity in my business?"

I replied, "Absolutely, let's experiment!"

Since I knew him well, I suggested, "I believe the antidote to your limitation is prosperity and righteousness. Prosperity is to overcome some shortfalls and righteousness is to reposition you in confidence to receive from God." The process of creating heart beliefs through biblical meditation was new to him so I gave him biblical meditation CD's on Righteousness and Prosperity. I said to him, "I want you to listen to the *Barrier Buster Meditation* CD on Righteousness in the morning when you wake up and the Prosperity CD before you go to sleep at night. Do this for 30 days. I also want you to create a confession list to rehearse positive affirmations daily."

Then, I gave him some guidelines. "First, make sure your biblical confessions are personal. Start with the two most powerful words in the English language, 'I am.' The soul in the subconscious mind takes all 'I am' statements as a command, a directive or authorization to make it come to pass. Remember, God's name is 'I am.' We see this in Exodus 3:14 and John 8:58.

"It's also important to make your confessions about yourself, not others. For instance, don't say, 'I am believing my sales force is successful.' Instead say, 'I am effectively communicating (power verb) to my sales force about success.' Adding a power verb evokes 'new images.' Instead of saying, 'I am prosperous,' say, 'I am excited (emotion) about the fact that I am prosperous (add a financial goal or a specific amount of money amount).' Describe what you want as though you already have it. This is called faith in Romans 4:17."

Here is another critical guideline I explained to my friend. Always state your confession in the positive. The **subconscious mind** does not hear "No" or "Not." This means if your confession contains "No" or "Not" the **subconscious mind** actually hears the opposite.

- Wrong: "I do not have fear." Such confession evokes the opposite of what you want.

- Right: "I am full of love" (and/or faith).

- Wrong: "I am having no more losses."

- Right: "I am thrilled with my company increasing by ___%." (Now see it! What does it look like? How does it make you feel?).

- Keep it brief. Make it specific. Make it realistic (for you). Vague confessions create vague results.

- Wrong: "I am believing for increase."

- Right: "I am enjoying making (a certain amount of money) per month."

- Wrong: "I am maintaining my weight of 175 pounds."

- Right: "I am feeling fit at 175 pounds."

Also, remember to add emotion and feeling words. This sets the process in motion to transform your Personal Belief System. You eliminate self-limiting beliefs and reinforce faith according to the truth.

My friend took my advice seriously. After the seminar in November, he began this process faithfully. The following April he announced to me that his business had tripled in the first three months of the year over what he had done the entire previous year. Why? When he believed his destiny in his heart, he found new, inventive ways to conduct business. He recognized people, ideas and resources he had missed up until this time.

I want to take a moment to tell you how this principle relates to the amazing miracle healing of Dodie Osteen. Dodie is the mother of Lakewood Church Pastor Joel Osteen. In 1981, Dodie was diagnosed with metastatic liver cancer. It has been my privilege to be casually connected to Dodie and more intimately with other members of the family.

In October of 1981, Dodie had a series of tests run at the City of Faith Hospital in Tulsa, Oklahoma. The tests included a grueling schedule of CT scans, upper and lower GI, bone marrow biopsy and uterine biopsy.

Then came the haunting words, "Your cancer is malignant." As you can well imagine, the emotions ran from astonishment to denial. Then came the seemingly final pronouncement that even with chemotherapy she only had a few weeks to live.

In the midst of the ensuing struggle, Dodie realized it was not the faith of her "famous" friends or husband that would deliver her. It was her own belief that would turn the tide. It wasn't the faith of Oral Roberts, Kenneth Hagin or her husband, John, that would set her free, but her own personal belief system.

She began her fight by refusing to lie in bed, letting others take care of her. She was committed to not act sick.[1/2] In fact, she set the "Law of Attraction" into action by grabbing a hold of James 5:16, "Pray for one another that you may be healed," and Luke 6:38, "Give and it will be given to you." Dodie began to extend herself to others, and her reaction was, "When I forced myself to pray for someone else, my health came back to me."[2/3]

She began to establish in her heart that God could not lie. If His Word said it, then it was true. The process, however, was a war. She said she never wavered in her heart, but she did in her head. According to Hebrews 4:12, her soul and spirit sometimes warred. There were times to deal with fear and times to cast down imaginations (2 Cor. 10:5). She laughed at symptoms but warred against thoughts. She disassociated (disconnected) herself from thoughts of the worst-case scenario with new empowering thoughts of God's Word. The greatest struggles came in the lonely moments during the middle of the night.

During this time, her family treated her as if she were normal. It kept the *pity parties* minimized and helped her focus on God (the truth). She meditated on forty scriptures every day before beginning her day. She made herself congruent with heaven's will. The truth permeated her mind and heart. Confession was a daily ritual, as well as a struggle. She watched over the words of her mouth. She confessed, "*I am* healed." She began to see it in her heart. Finally, in November 1983, her doctor, Reginald Cherry, pronounced her healed.[3/4]

What happened in this miracle moment? Dodie enacted the tenets, the principles of Romans 12:2. She wasn't conformed to the world's system. She was transformed by the renewing of her mind and establishment of her heart. Suddenly, she *proved* the good, acceptable and perfect will of God. Dodie identified her boundary, sickness. She then identified her antidote, healing. Pursuing its end, she meditated on the truth repetitively until it imprinted an image on her heart. Her rethinking attracted God's already existing provision from the Kingdom of heaven. What an incredible story of God's provision and a person's belief to activate the Law of Attraction and attract healing based on God's Word.

Let me tell you the story of a woman in one of my seminars. Often people come to me with desperate, debilitating situations. She looked haggard and exhausted from not sleeping through the night in ten years. Her view of life was filtered through pain caused by fibromyalgia. At seventy-two years old, life was something to be endured, not something to look forward to each day because of the constant pain.

She took two biblical meditation CDs from my *Barrier Busters Series*, one on Peace and the other on Healing. The CDs took her through the five steps of biblical meditation. As she got *still*, she positioned herself to receive new truth. As she listened to the Peace CD, within two weeks she was sleeping through the night.

She then listened to the CDs on Healing. Repetitively day and night she heard the truth on healing. She then began to see herself according to the truth. She not only saw herself well, but well enough to reach out and help her peers. She began to strategize her future by taking Bible school classes. She was increasing her capacity. She started confessing the truth: "I am excited about feeling whole as I minister to my peers in Tulsa."

She began to thank God for her healing. Similar to Judge Lee's healing, she saw the pain eradicated and her future was secured. She attracted to herself the **Kingdom** of heaven and its provision.

How's That Working for You?

Recently, in a place where I was speaking, I sat with a woman who was having a number of problems in her life. She was struggling with her weight, struggling with relationships, and just struggling to have any sense of victory in her life. I would make some suggestions about renewing her mind and God's Kingdom laws, and it was always met with this phrase, "I believe that but..."

In the midst of her telling me what she believed, suddenly the spirit of Dr. Phil came on me, and I interrupted with, "How's that working for you?"

She looked at me inquisitively, and then it hit her. She was more interested in defending what she believed than changing to a life of productivity and fulfillment. "You see, I'm not interested in winning the debate," I told her. "I'm interested in helping you."

The impact of what I had said hit her, and she began to weep. What she was doing wasn't working for her. Somehow, in this country, everything has been reduced to the bottom line of winning. Politics is all about winning. It has stopped being about new ideas to help people and has taken on the identity of winning at the cost of impugning anyone not like you. In certain corridors of the church, we defend the truth we have always been taught (the defense of truth is important), and we attempt to crucify new phraseologies and methods that attempt to help people. Sometimes we break tradition, and it upsets our comfort zones. The participants in the first move of God are calling people back to *what they had*, while God is getting ready to do a new thing (at least for us). People defend where they are even if it is mired in mediocrity, or worse, defeat. We huddle in our sanctuaries of truth, without realizing we reflect more of the world's system than God's. Our divorce patterns are the same as the world. Our lifestyle patterns reflect everyone else's. We are caught at the same place in our life year after year, yet we are caught defending what we've always been taught.

That is when I looked at this woman and said, "What if I told you there was a 'secret,' a missing ingredient that could change your life? What if I told you there were truths in God's Word that have been overlooked in our generation, but once we grasp them, they will change everything in your life? Would you be interested?" In the midst of tears and laughter, her life has been on a new course ever since. She has had some setbacks, she sometimes struggles with identity, but in the midst of three steps forward and two steps back, she is finding herself moving one step forward. And, for the first time in years, she is both fulfilled and productive.

I will never forget helping one of my former staff members through this process. She was a beautiful and intelligent young woman. She was bright and very capable. Tragedy out of her past left her feeling unloved and abandoned. She always felt she never measured up to God's standards. She felt unacceptable. She viewed herself as inferior, and in her eyes she believed God was mad at her.

After some hours of consulting with her, I showed her how to do biblical meditation on love and righteousness. (Not understanding *righteousness* is often a symptom of people feeling that God is angry with them.) Over a period of about a month, I started seeing a tremendous change in her. No longer was she up one day and down the next. She didn't feel *in* one time and *out* later. Her confidence started to soar. She was more relaxed. I noticed she wasn't trying to be accepted by performance, but she was performing at a higher level. When she left our ministry, she left a whole person, fulfilled, and feeling loved. Today, she has her own ministry and she is thriving.

Perhaps this book is best summed up in the experience of Jesus in the synagogue in Nazareth (Lk. 4:18ff). Jesus walked into a service one day and unrolled the scriptures to Isaiah 61, where it says, "The Spirit of the Lord is on me, because he has anointed me to preach good news to the poor. He has sent me to proclaim freedom for prisoners and recovery of sight to the blind, to release the oppressed, to proclaim the year of the Lord's favor."

God has made you to live a life without limits! It is time to discover who you really are and experience abundance! It is time for productivity theology—a practical faith that works! It is time for you to step into your destiny! *Remember, you are unstoppable!*

Keys for Reflection

Reset set-points by:

- Identifying self-limiting beliefs
- Establishing your antidote
- Meditating on the antidote
- Making a confession list
- Employing new empowering beliefs

EPILOGUE

John 3:3 states, "I tell you the truth, no one can see the kingdom of God unless he is born again." Being *born again* is essential to entering into the kingdom of God, or heaven. If you have never done that, I am going to include a prayer at the end of this epilogue, so that you can make that decision.

However, notice something of monumental importance in this verse. The reason you get born again is to see the kingdom of God. It is important to go to heaven, but it is more important to get heaven in you. If heaven is in you, you will go to heaven.

It is like a story my dear friend Myles Munroe told me some time ago about a shoe store. The shoe store contained the finest shoes in the land. He had a great variety of styles and colors with fair prices. Everyone who saw his store agreed what a great bargain those shoes were. He placed a great door to the entrance of his store on which he advertised his shoe store. When he advertised his shoe store, he talked about what a great door he had without mentioning his shoes. He wondered why more people didn't come to his shoe store.

If we are not careful, this is what we do in the church. We tell everyone about the door (Jn. 10:7), but not the content of His Kingdom. The most important decision you will ever make is to walk through that door, but understand it allows you to see the Kingdom of God's copious provision in your life.

If you have never accepted Christ as your Lord and Savior, pray this prayer with me: *Jesus, I receive you in my life, as Lord and Savior. I say yes to your ways and system. I submit myself to you afresh. From this day forward I will live for you. All that I say, do and am belongs to you. You are my Savior and Lord! Amen!*

Now, by grace through faith receive His kingdom! If you prayed that prayer, please contact our ministry team at:

ronmcintoshministries.com

connect@ronmcintoshministries.com

Glossary	
Word	**Definition**
Arguments	Two contrary opinions.
Attitude	A mental conditioning that determines my interpretation and response to an environment.
Blessed	Having the ability to use God's ability to meet my need.
Capacity	Ability + Resources + Attitude + Stewardship = Capacity
Cognitive Restructuring	Rehearsing your new truth, thought or identity over and over again, until you create a new perception, habit or thought process (heart belief).
Cognitive Dissonance	Mental discord.
Conation	To make an effort or to pursue a think or to act on what is known.
Confession	Declaring the truth of God's Word; picture yourself according to the truth and say and feel the emotion of the goal or result as a finished reality. This is calling the things that are not as though they were (Rom. 4:17).
Disassociate	Disconnect yourself from self-limiting beliefs; see yourself differently than what you are conditioned to do or be.
Emotional Implantation	A divine encounter with God or a revelation of truth that alters your perception.

Faith	The substance of things hoped for, the evidence of things unseen (proof of things already done in the mind's eye); faith is belief in your heart that trusts the character and motive of God. Faith = Belief + Expectation + Corresponding Action
Genius	Passion + Talent + Values + Destiny = Genius
Heart Beliefs	Information + Emotions + Consistency = Heart Beliefs (see identity)
Humility	To submit to the view and opinion of God.
Ideal Self	The self I want to become.
Identification	Identifying your set-points or self-limiting beliefs.
Identity	Knowing who God is, what He's already done and who He has made you to be. (see heart beliefs)
Imaginations	Negative internal images and stresses.
Impartation	What is realized must become a part of you.
Incubation	This is the principle of Biblical meditation that allows you to intentionally increase your faith or to attract God's Kingdom.
Individual Perception	Each person has a different vantage point or perception of what happens, so will interpret the experience differently.
Intention	I + M = R (Intention + Mechanism = Results) F + CA = R (Faith + Corresponding Action = Results)

Kingdom of God	The rule and reign of God; the location and resources of God
Manifestation	What is on the inside of you reveals itself on the outside of you.
Negative Filtering	Allows you to filter noisy, unimportant or negative things out of your thinking.
Positive Focusing	Causes you to focus on what is important for the moment according to your dominant thoughts.
Pretension	Something based in assumption.
Productivity Theology	A practical theology that produces results in your life.
Revelation	Something you always knew but never realized.
Reticular Activating System	The part of the brain that filters out unimportant information and focuses on what you consider to be meaningful facts or opportunities.
Self-Esteem	How you feel about yourself.
Self-Image	How you see yourself mentally and spiritually.
Self-Worth	How you value yourself.
Strongholds	Anything that makes you feel powerless to change, though it is contrary to the Word of God.
The Law of Attraction	You attract to yourself people, ideas and resources according to your most dominant thoughts.
The Law of Belief	What you believe in your heart with confidence becomes your reality.

The Law of Capacity	A person can only receive from God in direct correlation to his ability to receive from God.
The Law of Cause & Effect	Everything happens for a reason.
The Law of Control	People are positive in life to the dimension that they are in control of their lives.
The Law of Correspondence	Your outside world corresponds directly to your inside world.
The Law of Entropy	Things left unattended tend toward a state of chaos.
The Law of Expectation	What you expect in your heart with conviction becomes self-fulfilling prophecy.
The Law of Hysteresis	The tendency of material to revert back to its original shape, once the pressure changing it is removed.
The Law of Motion	Anything in motion stays in motion, unless acted upon by an equal force.

Chapter 1 Endnotes

[1] T. Harv Eker, *Secrets of a Millionaire's Mind* (Harper Collins Publishers, New York, 2005), p.2.

[2] Joseph H. Thayer, *Thayer's Greek-English Lexicon of the New Testament* (Baker Book House, Grand Rapids, Michigan, 1977), Entry 2222, p. 273.

[3] *Thayer's*, 4500,4501,4502,4503,4504, p. 505-506. Noah Webster, *American Dictionary of the English Language*, First Edition, (Foundation for American Christian Education, San Francisco, 2002), p. 43. *American Dictionary of English* Language p. Abundant.

[4] *Webster's New World Dictionary* (World Publishing Company, Cleveland & New York, 1957) p. 516, "extraordinary."

[5] *Thayer's*, #266, p. 30 "hamartia."

[6] Jack Canfield, *The Power of Focus* (Health Communications, Inc., Deerfield Beach, FL, 2000) p. xx.

[7] Brian Tracy, Mark Victor Hansen, Les Hewitt, *Maximum Achievement* (Simon & Schuster, New York, 1993) p. 4.

[8] Ibid p. 45.

[9] Ibid, p. 48.

[10] Ibid, p. 53.

[11] Brian Tracy, *Getting Rich Your Own Way* (John Wiley & Sons, Inc., Hoboken, NJ, 2004), p. 73.

[12] Stephen Scott, *Mentored by a Millionaire* (John Willy & Sons, Inc., Hoboken, NJ, 2004), p. 3, 4.

[13] Tracy, p. 241.

Chapter 2 Endnotes

[1] T. Harv Eker, *Secrets of the Millionaire Mind* (Harper Business, 2005) p. 7.

[2] *Webster's New World Dictionary*, College Edition (The World Publishing Company,
USA, 1957), p.43.

[3] Ibid, p. 568.

[4] Kenneth S. Wuest, *Wuest's Word Studies from the Greek New Testament, Volume 2,* (Wm. B. Eerdmans Publishing Company, Grand Rapids, Michigan, 1973), p. 207.

[5] James Strong, *The New Strong's Exhaustive Concordance of the Bible, Greek Dictionary of the New Testament* (Nashville: Thomas Nelson Publishers, 1984) Entry #4964, p. 70.

[6] Strong's, Greek p. 47, #3340; Joseph H. Thayer, *Thayer's Greek-English Lexicon of the New Testament,* (Baker Book House, Grand Rapids, Michigan, 1977), p. 405, #3340

[7] Webster, "sovereign," p. 1395.

[8] Noah Webster, *American Dictionary of the English Language,* First Edition (Foundation for American Christian Education, San Francisco, 2002), dominion, dominate p. 433. Strong's, Heb #7287. Gesenius, *Hebrew-Chaldee Lexicon to the Old Testament* (Baker Book House Co., Grand Rapids, 1979), Entry 7287, p. 58.

[9] Paragraph loosely based on Dr. Myles Munroe book, *Understanding the Power of Prayer,* (Whitaker House, New Kensington, PA 15068, 2002), p.14.

[10] Webster, p. 244, *American Dictionary, p. 35.*

[11] Webster, *American Dictionary,* p. 97. Webster, *New World Dictionary,* p. 1546, Strong, *Greek Dictionary of the New Testament,* Entry #342, p. 11. Thayer, p. 405.

[12] Strong's *Greek* #342, p. 11

[13] Brian Tracy, *Maximum Achievement* (Simon & Schuster, New York, 1993), p. 17

[14] Strong, *Exhaustive Concordance of the Bible, Hebrew and Chaldee Dictionary,* Entry #8176, p. 119.

[15] Ibid, Entry #8444, p. 123. Webster, *American Dictionary,* p. 124.

[16] R.C.H. Lenski, *The Epistle to Hebrews and the Epistle of James*, (Augsburg Publishing House, Minneapolis, 1966).

[17] Kenneth S. Wuest, *Wuest's Word Studies from the Greek New Testament, Volume 2* (Wm. B. Eerdmans Publishing Company, Grand Rapids, Michigan, 1973), p. 20.

[18] Lenski, p, 145. Lenski says of Hebrews 4:12, in place of soul and spirit the writer of Hebrews now uses heart for the center of our being.

[19] I.V. Hilliard, *Mental Toughness for Success* (Light Publications, Houston, Texas, 2003), p.47.

[20] Webster, Intent and Intention, p. 761

[21] Robert K. Cooper, "The other 90%" – (Three Rivers Press, New York, New York, 2001) p. 24.

[22] Doc Childre and Howard Martin, *The Heart Math Solution (Harper Collins Publishers, 1999)* p. 4, 17.

[23] Ibid.

[24] Ibid.

[25] Dr. Caroline Leaf, *Switch on your Bra*in (Baker Books, Grand Rapids, Michigan, 2013) p. 32.

[26] Ibid.

[27] Ibid, p. 35.

[28] Ibid.

[29] Strong's Greek #1381 p. 24, Thayer's Greek p. 1172

Chapter 3 Endnotes

[1] James Moffat, *The Holy Bible Containing Old & New Testaments* (Doubleday & Co., Inc., New York, New York, 1926), "conceive," Ephesians 3:20. *The New English Bible* (Oxford University Press, Oxford England, 1961), "imagine", Ephesians 3:20.

[2] James Strong, *The New Strong's Exhaustive Concordance, Greek Dictionary of the New   Testament,* (Thomas Nelson Publishers, Nashville, 1990), Entry #1410, p. 24, "able". Joseph H. Thayer,

Thayer's Greek–English Lexicon of the New Testament, (Baker Book House, Grand Rapids, Michigan, 1977), #1411, p. 159.

[3] Noah Webster, *American Dictionary of the English Language*, First Edition (Foundation for American Christian Education, San Francisco, 2002), p. 428. Webster's 1428, "do."

[4] Ibid p. 506

[5] Thayer's 4036, p. 505,506 Strong's 4053, 4054, 4055, p. 57.

[6] PreceptAustin.org Ephesians 3:20-21

[7] *Webster's New World Dictionary*, College Edition (The World Publishing Company,
    USA, 1957), p.143, "beyond."

[8] Myles Munroe, *Understanding Potential*, (Destiny Image Publishers, Shippensburg, Pennsylvania, 1991), p. 145.

[9] JowettPreceptAustin.org Eph. 3:20, 21

[10] Webster, p. 1515, "think."

[11] Webster's p. 725, "imagine" Strong's Heb. #1897, p. 32

[12] Webster's p. 9, "accomplish"

[13] PreceptAustin.0rg

[14] Strong's Greek #1411, p. 24

[15] RuthPasonPreceptAustin.org

[16] Strong's Greek #2842, p. 42.

[17] Strong's #1756, p. 29.

[18] PreceptAustin.org 2 Cor. 5:17 Vineom Kainos

[19] Message by Jerry Savelle

[20] pepweb.org/Anthony Robbins, *Awaken the Giant Within* (Free Press, New York, 2003), p.66.

[21] Cooper, "The Other 90%", p. 24.

[22] Dr. Caroline Leaf, *Switch on Your Brain* (Baker Books, Grand Rapids, Michigan, 2013), p.150.

[23] Ibid.

[24] Brian Tracy, Change Your Thinking (John Wiley & Sons, Inc., Heboken, NJ) p. 187.

[25] Lou Tice tape series

[26] Strong, Greek Dictionary, Entry #4982, p. 70.

[27] *Webster's New World Dictionary, College Edition* (The World Publishing Company, USA, 1957), p.302.

[28] Conversation with Mike Stephens

[29] Myles Munroe, *Understanding Potential*, (Destiny Image Publishers, Shippensburg, Pennsylvania, 1991), p. 145.

Chapter 4 Endnotes

[1] 2 Corinthians 10:5 (KJV) James Strong, *The New Strong's Exhaustive Concordance of the Bible, Greek Dictionary of the New Testament* (Nashville: Thomas Nelson Publishers, 1984), Entry 3053, p.45.

[2] Alex Loyd, *The Healing Code* (Grand Central Life and Style, New York, 2010), p.109.

[3] Ibid, p. 111.

[4] Ibid, p. 23.

[5] Ibid, p. 156.

[6] Ibid, p. 112.

[7] Ibid, p. 160.

[8] Ibid, p. 203.

[9] Ibid, p. 38.

[10] I.V. Hilliard, *Mental Toughness for Success* (Light Publications, Houston, 1996) p. 185.

[11] *Webster's New World Dictionary*, College Edition (The World Publishing Company, USA, 1957), "nature," p.978.

[12] Ibid, "function", page 586.

Chapter 5 Endnotes

[1] Maxwell Maltz, *Psycho-Cybernetics*, (Prentice Hall, Inc.,1960) p. vii.

[2] Ibid, p. ix.

[3] Ibid, p. 2.

[4] Ibid.

[5] Ibid, p. 24

[6] Ibid, p. 31

[7] Ibid, p. 12

[8] T. Harv Eker, *Secrets of the Millionaire's Mind* (Harper Business, New York, 2005), p. 107.

[9] Brian Tracy, *Change Your Thinking, Change Your Life* (John Wiley & Sons, Inc., Hoboken, NJ, 2003), p. 3.

[10] Ibid.

[11] Eker, p. 111.

[12] Gesenius, *Hebrew-Chaldee Lexicon to the Old Testament* (Baker Book House Co., Grand Rapids, 1979), Entry 7181, p. 746.

[13] Lou Tice tape

[14] Joseph H. Thayer, *Thayer's Greek-English Lexicon of the New Testament*, (Baker Book House, Grand Rapids, Michigan, 1977), Entry # 1097, p. 117.

[15] Noah Webster, *American Dictionary of the English Language*, First Edition, (Foundation for American Christian Education, San Francisco, 2002), p. 45. *Webster's New World Dictionary, College Edition* (The World Publishing Company, USA, 1957), p.1170. James Strong, *The New Strong's Exhaustive Concordance, Hebrew Chaldee Dictionary,* (Thomas Nelson Publishers, Nashville, 1990), Entry #835, p. 18. Creflo Dollar message at Mabee Center, Word Explosion.

[16] Gesenius, Entry # 2556, p. 296.

[17] Strong, *Hebrew-Chaldee Dictionary,* #1897, #1899, p. 32; Webster's, *New World Dictionary*, p. 914.

[18] Rhonda Byrne, *The Secret* (Atria Books, Beyond Words Publishing, Hillsboro, Oregon, 2006), p. 21.

[19] Strong, *Hebrew Chaldee Dictionary*, Entry #7503, p. 119; Gesenius, #7503, p. 776.

[20] Brian Tracy, *Million Dollar Habits* (Entrepreneur Media Inc., Canada, 2004), p. 48.

[21] Eker, p. 166-167.

[22] Ibid, p. 167.

[23] Byrne, *The Secret*, DVD

[24] Ibid.

Chapter 6 Endnotes

[1] Brian Tracy, *Maximum Achievement* (Simon & Schuster, New York, 1993), p. 4.

[2] Tracy, *Maximum Achievement*, p. 45.

[3] Ibid, p. 48.

[4] Brian Tracy, *Create Your Own Future* (John Wiley & Sons, Inc., Hoboken, NJ, 2002) p. 17.

[5] Jack Canfield, *The Power of Focus* (Health Communications, Inc., Deerfield Beach, FL, 2000) p. xx.

[6] Myles Munroe at conference at Transformation Church, Tulsa, Sept. 12, 2005.

[7] Unknown source in file system of research, *likeness*

[8] Joel Osteen, *Your Best Life Now* (Warner Faith, Time Warner Book Group, Ne York, 2004).

[9] I.V. Hilliard, *Mental Toughness for Success* (Light Publications, Houston, 2003).

[10] Maxwell Maltz, *Psycho-Cybernetics* (Pocket Books, New York, 1960), p. ix.

[11] Ibid, p. 2.

[12] Ibid, p. ix

[13] Ibid, p. 4

[14] www.barna.org, *Barna Update*, Barna by Topic, "Stewardship," April 5, 2000.

Chapter 7 Endnotes

[1] www.inovationtools.com

[2] Joseph H. Thayer, *Thayer's Greek-English Lexicon of the New Testament*, (Baker Book House, Grand Rapids, Michigan, 1977), Entry #932, p. 96-98.

[3] James Strong, *The New Strong's Exhaustive Concordance of the Bible, Greek Dictionary of the New Testament* (Nashville: Thomas Nelson Publishers, 1984), Entry #1484, p.25. Thayer, Entry #1484, p. 169.

[4] Brian Tracy, *Create Your Own Future*, (John Wiley & Sons, Inc., Hoboken, NJ, 2002), p. 17.

[5] Brian Tracy, *Change Your Thinking, Change Your Life* (John Wiley & Sons, Inc., Hoboken, NJ, 2003), p. 3.

[6] Harry Beckwith, *Selling the Invisible* (Warner Books, New York, 1997), p. 185.

[7] Webster, *Webster's New World Dictionary*, College Edition (The World Publishing Company, USA,1957) p.1439.

[8] Ibid, p. 799.

[9] Dr. James Richards, *Grace the Power to Change* (Whitaker House, New Kensington, PA, 1993), p. 36.

[10] Matthew 11:28-30.

[11] Strong, *Greek Dictionary of the New Testament*, Entry #5485, p. 77. Thayer, Entry #5485, p. 666.

[12] Dr. James Richards, *Grace the Power to Change*, p. 36.

[13] Ibid, p. 70.

[14] Conversation with Dr. Jim Richards

Chapter 8 Endnotes

[1] James Strong, *The New Strong's Exhaustive Concordance of the Bible, Greek Dictionary of the New Testament* (Nashville: Thomas Nelson Publishers, 1984), Entry 4991, p. 70.

[2] Ibid, 4103, p. 58

[3] Strong's, Greek, Entry 5287, p.74; Joseph H. Thayer, *Thayer's Greek-English Lexicon of the New Testament*, (Baker Book House, Grand Rapids, Michigan, 1977), Entry 5287, p. 645.

Noah Webster, *American Dictionary of the English Language*, First Edition, (Foundation for American Christian Education, San Francisco, 2002), Substance, p. 1454. R.C.H. Lenski, *The Epistle to Hebrews and the Epistle of James*, (Augsburg Publishing House, Minneapolis, 1966), p. 375.

[4] Strong's Entry #4100; *Webster's New World Dictionary*, College Edition (The World Publishing Company, USA, 1957), p.1028.

[5] Thayer, Entry #4224, p. 534.

[6] Strong's, Entry #5485, p. 77. Thayer, Entry #5485, p. 665.

[7] Thayer, Entry #5485, p. 666.

[8] Thayer, Entry #5485, p. 667.

[9] Webster, "hope"

[10] Webster, p. 504.

[11] scribd.com 15961499

[12] Webster's, p. 882.

[13] Andy Andrews, *The Traveler's Gift* (Nashville: Thomas Nelson Publishers, 2002), p. 154.

[14] Ibid, p. 155

[15] Ibid, p. 157

[16] Derived from a conversation from someone who heard an Andrew Womack message.

[17] Andrew Womack, *Hardness of Heart* (Colorado Springs, 1991), p. 13.

[18] Ibid pragma

[19] Strong's, Entry #1252, p. 22.

[20] Strong's Hebrew #6419, p. 95

Chapter 9 Endnotes

[1] *Webster's New World Dictionary*, College Edition (The World Publishing Company, USA, 1957), p.721.

[2] wikipedia.org wiki/Martin Seligman

[3] James Strong, *The New Strong's Exhaustive Concordance, Hebrew Dictionary of the Old Testament*, (Thomas Nelson Publishers, Nashville, 1990), Entry #3519, p. 54. p. 32, #1935; Strong's, *Greek Dictionary of the New Testament*, Entry #1391, #1392 p. 24.

[4] Joseph H. Thayer, *Thayer's Greek-English Lexicon of the New Testament*, (Baker Book House, Grand Rapids, Michigan, 1977), Entry 1391, p. 155.

[5] James Strong, *The New Strong's Exhaustive Concordance, Greek Dictionary of the New Testament*, (Thomas Nelson Publishers, Nashville, 1990), Entry #4152, p. 59.

[6] Strong's, #2124, p. 33.

[7] Strong's #4982, #4991, p. 70. Thayer's #4982, p. 610.

[8] Webster's, p. 299.

[9] Thayer's, #1391, p. 155.

[10] R.C.H. Lenski, *The Epistle to Hebrews and the Epistle of James*, (Augsburg Publishing House, Minneapolis, 1966), p. 375.

[11] Thayer's, #1922, p. 237.

[12] Strong's, *Greek Dictionary*, #2222.

[13] Thayer, #1391.

[14] Ibid, #2663, p. 335.

[15] Strong's Greek, #4137, p. 58.

[16] Dr. James Richards, *Moving Your Invisible Boundaries* (True Potential Publishing Travelers Rest, SC 29690, 2013).

[17] Richards, p. 196.

[18] Ibid, p. 197.

[19] Richards, p. 198.

[20] Thayer's, #1391, p. 156.

[21] Ibid, #1391, p. 195.

[22] Blue Letter Bible.org #5426 Colossians 3:1-3

[23] breakingchristiannews.com/articles/display-artatml?id=12893

[24] Strong's Greek, #308, p. 10

Chapter 10 Endnotes

[1] Adapted from the Slight Edge

[2] James Strong, *The New Strong's Exhaustive Concordance of the Bible*, *The Greek Dictionary of the New Testament* (Nashville: Thomas Nelson Publishers, 1984), Entry #4051,4052, p.57.

[3] Jeff Olson, *The Slight Edge* (Success Books, Lake Dallas, Texas 75075, 2005), p. 34

[4] Ibid, p. 34.

[5] Ibid, p. 35.

[6] *Webster's New World Dictionary*, College Edition (The World Publishing Company, USA,1957), "store", p. 215.

[7] Ibid.

[8] Lottery winners - About 70 percent of people who suddenly receive a windfall of cash will lose it within a few years, according to the National Endowment for Financial Education.

[9] Webster p. 3

[10] Ibid p. 1240

[11] Noah Webster, *American Dictionary of the English Language*, First Edition, (Foundation for American Christian Education, San Francisco, 2002), Substance, p. 83.

[12] Mark Victor Hansen & Robert G. Allen, *One Minute Millionaire*, (Harmony Books, New York, 2002), p. 58.

[13] Webster, *American Dictionary*, p. 33. Webster, *New World Dictionary*, p. 1069.

[14] Brian Tracy, *Create Your Own Future* (John Wiley & Sons, Inc., Hoboken, NJ, 2002), p. 59.

[15] Ibid, p. 63

[16] knowledge

[17] Dr. James Richards, *Moving Your Invisible Boundaries* (True Potential Publishing Travelers Rest, SC 29690, 2013), p. 255.

[18] Strong's, Greek, #3340 p. 47.

[19] awmi.net Ephesians 4:23

[20] Winston Churchill – Courage

[21] Webster, p. 415

[22] Andy Stanley, *The Next Generation Leader* (Multnomah Publisher, Sisters, Oregon, 2003), p. 53.

[23] Brian Tracy, *Change Your Thinking, Change Your Mind (John Wiley & Sons, Inc., Hoboken, NJ, 2003), p. 143, 144.*

[24] Webster, p. 1431.

[25] Bob Harrison Newsletter, May, 2007.

[26] Rhonda Byrne, *The Secret* (Hillsboro, OR: Atria Books, Beyond Words Publishing, 2006), p. 107.

[27] Ibid.

[28] Ibid., p. 103.

[29] David Bach, *Start Late Finish Rich* (New York: Broadway Books, 2006), p. 7.

[30] Ibid.

[31] *The Automatic Millionaire* (New York: Broadway Books, 2004), p. 97.

Chapter 11 Endnotes

[1] Dodie Osteen, *Healed of Cancer* (Lakewood Church Publication, Houston, TX, 1986),

p. 15.

[2] Ibid, p. 18.

[3] Ibid, p. 29.

p. 29.

ABOUT THE AUTHOR

Ron McIntosh is an international speaker, author, director of a Bible College and a consultant and coach to many organizations. His message on leadership and productivity has been heard the world over.

He is the President of Ron McIntosh Ministries and I.M.P.A.C.T., a leadership and consulting ministry. He is also the Executive Director of Victory Bible College in Tulsa, Oklahoma. Ron is the former Campus Pastor of Oral Roberts University and the author of 4 books, including best sellers such as *The Greatest Secret* and *Quest for Revival*. *Quest for Revival* has now been translated into four languages around the world. Ron serves on several boards including Impact Productions. He has been a guest on multiple television shows and has a gift for revealing principles of leadership, productivity and the move of God's Spirit to this generation. Ron's unique blend of insight and practical application inspires people to find the life they were born to live.

Ron has a Bachelor of Science in Christian Education and a Masters of Divinity from Oral Roberts University. He and his wife, Judy, live in Tulsa, Oklahoma and are the proud parents of three children. Learn more about Ron at ronmcintoshministries.com.